SHAPING THE C

*Here in this brilliant book, congregational s
cultural studies, all under the innovative heading of implicit theology . Percy
writes with wit, originality, wisdom, and profound insight. As a result of reading
this book, one looks at the relationship of church and the world in a deeper and
richer way. There is no doubt in my mind that this will be one of the great books
of the decade; it will be recognized as a 'classic'. A must read.*
Very Revd Dr Ian Markham, Dean and President, Virginia Theological
Seminary, USA.

Martyn Percy's Shaping the Church*, offers readers a fascinating and lively
account of ecclesial life from the underside. He shows that the forces that shape
the church, its sacramental practices and ministry for the greater part operate
at the implicit level in the 'benign and insignificant peripheries and artefacts
of ecclesial life.' Percy is equally at home in theology, sociology, and cultural
studies. He has a feel for the church and its life in the world and he communicates
it with verve, wit and insight. His work combines sharp analysis and critique
with shrewd theological judgements on important issues in contemporary church
life. A first-rate theologian and cultural commentator; this book will stimulate,
challenge and reward.*
Rt Revd Associate Professor Stephen Pickard, Assistant Bishop, Diocese of
Adelaide, Australia

This book seeks to dynamically alter the way that theologians, ecclesiologists,
students of religion and ministers look at the church. Taking the ideas of
composition, formation and vocation as basic ecclesial categories, Martyn
Percy explores how apparently innocent and incidental material is in fact highly
significant for the shaping of theological and ecclesiological horizons.

The Introduction sets the tone, with a meditation on how the apparently ordinary
scent of a country church can be redolent with meaning, setting the tone of
expectation in relation to subsequent worship. This book is not, however, simply
about reading meanings into events, ideas, conversations and contexts. Rather, it
sets out to faithfully interpret much of the material that surrounds us, yet is often
taken for granted, or more usually unnoticed. The book is an invitation to involve
the scholar or minister, paying close and patient attention to beliefs, language,
artefacts, rituals, practices and other material – all of which are constitutive for
ecclesial life and theological identity.

Explorations in Practical, Pastoral and Empirical Theology

Series Editors: Leslie J. Francis, University of Warwick, UK
and Jeff Astley, Director of the North of England
Institute for Christian Education, UK
Martyn Percy, Ripon College Cuddesdon and
The Oxford Ministry Course, Oxford, UK

Theological reflection on the church's practice is now recognised as a significant element in theological studies in the academy and seminary. Ashgate's new series in practical, pastoral and empirical theology seeks to foster this resurgence of interest and encourage new developments in practical and applied aspects of theology worldwide. This timely series draws together a wide range of disciplinary approaches and empirical studies to embrace contemporary developments including: the expansion of research in empirical theology, psychological theology, ministry studies, public theology, Christian education and faith development; key issues of contemporary society such as health, ethics and the environment; and more traditional areas of concern such as pastoral care and counselling.

Other titles in the series include:

Shaping the Church
The Promise of Implicit Theology

MARTYN PERCY
Ripon College Cuddesdon, UK

ASHGATE

Published by
Ashgate Publishing Limited
Wey Court East
Union Road
Farnham
Surrey, GU9 7PT
England

Ashgate Publishing Company
Suite 420
101 Cherry Street
Burlington
VT 05401-4405
USA

www.ashgate.com

British Library Cataloguing in Publication Data
Percy, Martyn.
   Shaping the church: the promise of implicit theology. – (Explorations in practical, pastoral and empirical theology)
   1. Implicit religion. 2. Christianity and culture. 3. Religion and sociology. 4. Theology, Practical.
   I. Title II. Series
   261–dc22

Library of Congress Cataloging-in-Publication Data
Percy, Martyn.
   Shaping the church: the promise of implicit theology / Martyn Percy.
      p. cm. – (Explorations in practical, pastoral and empirical theology)
   Includes bibliographical references and index.
   ISBN 978-0-7546-6600-4 (hardcover: alk. paper) – ISBN 978-0-7546-6605-9 (pbk.: alk. paper) – ISBN 978-1-4094-0852-9 (ebook) 1. Church. I. Title.
   BV600.3.P47 2010
   260–dc22

2010005810

ISBN 9780754666004 (hbk)
ISBN 9780754666059 (pbk)
ISBN 9781409408529 (ebk)

Mixed Sources
Product group from well-managed forests and other controlled sources
www.fsc.org Cert no. SA-COC-1565
© 1996 Forest Stewardship Council
FSC

Printed and bound in Great Britain by
MPG Books Ltd, Bodmin, Cornwall.

For Stewart, Nick and Tim

Contents

Acknowledgements

I am grateful to friends and colleagues for help with this volume, and with conversations and comments on chapters at earlier stages. In particular, thanks are due to Paul Avis, Helen Cameron, Mark Chapman, Jenny Gaffin, Gareth Jones, Ian Markham, David Martin, Emma Percy, Stephen Pickard and Alistair Redfern. The division of the book falls into three parts – concerned with sacraments, church and ministry – and follows the contours of a course taught by Dan Hardy when Van Mildert Professor of Divinity at Durham. Like many other students of his, my debt of gratitude to him as a mentor is immense.

The first part of the book – concerned with sacraments in contemporary life and practice – begins with an essay that was originally given as a paper at a Meissen Commission gathering in 2005, and subsequently refined for the 'Blurred Encounters' conferences, and eventually published in the series (with John Reader and Chris Baker). The second and third chapters draw on much earlier reflections which have been given as papers, and recently re-worked for this volume.

The second part of the book – on the nature of the church – draws on my continuing work in the field of contemporary ecclesiology. The material on 'fresh expressions' was originally published in the *Journal of Implicit Religion*, following the Windsor Colloquium of 2007. The material on liberal churches and organic church growth is drawn from a recent symposium on rural ministry, and some earlier work (see Ian Markham and Martyn Percy, *Why Liberal Church are Growing*, Continuum, 2005).

The third part of the book – on ministry – draws on more recent work that is concerned with formation, leadership and the practice of polity. 'Herding Cats?' was a paper that first saw the light of day almost a decade ago, but has been revised and updated in the light of recent ecclesial developments. An earlier version of 'Sacred Sagacity' was first published in the Lambeth Conference edition of the *Anglican Theological Review*, whilst 'Feeling for the Church' is very much work in progress, although an earlier version of this work first appeared in a festschrift for Wesley Carr, published in 2004.

Lastly, I once again thank my family for their forbearance during the writing of this book. My wife Emma, in particular, has been a patient and wise companion in many a conversation, as she develops her own work. Their love and support is, as always, beyond measure.

Introduction
The Promise of Implicit Theology

The genesis of this book lies in a long-standing fascination with ecclesial formation. What exactly are the forces, currents, practices and ideas that shape the church? How does a congregation or a denomination understand its identity, on the one hand, in relation to the providence and revelation of God, and on the other, in relation to the context and culture in which ecclesial composition inexorably occurs? What is the relationship between the acknowledged propositional truths that order ecclesial identity, and the more hidden and mellifluous currents that might shape the life of the church? One does not need to be a sociologist to understand that class, ethnicity, gender, age and aesthetics all exercise powerful influences on the theological construction of reality that comprise ecclesial cosmologies. The late James Hopewell, in his modest yet prescient study of ecclesiology, notes that

> As slight and predictable as the language of a congregation might seem on casual inspection, it actually reflects a complex process of human imagination. Each is a negotiation of metaphors, a field of tales and histories and meanings that identify its life, its world, and God. Word, gesture, and artefact form local language – a system of construable signs that Clifford Geertz, following Weber, calls a 'web of significance'. Even a plain church on a pale day catches one in a deep current of narrative interpretation and representation by which people give sense and order to their lives. Most of this creative stream is unconscious and involuntary, drawing in part upon images lodged long ago in the human struggle for meaning. Thus, a congregation is held together by much more than creeds, governing structures and programs. At a deeper level, it is implicated in the symbols and signals of the world, gathering and surrounding them in the congregation's own idiom. (Hopewell, 1987, p. 11)

Here, Hopewell (and following Clifford Geertz) is more than hinting at the implicit forces that shape ecclesial life. He is extending a rather novel invitation to theologians: to explore far more than the (set) propositional texts that churches appeal to in order to construct and justify their identity, and to consider the apparently benign and insignificant peripheries and artefacts of ecclesial life. Essentially, this volume is a cautious response to that invitation, namely to ponder the implicit aspects of ecclesial life, and thereby explore the composition of congregations and denominations in a new light.

The very word 'implicit' is suggestive. Normally used as an antonym with 'explicit', the terms have a complex etymological history. 'Implicit' is derived from the Latin *implicitus*, meaning to implicate – a term, in turn, that suggests involvement, interweaving, and entanglement. The Latin word *implicatus,* expresses this, with *plicare conveying the notion of 'folding' – in the sense of mixing and combining, rather as one might expect to 'fold' an ingredient into a recipe. Thus,* 'implicit' means the meaningful folding together and close connecting of a variety of strands. Correspondingly, 'explicit' is the un-folding, un-ravelling or explaining of the miscible. It is bringing order from apparent chaos and clarity from complexity.

In one sense, then, doctrine can be said to be an 'explicit' form of theology – a concrete mode of discourse in which meaning and truth has been distilled from story, debate and conjecture. There can be no argument that this is at least something of what it means to inherit a tradition in ecclesial life: the wilful propagation of truth, putatively, across space, time and cultures. What is implicit in theology or ecclesiology, therefore, is more open to debate and challenge. For example, what part does aesthetics or social class play in the construction of Anglican identity? What is the difference between the culture and the content of authority in Roman Catholicism? What kind of influence does contemporary consumerism exercise in 'fresh expressions' of the church?

In exploring implicit theology, therefore, we are embarking on something of a journey. On the one hand, it is examining the basic-but-nascent theological habits (e.g., language, culture, worship, practice, etc) that more properly account for the daily life of churches, congregations and denominations. On the other, it is guessing at the hidden meanings in structures and practices that on the surface appear to be benign and innocent. Fundamentally, the invitation to engage in the exploration of implicit theology is centred on the premise that not everything that shapes the church can be or is plainly expressed. There is something natural about the implicit too; premises rest on authorities or sources that are rarely surfaced or challenged. Credulity, and a degree of faith in any ecclesial body, depend, to some extent, on the implicit being present and yet unquestioned. Dress codes in any church, for example, even amongst the laity, carry and convey unspoken messages about the ethos of worship – the extent to which it is formal or informal, perhaps – that are seldom articulated.

Explicitness irons all these folds out, and reveals what has been hidden. But as anyone who has ever studied churches or denominations will know, the complexity, density, extensity and intricacy of a congregation contains manifold layers of complexity. Whilst the task of theology is, on one level, to distinctly express all that is meant, ecclesial life, by its very nature, contains much that is seemingly indistinct and apparently un-meant. There is much to ecclesial life that is merely implied, and seldom made explicit. The burden of this brief and explorative monograph is therefore one of exposure: drawing attention to those things that are taken for granted or overlooked, and raising them to their proper place within the life of the church and theological investigation. Rather like C.S. Lewis, the book is wilfully absorbed with the apparently tangential and tacit; with the seemingly oblique and obtuse. For underneath this lurks a conviction; namely that what is natural, given and ordinary is also imbued with meaning and value that is a form of theological currency.[1]

James Nieman offers an example of this in his essay, 'Attending Locally':

> Consider a dispute in a church council about how to conduct business. One group relishes long meetings with extensive discussions of details, while another group insists on brief meetings only as needed, trusting members to carry out assigned duties between times. Simply to reduce such a situation to questions of managerial style can completely miss the serious theological claims by each group about the nature of the church and the commitment to it. The former sees the church in terms of familiar associations, so that commitment requires shared time. The latter sees the church in terms of operations, so that commitment is shown by productivity. Deeper still, both groups *implicitly assert a view of God* (emphasis mine) through how they want to conduct church business. Failure to recognize this not only does violence to the situation but also subverts the chance for both groups to discern what is mutually at stake for them in being church. (Nieman, 2002, p. 202)

In articulating and positioning the promise of implicit theology in this way, it is important to acknowledge that although there are some helpful overlaps with the kinds of agenda pursued by those engaged in the 'implicit religion project', the two are not to be confused. Implicit religion, as an academic concept, can locate its roots in discussions of 'folk', 'civic' and 'popular' religion. James Frazer, Mircea Eliade, Clifford Geertz, Mary Douglas and Gunther Heimbrock have all done important anthropological work in this field, exploring the relationship between implicit faith practices and formal religion. From a historical perspective, the writings of Keith Thomas (1978) continue to have significant resonance. More recently, writers such as Edward Bailey (1998), Leslie Francis (2007), Timothy Jenkins (2001), Anton Wessels (1994), John Reader (2005) and John Drane (2003) have served the academy and the church by drawing on Peter Berger and Thomas Luckmann's notion of 'invisible religion' (Berger and Luckmann, 1967; Luckmann 1967), and Robert Bellah's articulation of civil religion (Bellah, 1967).

Additional supporting paradigms for the conceiving of implicit theology can be drawn from other sources too. One immediately thinks of the attention paid by scholars to the more formal aspects of civic religion in European culture,[2] and to the no less significant modes of operant religion in the same context. Or one could consider Wade Clark Roof's distinction between 'formal' and 'operant' religion. Or of Ursula Le Guin's distinction between 'father' and 'mother' tongue; the former referring to the formal language of ecclesial authority, and the latter to the vernacular discourse that shapes much of congregational and denominational life. Or of Nicholas Healy's distinction between 'blueprint' and

---

[1]   For an illuminating discussion of this in relation to C.S. Lewis, see Ward (2008).

[2]   See Kenneth N. Medhurst and George H. Moyser (1988).

'concrete' ecclesiology, and between 'ideal' and 'real' (or 'earthed'). Finally, of George Lindbeck's notion of theology as a 'cultural-linguistic' system (1984); and more recently of Jeff Astley's exploration of 'ordinary theology' (2007).

The debt that this book owes to such sources should not be in any doubt. However, this book intentionally builds on some earlier work of mine in the same series (Percy, 2006b) and takes a deliberate interest in ecclesial formation, as well as being shaped by practical theology and Anglican identity. Whereas the first volume was rooted in anthropology, sociology and cultural studies, this one is more firmly focused on missiology, ecclesiology and pastoral studies. And yet in a similar sense, this monograph is a continuation of the discussions, beginning with a premise that Christianity is about much more than beliefs, propositions and formally sanctioned practices.[3] Indeed, this is a deep misunderstanding about the nature of Christian life. The belief that God is Father, Son and Holy Spirit is not an arid set of directives, but rather a faith that is embedded in a community of praxis that makes beliefs work, and gives shape and meaning to the lives that believe. So religious belief is not simply some kind or arcane metaphysics; it is, rather, performed – much as one might perform a play. Indeed, the beliefs must be performed in order to comprehend the drama. Simply reading the scriptures as a text is about as effective as reading a play as a text. To understand the life of the drama and the intention of the author, the play needs to be witnessed as a performance. Christian faith is, first and foremost, the performance of God's drama. And such performances occur each week, locally.

To be sure, the whole history of denominational difference and identity is a struggle to define what constitutes a faithful performance. Some denominations think others have 'lost the plot', so to speak. Others acknowledge, more charitably, that whilst their performance is of a type, others are no less faithful and legitimate. So without wanting to labour the analogy further, the relevance of this to implicit theology should be reasonably obvious. In adopting the notion of implicit theology as a lens through which to consider the more performative aspects of ecclesiology, we are able to privilege style, not just substance, as theologically significant. Apparently innocent ecclesial structures and gestures emerge as an expression of value, not as mere artefacts.[4]

For example, many congregations understand the value of what I would term 'truthful duplicity' – and not necessarily in negative ways, either. The word *mokita* refers to what everyone knows but no-one says. 'The Vicar can't preach' would be an explicit case in point – but where the congregation nonetheless understands that the pastoral, organizational and other gifts offered by the Vicar more than outweigh his or her under-performance in the pulpit. It is also the case that just below the

---

[3]   The volumes can be read quite independently. However, a third monograph in this series, and to complete the trilogy, is currently being written which will focus on the role of the church in public life.

[4]   On churches and structures as expressive of values, for example, see Long Jnr. (2001). See also Kim and Kollontai (2007).

surface of discourse there can be many kinds of implicit contracts between several parties operating in congregations or denominations. 'We deliberate but we don't or won't decide' would, I suppose, be an obvious understanding that resonates with many Christians. The phrase is never uttered: but it is understood, and may indeed, as value, be cherished in certain instances. The purpose of un-decidability is to give everyone time and space: there is an element of *chronos* and *kairos* in harmony here.

Or consider 'theological graffiti', which is abundantly present in the life of the church. Here one thinks of sayings that appear to be rooted in the core tradition (e.g., scriptures) but are in fact expressing resonant but rather attenuated values. 'The priesthood of all believers', 'the ministry of the whole baptised people of God' – rather like 'God helps those who help themselves' – are not biblical phrases, but rather ones that are merely vested with quasi-biblical mystique. Similarly, the sub-headings that often intrude in versions of the bible then become the lens through which the text is read. Strictly speaking, there is no 'Great Commission' in Matthew 28: the added headline now shapes the implied meaning of the text in ways that are directive and restrictive.

In parishes, magazines and notice sheets will often convey the core theological values of a congregation without even realizing it. An appeal for money or help; an advertisement or announcement – all will in some sense witness to the theological construction of reality that is behind the apparently innocent, just as memorial plaques and gravestones have done in the past, and continue to do so.

So we can begin to see here that the sense of the aesthetic might also occupy some of the theological foreground and assume some character, instead of being relegated to the background.[5] A simple example can illustrate this. In the early *Acts of the Christian Martyrs*, the death of Polycarp in 155 AD, we are told, was witnessed by many faithful devotees who described his execution at the hands of the authorities in the most colourful terminology:

> '... the men in charge of the fire started to light it. A great flame blazed up and those of us to whom it was given to see beheld a miracle ... for the flames, bellying out like a ship's sail in the wind, formed into the shape of a vault and thus surrounded the martyr's body as with a wall. And he was within it not as burning flesh, but rather as bread being baked, or like gold and silver being purified in a smelting furnace. And from it we perceived such a delightful fragrance as though it were smoking incense or some other costly perfume ... ('Martyrium Polycarpi' – *9.3; 21, Acta Martyrum*)

Christianity is a faith of the senses. There are things of beauty to see and texts to read; sounds and words to hear; artefacts and objects to touch; and sacraments to taste and savour. We rarely think of our faith in terms of its sense of smell. But this is all rather surprising when one considers just how important the olfactory

---

[5]   See Klassen ed. (2006) and LaMothe (2008).

imagination is in the ancient world: the scent of salvation, to borrow a phrase from one Susan Ashbrook Harvey (Harvey 2006, p. 7). For in the scents, smells and odours of scripture, tradition and church, we have intimations of the divine. As one anthropologist, Clifford Geertz, says, 'religious symbols *reek* of meaning' (Geertz, 1973). And sometimes they literally do reek – the message is in the smell.

In the account of the martyrdom of Polycarp, we are introduced to the resonances between scent and meaning: the aroma of baking bread is a Eucharistic hint, and the smell of gold or silver being purified a promise for believers. Here, in Polycarp's death, we have the hint of salvation and eternal life for all believers. But in the smell of freshly baked bread, we are also given another hint – that of home, and linking the place of our birth and upbringing with our eventual home, namely heaven. In this waft of a scent, we are introduced to the possibility of implicit theology. The smell of a country church (flowers, polish, of old prayer books and a slightly musty hint) is a reassuring scent – one that is so deep – that it conveys a sense that informs our theology and shapes our ecclesial horizons.

Correspondingly, when the concept of implicit theology is understood and valued as part of the heritage of Christianity, theology itself can be reconceived as commonplace – an everyday performance and practice (so yes, linguistic), and not merely discipline reserved for a select few. In other words, the authority of ideas, valued behaviour, structures and concepts is implied without being questioned; implicit theology is, therefore, that which is deduced from operant religious practice (which would include a variety of expressions of faith and belief) rather than formal religious propositions. Its authority rests upon the fact that it need not make itself explicit.

Perhaps another way of expressing this would be to reclaim the word 'natural' as a useful prefix for theology. Ellen Clark King's *Theology By Heart* (2004) draws attention to the 'natural' ways in which women speak about God on deprived working-class estates in the northeast of England, demonstrating admirably the theological prescience of vernacular and lay spiritual language. In some respects, Daniel Hardy can also be understood as an ally in this project. Towards the end of his life, he came to understand all theology as 'natural' – not in the sense that the Deists of previous centuries had meant, but rather as an acceptance that the 'texts' modes and methods of theology could not and should not be confined to the formal, propositional and those invested with the status of 'official'. There is something entirely natural about the range and scope of theology, and the material it is engaged with. It covers our world and the wider cosmos; it is ecologically attuned to all the environments in which God may be manifest. Effectively, it excludes nothing. In affirming 'natural theology', Hardy invites us to contemplate all the ways in which God may be encountered.[6] In this sense, the burden of the book, as well being about shifting the foci of theological texts from the formal and propositional to the informal and relational, is also centred on the advocacy of interpretation and discernment. As Rowan Williams puts it:

---

[6]   For fuller discussion, see Hardy (2002 and 1996).

And this leads into (another) kind of responsibility, that of being an interpreter – by which I mean not primarily someone who interprets culture to and for the Church or interprets the Church's teaching to the world outside, but someone who has the gift of helping people make sense to and of each other. Communities, in spite of the sentimental way we sometimes think of them, don't just happen. They need nurture, they need to be *woven* into unity … If the unity of the Church is not that of a mass of individuals with a few convictions in common but that of a differentiated organism where the distinctiveness of each is always already in play, then for the Church to be consciously itself, it needs people to see and show how diversity works together … Put more theologically, it is about helping believers to see Christ in one another. The interpretative work of the priest looks first at how to uncover for one person or group the hidden gift in another – especially when the first impression is one of alienness and threat.[7]

This observation prompts a word or two about the range and scope of discernment that can be offered in a modest volume such as this. Clearly one route that could be taken in a volume of this kind is to find spiritual or theological meaning in non-traditional texts. There is a plethora of resources and books that will, for example, attempt this with contemporary culture. Ambitious projects have been undertaken by theologians that 'find' God and meaning in popular music, films, novels and other artefacts of contemporary consumer culture.[8] One could also conceive of a project in which implicit theology surfaced, that was primarily concerned with aesthetics that were more extrinsically linked to ecclesiastical proclivities.[9] Or, for that matter, of the fascinating pastoral theological attention given in recent years to both deafness and blindness, and the consequences of this for theological subtexts in congregations and denominations that merit surfacing and analysing.[10] This, however, is not our purpose here.

Rather, our concern is with the hybridity of culture and theology within ecclesial communities, and the consequences of this for subsequent ecclesial contouring. Think, for example, of Pugin, whose church architecture emerged out of his (misplaced?) sense of anxiety about the decay and imminent death of the Church of England. He believed that he lived in degenerate times, and therefore sought to create sacred spaces that restored the renaissance – and a romanticized notion of the middle ages – in order to rescue society from its moral implosion. Pugin, in effect, attempted to return architecture to a 'natural' age, and away from the brutalism of industrialization. In doing so, of course, he simply leant on a romantic myth – albeit one with some substance – that could raise morale amidst 'those dark satanic mills' that Blake and his contemporaries had also set their

---

[7]   'The Christian Priest Today': lecture on the occasion of the 150th anniversary of Ripon College Cuddesdon.

[8]   See for example Cobb (2005); Garrett (2007); Deacy and Arweck eds (2009).

[9]   See, for example, Brecht (1999).

[10]   See Hull (2001) and McClintock Fulkerson (2007).

faces against. So, Pugin's architecture is rooted in his (flawed, but understandable) implicit theology: modernity was brutalizing and evil, and had to be driven out by art and beauty. The principles of his architecture were governed by his theological presumptions, which in turn became the means whereby new worlds were ordered for others. Pugin's implicit theology shaped his architecture. His architecture, in turn, shaped the new generation of romantic renaissance thinking in the church which quickly found expression in Anglo-Catholicism (Hill, 2007, pp. 114ff and 243–7). It is no accident that the Radical orthodox movement, championed by John Milbank and others, follows closely in this vein.

There are also quite concrete ways in which implicitness can be discerned in the shaping of ecclesial polity. Consider again, for example, the myriad of ways in which Anglican identity is formed. In *The Ancestor's Tale: A Pilgrimage to the Dawn of Life* (2004), Richard Dawkins uses the structure of Chaucer's *Canterbury Tales* to reflect on the origins of life. The species in the book travel backwards through time, and meet at the points of convergence and diversification, in order to find their 'concestor' – the common species from which they originate.

For religious traditions, this lens of evolution, albeit deployed analogically, raises some fascinating questions. Where does a denomination obtain its traits from? Why is there diversification, disagreement and difference across the 'species'? Is the shape of Christian identity about nature or nurture? If we were speculating upon Anglican identity, we could consider some of the different ways of describing Anglican polity – a kind of ecclesial DNA, as it were. The hidden forces, factors and codes that shape its life (both inner and outer) might include behaviours associated with class, race and gender.[11] One might also detect attitudes associated with manners, irony, breadth, humour; characteristics that are associated with ethos, including passion, conviction, ambivalence and reticence, that find expression in worship, structures and various modes of discourse, including doctrinal debate.[12]

Thus, and as Urban Holmes remarked many years ago, Anglicans can hardly ever resist the pairing of two three letter words: 'Yes, but ... .' Anglicanism seems to have an 'in-built' reflexivity which is almost part of its DNA. Moreover, it is a kind of peaceable polity in which 'speaking across differences' matters; indeed, one might say that style is as important as substance. But what happens when that polity is tested to its limits? What happens when its elasticity begins to lose its capacity to somehow hold competing convictions together? These issues raise profound questions for Anglicans – on the nature of authority, on the right level of self-conscious identity required for holding manifest cultural diversity and negotiating theological differences. In attempting to address such questions, it is clearly important that Anglicans are able to excavate both their explicit and implicit theological roots.

---

[11]   See Niebuhr (1929).
[12]   See Percy (2006).

Yet today, whatever the word 'Anglican' might mean culturally, theologically or liturgically, it is its ecclesiological use that is the most elastic. So much so, in fact, that the term 'Anglican' has become a cipher for linking a series of opposites or polarities, that in turn express its diversity. So, if one was to look for correlative vocabulary from *Roget's Thesaurus* in respect of 'Anglicanism', what words might be added that complement the noun? I am reasonably sure that single words would not do; only thesis and antithesis; Hegelian dialect in action. Thus, solid, yet flexible; strong, yet yielding; open, yet composed; inclusive, yet identifiable: all might work. And the list could certainly go on. But I suppose that in pointing out the connection of opposites, I am suggesting that Anglicans have an innate capacity for un-decidability and elasticity, in the very midst of concreteness. Anglican identity only begins to make proper sense when it is related to its mirror image or opposite number; it partly knows what it is by what it isn't. No one wing or facet of the church can begin to be true without relation to its contrary expression. As the popular Christian writer Brian McLaren notes,

> Generous orthodoxy is … the practice of dynamic tension – you can resist the reductionist temptation to always choose one thing over another, and you learn to hold two or more things together when necessary … Anglicans have demonstrated this both and beautifully in relation to scripture … it is never *sola* [scripture] – never the only factor. Rather, scripture is in dialogue with the tradition, reason and experience … None of them *sola* can be the ultimate source of authority … When these [the four] agree, Anglicans move forward with confidence … When they don't agree, Anglicans seek to live with the tension and the tolerance, believing that better outcomes will follow if they live with the tension rather than resolve it [prematurely?] by rejecting one of the four values … all are gifts from God, and none should be rejected. Compromise … Anglicans make room for one another when scripture, reason, tradition and experience don't line up for everyone the same way … When conceptual agreement fails, [Anglicans] will tell you they are brought together by liturgy … but not just words on a page. Rather, it is their deep appreciation for the deep beauty of liturgy that helps them to make room for one another. (McLaren, 2004, p. 235)

Some of the most decisive splits in Christianity appear to be grounded solely in doctrinal disputes. However, when inspected more closely, the cultural aspects of separation can also emerge to give a richer account of the shifting tectonic plates of denominationalism. For example the first great schism in Christianity is not only doctrinal; it is also between the centres of power and culture in both the East and West. The second great schism – the Reformation – owes much of its energy to theological disputes. But the Reformation must also be read as a symptom of emerging nationalism and states within Europe, that increasingly wish to order their own temporal and spiritual affairs, and develop a genuinely vernacular religious expression of Christianity.

These sizeable paradigm shifts have led to the creation of the great continents of Christendom – Protestant, Roman Catholic and Orthodox – and their evolution since the sixteenth century tells an important story about their capacity to develop in places beyond their original context. In that respect, South America remains one of the most fascinating arenas of study that focuses on the development of religion, as both Roman Catholicism and Protestantism vie for pre-eminence within a highly variegated ecology.

The twentieth century has, of course, seen the seedlings of a third schism, namely that between conservatives and liberals, or between traditionalists and radicals. The fault lines in this scenario are complex to trace, but the early indications are that this is less about the creation of a further continent than it is about the emergence of new ecclesial islands caused by denominational erosion and more local ecological calamities or geological catastrophes. To some extent, the emergence of the Southern Baptists – as distinct from (North) American Baptists – serves as some kind of paradigm that warns ecclesiastical communities about the price of failing to cohere. Such divisions, when they emerge, produce fresh expressions of ministry which are then traced inductively to some (mythic) point of origin. This theological 'result' is then, typically, adopted as a point of departure for deductive theological reasoning; thereby allowing the 'new' church to imagine itself as the 'original'. The fact that the two strains deriving from the single breed are likely to still remain very closely related in both structure and form, can be a cause of acute anxiety for future generations of ministers and believers. (Witness the distance Mormons try to put between themselves and Reformed Latter Day Saints: the actual differences are lost on all but the shrewdest observer with an eye for detail).

A more culturally-informed theological reading of ecclesial polity and ministerial praxis can also throw some light on how theological divisions are in fact symptoms rather than causes of ecclesial fracture. Take the worldwide Anglican Communion, and its current difficulties in holding together as a meaningful and purposeful body. On the surface, the manifest difficulties appear to be centred on issues such as sexuality (i.e., the place of lesbian and gay people, whether as ordained or laity), gender (i.e., women bishops and women priests), the right use of the bible (i.e., are ethical issues resolved principally by reference to scripture, or does reason, culture and experience have a part to play in ethical decisions?) and the appropriate interpretation of scripture (i.e., does it have one plain meaning, or several possible competing meanings?). It is therefore possible to narrate the schismatic tendencies in Anglicanism with reference to authority, theology and ecclesial power. But on its own, as a thesis, this is clearly inadequate, as such tensions have existed within Anglicanism from the outset. There has not been a single century in which Anglicanism has not wrestled with its identity; it is by nature a polity that draws in a variety of competing theological traditions. Its very appeal lies in its own distinctive hybridity, and indeed, in implicitness:

The *via media*, in historcial terms, was John Donne's phrase whose heritage dates back to Aristotle's 'Golden Mean'. It is striking that in Anglican history, the focus has been on the method, rather than a distinct theology or creed. Perhaps the most important thing about Hooker is that he wrote no *Summa* and composed no *Institutes*, for what he did was to outline method. What is distinctively Anglican then is not a theology but a theological method ... (McConnell, 1983, p. 43).

So, central to the understanding of implicit theology is the recognition that practices shape beliefs and religious beliefs also shape practice; this should not surprise us. As Kathryn Tanner notes,

religious beliefs are a form of culture, inextricably implicated in the material practices of daily social living on the part of those who hold them ... in the concrete circumstances in which beliefs are lived ... actions, attitudes, and interests are likely to be as much infiltrated and informed by the beliefs one holds as beliefs are to be influenced by actions, attitudes and interests ... (Tanner, 1992, p. 9)

Here, doctrines are 'dramatic scripts' which Christians perform and by which they are performed. Doctrines 'provide a scripted code for the motions of a Christian's life in much the same way that broader cultural codes and linguistic patterns structure the self'. In other words, doctrines practice us; practices are not just things that Christians do in the light of doctrine: 'practices are what we become as we are set in motion in the space of doctrine' (Volf and Bass, 2002, p. 75). In this sense, we are once again close to Lindbeck's theory of theology – its performative dimension as something that is 'cultural-linguistic': it (i.e., doctrine, belief, etc) 'gains power and meaning insofar as it is embodied in the total gestalt of community life and action' (Lindbeck, 1984, p. 36). There is the irony for the theologian, and for the church. For in gaining an understanding of how the world beliefs and practice begin to cohere, one immediately sees that they, in fact, do not. As Tanner says,

Christian practices do not in fact require (1) much explicit understanding of beliefs that inform and explain their performance, (2) agreement upon such matters among the participants, (3) strict delimitation of codes for action, (4) systematic consistency among beliefs or actions, or (5) attention to their significance that isolates them from a whole host of non-Christian commitments. More often than not, Christian practices are instead quite open-ended in the sense of being undefined in their exact ideational dimensions and in the sense of being always in the process of re-formation in response to new circumstances. (Volf and Bass, 2002, p. 229)

So in that case, what might *Anglican* practices and beliefs be? In terms of implicit theology, I take them to be 'resonances of God's engagement with the world'

(Volf and Bass, 2002, p. 260). And in this respect, we might then want to argue that theology should be in a much deeper relationship with operant practices and beliefs – something to do with 'real life', the 'concrete church' and the context of 'operant' or 'vernacular' religion. It is through the study of implicit theology that the theologian will find individuals and communities 'working out their own salvation' (Philippians 2: 12). It will mean careful attention to the roots and ancestry of our polity – to the common stories that bind a species together, even as it diversifies and flourishes in emerging and new contexts. The Anglican Church, as Michael Ramsey reminds us, has credentials: 'incompleteness – with tension and travail in its soul'. Or as a more contemporary bishop puts it, 'we are a school of relating'.

In view of these remarks, it should be stressed that *Shaping the Church* seeks to make a nuanced case for the primacy of pastoral-practical theology (methodologically): as a pivotal and creative mode of theological engagement and discernment, that can truly discern the significance of everyday implicit theology. In other words, to shift the theological foci to those ideas, values and practices that shapes the life and witness of Christians and the churches. The book gives some space to the place of 'congregational studies' as a major focus for the discernment of implicit theology, and as an essential companion for understanding the relational gap between the ideal and real theology, together with the formal and operant theology: the latter in each case being more commonly practised and understood.

Much has been written about the theology of certain movements in order to explain their power and appeal. There is no doubt that familiarity with the formal theological propositions or the ideological formulations of a specific ecclesial movement are essential to an understanding of any church. But the central foci with which we are concerned is how might we locate an implicit theology within a church, denomination or congregation, particularly if it is hidden? Most studies of the church tend to suggest that the theology of a given congregation or denomination can be located in the dogmatic creeds, principles and formulations that it advances to the world. But as we have already been suggesting, very few of the members of a congregation or denomination have a specific or conscious knowledge of such articles of faith; their grasp of such things is tenuous at best.

One could identify dozens of examples of implicit theology which guide and direct ecclesiology in ways that are deeper than the formal propositions of explicit theology. This hypothesis will be explored and tested in three distinct but overlapping parts: church, ministry and sacraments.[13] The first section – Church – offers a consideration of the value placed on modes of behaviour and practice in formal and informal (or 'fresh expressions') of ecclesial polity, the missiological practice of liberal churches, and the more general question of church growth. There are currently few obvious explicit theological treatises that address such

---

[13]   The 'Church, Ministry and Sacraments' distinction is derived from a course of lectures taught by Daniel Hardy whilst Van Mildert Professor of Theology at Durham University.

issues. The second section – Ministry – explores some of the softer and more mellifluous values that shape polities, including an appreciation of the ways in which manners and other diplomatic codes of behaviour govern the cadence and timbre of its ecclesiology, and of leadership in ecclesial communities. The third section – Sacraments – returns the agenda of implicit theology to something like the territory more usually associated with implicit religion: the practice of faith in everyday life. It explores the place of sacraments in contemporary culture, and thereby explores the implicit ways in which sacred moments and tokens continue to communicate with meaningful social resonance.

Taken as a whole, *Shaping the Church* notices and gives due attention to the theological and ecclesial significance of details that can appear to be trivial or inconsequential, recognizing that they are in fact indicators of deeply held convictions, contested theologies and changing ecclesial structures. Drawing on a broad range of experiences and roles within the church, the implicit is given space to emerge from within a myriad of apparently unrelated manifestations of Christian life as the text of Church life is presented and read in all its richness and complexity. The insights that emerge from immersion in the detail of church life in the early parts of the book are then used to explore questions of leadership and ecclesiology in the latter part.

The scope of this book is deliberately broad, covering topics as diverse as fresh expressions, theological formation, and baptism policies. This breadth is necessary because when we are immersed in our own small corner of the Anglican Communion it can often be difficult, if not impossible, to understand the profound connections between the details of church life and the broader ecclesial structure. One of the privileges of having occupied a variety of roles within that structure – as curate, researcher, teacher and Principal of Ripon College Cuddesdon – is that it has allowed me to recognize and delight in those connections, and to appreciate their significance as together we continue to shape the church. So the intention of the book is not to make decisive pronouncements on the individual subjects I raise, so much as to draw together material from diverse parts of the church in order to set off a set of resonances, revealing how the details illuminate and influence and belong within the communion as a whole. In a sense, this is a deliberately open-ended book. It is my hope that readers will not so much agree or disagree with my argument, as inhabit the pages of the book with me, revelling in their deepened appreciation of the wide-reaching theological and ecclesial import of the details of their own lives in the church.

It is perhaps important to keep in mind that as we seek to interpret the life of the church around us, the 'texts' that we are concerned with are not the obvious ones, but rather, those that have implications for the shaping of polity. One thinks of mood, climate, *terroir*, structures and values, more than, say, formal reports or articles of faith. Very few Anglicans, for example, will have an explicit grasp of the distinctiveness and clarity of Anglican doctrine. Moreover, there are a number of Anglican theologians who have perceptively understood that that Anglican theology is carried less by its formal statements and more by the manner of how those statements are held. Thus, Michael Ramsay speaks of the Anglican tendency to 'understate' the Gospel, which he suggests is superior owning clarity in method and direction in theology, which leads to 'confessionalism'. Put another way, it is the openness (some would say haziness) of Anglican polity, in both style and substance, that enables comprehensiveness. And critically, that comprehensiveness is the by-product of living a tradition rather than explicating a form or confessionalism. Naturally, of course, this means that Anglican polity is susceptible to attack – especially in fondness for comprehensiveness – since most of its ordering arises out of implicit theological living rather than anything especially explicit.

So the theological programme that emerges from the discussion invites theologians to take more notice of local contextual ecclesial and operant pastoral practice as *primary* theological material, rather than such praxis merely being seen as the outcome of discerning and interpreting formal theological or denominational propositions. Furthermore, that attention to implicit theology would help bridge the gap between the academy and the parish; it would help students of theology and trainee ministers make the right connections between what they learnt and what they experienced. Currently, they tend to jettison either the academy (and go 'native' in the parish) or they retreat from the parish, and wonder why it is so alien to what they learnt at seminary. This book seeks to provide a set of interpretative keys that helps to address this dilemma.

This set of chapters therefore explores the tension between theology and ecclesiological experience (i.e., composition, formation and vocation), and argues that the church stands in the gap between operant/formal religion and implicit/ explicit theology. This, in turn, can be construed as an expression of the incarnational life of the church. It argues that much of the (apparently) incidental and peripheral matter and concerns that shape church life needs to be taken more seriously as theologically and pastorally significant material. Only by understanding implicit theology can theologians gain an understanding of ecclesial evolution, pastoralia and faith development. The volume seeks to introduce academics, clergy and ecclesial commentators to something it in some sense already knows: that which is implicit is deep and formational for ecclesial life. The implicit therefore deserves to be treated as both an original yet familiar concept to the academy and church, which offers fresh insight on the apparently ordinary. Implicit theology opens up new vistas of enquiry in practical and pastoral theology that grapple with the perplexing, puzzling and perspicacious possibilities for ecclesial life.

PART I
Sacraments – Spiritual Life

1. Baptism: Belief, Practice and Culture
2. Confirmation and Conversion: Continuity and Change
3. Tripping Down the Aisle: Churchgoing, Culture and Contemporary Eucharistic Practice

The opening section of this book primarily focuses on spiritual and ecclesial phenomena that are normally taken for granted. In considering the sacramental life of the church, however, particular attention is drawn to the implicit and latent aspects of their practice. Drawing on cultural and historical studies, the chapters challenge the conventional theological monopolizations of our discourses in relation to the beliefs and practices of the church. The 'grounded ecclesiology' that emerges from these readings of sacramental life calls into question the habitual ways in which faithful spiritual Christian life is undertaken, and suggests that culturally and socially, Christian faith is far more widespread than is sometimes supposed in secular society. The first chapter examines baptismal practice and culture, and looks at some of the folk religious understandings that powerfully reinforce Christian tradition. The second chapter explores the link between Confirmation and conversion, and examines the implications of some of the cultural movements that simultaneously point to continuity and change in contemporary society. The third chapter offers a grounded ecclesiological reading of Eucharistic practice, which draws on historical insights to suggest new ways of approaching mission and ministry, and our understanding of ecclesiology.

Chapter 1
Baptism: Belief, Practice and Culture

Introduction

Strictly speaking, the vast majority of theology should be the study of the implicit rather than the explicit. For it is in the life of congregations and denominations that the gospel is discerned, interpreted and lived. Theology, for the most part, 'happens' in discipleship; it is not 'read' in textbooks. For example, reading the treatises of Martin Luther King Jr. can only form a small part of the process of assessing his contribution to theology and society. It is really only in hearing and experiencing his radio or TV broadcasts that one begins to get a sense of how his theology performed; how it moved and motivated his followers. The style of presentation matters at least as much as the substance of the message: the sensate and persuasive timbre of the rhetoric conveyed in the performance is itself theological material. Likewise, the key to understanding the theology of churches – their declared theological priorities – can never be a matter of mere textual analysis. Such an approach would miss the fact that 'church' is an interpretation and performance of theology that takes on a life of its own.

Churches seldom need to make formal or explicit theological statements in their public self-disclosure. They prefer to *imply* their identity and authority; power flows from the implicit more than the explicit. Even the most cursory reading of advertisements at the back of a church newspaper for clerical posts confirms this. One advertisement may invite applications for the post of Rector: '… liturgical; vestments worn; Sunday Eucharist 10am, Rite A'. Such advertisements make no explicit mention of the theological outlook that a congregation will be hoping for; it is implied in the text with reference to the liturgical preferences that have been expressed. Another advertisement, in the same paper, may have an entirely different feel: 'wanted … energetic young pastor for vibrant new church; home groups; family services; youth work and other outreach'. Again, no obvious theological priorities are identified in the advertisement; but most applicants will understand the coded nature of the text, even without the word 'evangelical' needing to be mentioned.

A commonplace observation relating to theologians is that most of those in the discipline who undertake or 'do' theology often discard valuable material (which is normally seen as ephemeral), and overly concentrate on texts and ideas that operate at a distance from the places where the majority of theological reflection and activity takes place. The husk is tossed away, and only the kernel analysed. In contrast, however, one might observe that the primary materials of theology are often not so much the formal statements of ecclesial bodies, but rather their operant practices, beliefs and interpretations. Attention to these reveals the deeper theological identity of churches and denominations, and also points towards theology re-imagining itself as a dynamically dialogical discipline.

To understand the use of the term 'implicit theology' more, it may also be helpful to have some acquaintance with the etymological roots of the word 'implicit', which is bound up in the idea of entanglement, of being entwined, and in the overlapping of involvement; together with the idea that those statements or concepts which have authority are often not plainly expressed. In other words, the authority of ideas, concepts or valued behaviour is implied without being questioned; implicit theology is, therefore, that which is deduced from operant religious practice (which would include a variety of expressions of faith and belief) rather than formal religious propositions. Its authority rests upon the fact that it does not need to make itself explicit.

One could identify dozens of examples of implicit theology that guide and direct ecclesiology in ways that are deeper than the formal propositions of explicit theology. Typically, this means theologians having the courage to begin with the miscibility and contingencies of 'story knowledge' rather than with formal theological propositions. Don Cupitt, in an influential essay (1992) has suggested theology has too often aligned itself with philosophy and the dominant power of non-narrative reasoning. In so doing, argues Cupitt, theology has concealed its origins in story and drama, and has correspondingly evolved into something like Platonism with a biblical vocabulary. In contrast, a concentration on implicit theology returns theology to the contexts, experiences and stories from which theological reflection emerges. Moreover, it is in paying attention to spiritual and ecclesial stories that theology begins to rediscover its primary material for study and reflection.

Implicit theology, then, and not unlike 'implicit religion' (a term coined by Edward Bailey, 1997),[1] understands that much of what is said and expressed in the name of God and the name of the church is a mixture of official and formal religion, together with operant and folk religion. Moreover, it is only in paying attention to local customs and linguistic accents that we can even begin to understand how God is *particularly* incarnate for this community or that congregation. Typically, one might say that implicit theology and implicit religion come together in the world of ritual, and most especially those rites of passage offered by the church.

It is here that the practical theologian will encounter individuals and communities 'working out their own (version of) salvation' (Philippians 2: 12). Something for which Don Browning calls the church and theology to account when he writes that:

> The theologian does not stand before God, Scripture and the historic witness of the church like an empty slate or Lockean *tabula rasa* ready to be determined, filled up, and then plugged into a concrete practical situation. A more accurate

---

[1]   See also Towler (1974).

description goes like this. We come to the theological task with questions shaped by the secular and religious practices in which we are implicated – sometimes uncomfortably. These practices are meaningful or theory-laden. (Browning, 1991, p. 2)

Thus, theologians and ministers eventually learn that they cannot rely on theological blueprints to determine how congregations could or should be in contemporary culture. In this respect, theology needs to work with fields such as congregational studies, by helping the church to become exegetes of texts, congregations and the local culture of a given context.[2] And, as Yust reminds us, this requires engagement with 'several social science disciplines ... [so that they can] describe congregational life in its thickness'. (2002, p. 241) This particular epiphany seems to lead us to agree with Roberts, who argues that theology itself, and most especially practical theology, is 'a practical process of discerning God's will ... a community activity requiring conversation and interaction' (Roberts, 2002, p. 184).

Interestingly, there are plenty of signs of such conversation and interaction in the praxis of the churches. The *Alpha Courses*, for example, which have become a global 'brand' of Christian initiation through the energy and creativity of Nicky Gumbel, have taken a decided therapeutic and relational turn considering its evangelical roots. Gone is the 'get up out of your seat and come to the front' style of crusading popularized by Billy Graham in large stadiums throughout the world for almost a century. Gumbel has replaced the big ritual of the old-fashioned revivalist rally with something more intimate, homely and personal. Here, the process of initiation has become modular, progressive and consumerist; a chance to 'sample' Christianity, then buy. Thus, we might say that the (implicit) theology of *Alpha* is primarily expressed in its style, not its substance.

These remarks, I should add, should not be read as a criticism of *Alpha*. They are, rather, an attempt to show how the practice of initiation remains stubbornly intra-related to social and cultural values. Moreover, those cultural values, whether expressed in social realms or in the informal and operant practices of the church, tend to speak of an implicit theology that requires a deeper kind of attention and interpretation from theologians if one is to understand how the church is engaging with the world. As I have suggested, such an understanding needs to conceive of theology as a mode of cultural conversation; speaking, listening, interpreting and belonging within the world, even as it seeks to be an agent of its transformation by virtue of being 'other-worldly'. Or, perhaps like anthropology, some kinds of theology actually *require* fieldwork, immersion and observation – or 'deep hanging out', in a memorable phrase coined by Clifford Geertz – if the underlying theological and ecclesiological composition of a church, congregation or movement is to be revealed and analysed.

---

[2]   For further discussion, see Percy (2005).

These opening three chapters model this 'deep hanging out', as the theology implicit in the particularities of people's changing attitudes to the sacraments is allowed to emerge through immersion in the detail. Chapter 1 reflects on what attention to implicit theology can teach us about changing understandings of baptism. Chapters 2 and 3 focus on Confirmation, and the Eucharist respectively.

Looking at Baptism

Looking at photographs, the literary critic Roland Barthes made a distinction between what he called the *Studium* and *Punctum*. The *Studium* is the photograph's overt agenda, which might include a view, the person, an event or a drama. This will be the reason why the photograph was taken: to catch an event and preserve it for others to see. But photography cannot control all the images it captures; the eye of the camera is indiscriminate, and may include things in the detail that the photographer never intended to capture in the final image. Quite often, something strange or unfamiliar will slip in, disturbing the *Studium*. Whatever it may be, it is often something that the photographer was not looking to include, but then becomes part of the focus of the viewer; it can become a transfixing point. Often the *Punctum* of a photograph can convey a message, which, if read and interpreted, gives a completely different slant to the *Studium*.[3]

One of my slightly stranger pastimes is reading old parish magazines. By old, I mean those dating from more than 50 years ago, since they often have revealing things to tell us about the ordinariness of parish life and the praxis of ministry, offering some kind of window into how Christianity, theology and contemporary culture were woven together in a bygone era. In the last parish in which I served as honorary curate, I would regularly read and re-read the parish letters sent out by previous incumbents, together with their notices of events and services in the parish. One could, for example, read the letters of Oliver Tomkins, who served as Vicar of Millhouses in Sheffield during the Blitz. Tomkins would write cheery letters to his parishioners, extolling the virtues of thrift and charity against a background of food rationing. The letters would often provide morale-boosting calls to the parish as a whole, urging them to be resilient and faithful in the midst of their hardships. These hardships would include the bombing of Sheffield, and the need to share their beloved building with the Methodists, who had lost the use of their building during the Blitz.

But in these magazines it was often the *Punctum* that caught my eye more than the *Studium*, and most especially when it came to notices about baptism. For here, Tomkins urged his parishioners to turn up promptly for baptism at two o'clock on Sunday afternoons, adding that a number of people are in the habit of turning up at 2:30 p.m., thereby missing the service entirely, and causing him to repeat it. In other words, the standard practice for the offering of baptism in the early 1940s

---

[3]   See Barthes (1977).

made the rite available outside of a normal church service, with the baptism service itself probably not lasting much more than 20 minutes. One can only presume that some parishioners were turning up a little later – possibly slightly the worse for wear after a good lunch – and were still hoping to have their child christened, even though they were half an hour late. Tomkins' notices to his parish clearly suggest that his parishioners were very much used to baptism on demand. Indeed, the rite is regularly referred to as a Christening, and as such, enjoyed considerable popularity just over half a century ago.

If one compares the practice of Tomkins to that of today's parish priests, one sees some considerable differences. First, the term 'Christening' is almost never used by the clergy, who uniformly prefer the term 'baptism'. Second, baptisms generally take place in the context of a normal act of worship on a Sunday morning. Third, there is little sense in which today's clergy would simply allow baptism parties to turn up with relatively little preparation, and allow the child to be baptised virtually on demand. Fourth, there can be no question that Tomkins baptised many more children with his 'open' policy, than have any of his successors with their more restricted policies.

There are doubtless many reasons why the numbers of children being baptised in England over the last 50 years have dwindled. The figures are in some ways startling. Even in the mid-twentieth century, more than half the population of England had been baptised by the established church. In 1994 the figure is 249 per 1000 live births. By 1997 the figure has dropped to 223 per 1000. The latest figures for 2002 show 181 per 1000. In less than a century, the Church of England has slipped from baptising more than 50 per cent of live births to less than one in five.[4] Some sociologists, such as David Martin, have pointed to too much liturgical renewal as being a factor, such that the rite of passage has become too distant from ordinary non-churchgoing culture. Others have suggested that secularization itself has removed the need for individuals to register the significance of birth (and the transformation or renewal of generational patterns) with institutional religion. Others have argued that a stricter baptism policy – insisting that applicants jump through more 'theological hoops' – has alienated the public at large.

There is some merit in all these theories, but I would suggest that the factor that is most worthy of attention is the relationship between socio-cultural expectations around birth, and the self understanding of the church in relation to baptism. Put another way, we might say that churches need to pay much greater attention to 'the sacred canopy' (a phrase coined by Peter Berger) – the totality of human awareness of the transcendent, especially in the experiences of birth, chance and decay, and death. In such an understanding, folk religion or common spirituality becomes as important as official, formal or denominational religion. Berger's thinking closely follows Thomas Luckmann's notion of 'invisible religion' – a term that was used positively to describe whatever falls outside the scope of organized religion.[5]

---

[4]   Source: *Church of England Year Book*, London, CHP, 1994, 1997 and 2005.
[5]   See Berger (1973) and Luckmann (1967).

It is not my place here to argue with Berger's or Luckmann's social theories. However, their work provides part of the foundation which underpins this chapter, namely an understanding that ideas about the significance and practice of baptism need to be studied not only from the perspective of theology and the formal position of the churches, but also from the vantage point provided by theorists of contemporary culture, who have a broader understanding of the purposes of ritual within society. To that end, I want to proceed by outlining a basic hypothesis that is concerned with 'implicit theology' – this will take up the first part of the chapter, with the second part outlining why attention to this area (focused on baptism) is important for the field of theology and the practice of the churches.

Implicit Theology and Baptism

With one or two rare exceptions, the place and significance of implicit theology or implicit religion in the life of communities and congregations has been better understood by sociologists than by theologians.[6] In David Clark's prescient study of a North East English fishing community (Staithes), he shows how the liminal qualities of the un-baptised infant are a matter of concern for all. He notes how baptism has been traditionally seen as a bridging point: it is a ritual that mediates between original sin and welcoming the child into the family of the church. It contains the idea of movement: from one social realm to another; from sin to forgiveness; and from being an outsider to being a member. Baptism brings to an end the liminal state of the child, who hovers between two worlds. The ritual brings resolution and aggregation, not only in theological terms, but also at the level of community and generational understandings, together with those ideas and sentiments that may proceed from folk religion (Clark, 1982, pp. 116ff).

Clark, drawing on the work of earlier sociologists, notes how people are often usually muddled and unclear about their reasons for having their children baptised. Invariably, individuals and communities have very strong feelings about the death and burial of un-baptised children, which largely rests on the ambivalence about the child entering a social world, and yet never becoming part of it. In other words, without their liminal state being resolved, they remain in an in-between state; a kind of social and theological limbo. This, Clark points out, accounts for why children in the earlier part of the twentieth century were often baptised at a very young age – often before they were two months old – in case illness lead to premature death. From the perspective of the parents and the community, it was desirable to make the infant belong to the world as soon as possible. Making them a member of the church – in a public and yet ambivalent way – could partially or mostly achieve this.

---

[6]   Amongst the exceptions within the English Anglican tradition, recent writers to single out are Wesley Carr, Paul Avis and Christopher Moody.

In Clark's fieldwork-based study, he suggests that baptism was often seen in a pragmatic and instrumental light. Baptisms were frequently carried out in the home – especially amongst those of Chapel-going families that felt removed from the stiffness and class-based austerity of the Anglican church. (Or at least this is how it was perceived.) The fact that baptising at home has not always been an unusual practice amongst Anglicans can be seen from the *Diaries of Parson Woodforde*. Woodforde not only baptised on home visits, but also did so in his own Rectory parlour (using a punch bowl), arguing that it was warmer and more intimate than his church. The baptism, by being conducted in the home, became an intimate ritual that had little ritual elaboration, but was nonetheless seen as a rite that protected the child in the afterlife in the event of dying in infancy. Correspondingly, the churching, or purification of women, took place when the new mother first went to church after the birth: this was the resolution of her liminality after a period of confinement – her re-emergence as a new social being, which also had social and cultural resonances as much as they might have been theological.[7]

For many in contemporary Western culture, underwritten as it is by all kinds of assumptions about the power and competence of medicine, churching women can either look quaint, or perhaps plain superstitious. But its function in ancient times (e.g., as 'purification' – see Luke 2: 22ff) was both ritualistic and medical. The 40-day period between birth and 'purification' is a biological and religious time-span; biological, since this is approximately the time it takes for the new mother's body to readjust after birth; religious, because of the connotations of passing through times of trial – also linked to the number 40. But in modern liturgies, churching or 'purification' has been misunderstood, and reconstituted as 'thanksgiving for the birth of the child'. Actually, the original rite celebrates the safe-keeping of the mother and her social re-aggregation. The rite carries and conveys more implicit theology than immediately meets the eye.

In both churching and baptism, the liminality of the mother and child is ended by a rite of passage. However, as Clark points out, (Clark, 1982, p. 123) the close of the twentieth century saw the virtual end of churching, and movement of baptism from the home to the Chapel, with a consequential increase in ritual activity. That said, aspects of folk religion persisted even in the twentieth century: gifts of salt (symbolizing preservation), an egg (symbolizing fertility) and a coin (symbolizing wealth) were still often brought to the new mother and baby, once they had returned from maternity hospital. The continuing practice of offering these gifts – almost certainly pre-Christian in origin, but now endowed with a meaning that has a Christian gloss – demonstrates a remarkable spiritual resilience.

Consider, for example, this ancient rhyme:

> The bairnie she swyl'd in linen so fine,
> In a gilded casket she laid it syne,

---

[7] For an interesting study of women's perspectives on churching, see King (2005).

> Mickle saut and light she laid therein,
> Cause yet in God's house it had'na been.

Here, salt and light are laid in the cradle to protect the infant prior to baptism. In this Scottish ballad, evil is kept at bay, because the Devil is thought to hate salt and light. Such superstitions led to a variety of practices in the medieval church, including children who had died before they could be baptised being smeared with salt on the neck, as a sign that they were indeed *intended* for christening. Even though the un-baptised could not be buried in consecrated ground, this marking signified that the parents meant the child to belong to God. Such practices continued through to the Reformation in England: 'it was uncrisned, seeming out of doubt, for salt was bound to its neck in a linen clout'.[8]

Other informal practices can also be observed in relation to birth. Clark again points out how folk customs persist – often stubbornly – in the face of the medicalization of birth. Crossing a child's palm with silver (a coin – for wealth), touching the forehead (for luck – but also an act of blessing) and 'wetting the baby's head' (toasting the child – but also a nod towards baptism) remain commonplace. The wrapping of the baby in a family shawl – often a valuable heirloom passed down from mother to daughter – establishes a pattern of generational continuity and a sign of God's continual bestowal of favour and fertility. The exchange of gifts establishes social hierarchies; the giver has seniority and status, and the receiver is dependent. The giving of silver plates, knives, forks, spoons and napkin rings has a resonance that is suggestive of longevity, and eventually taking one's place in the community. The practice of not welcoming an un-baptised baby into one's house also suggests a complex mixture of superstition and theologically-resourced ideas (i.e., original sin, etc); and churching – that whatever is 'unclean' in childbirth or conception – is resolved through ritual.

The baptism ritual then, taken as a whole, is more than the sum of the parts provided by the church or minister. The selection of godparents and sponsors can represent a realignment of families, their status and levels of responsibility. The gifts and their donors establish how the child is to be supported, or how this is to be symbolized. Who carries and formally names the child in a baptism ceremony also carries intimate social weight which is often invisible to the minister. The cutting of a Christening cake and the making of a wish (i.e., hope or luck for the future) point to a network of extended and informal rituals that last for a few or several months, which in turn have spiritual or 'folk religious' resonance. Granted, one may say that these informal practices have little to do with the church. But another way of regarding them is to see them as being related closely to the baptism, with the Christian ritual itself as the focal point in which the informal spiritual (or superstitious) practices actually find their proper place.

---

[8]   See the *History of the Family of Stanley*, which dates from the early part of the sixteenth century.

An understanding of implicit theology allows us to see that each of the gestures surrounding a birth has some kind of intention that points towards some higher spiritual, theological or social meaning. The actual gesture may not carry that meaning in any perfected manner, or in a way that has an obvious explicit theological purpose or indication. But that is not the point. The informal rituals and gestures are subtle, nuanced and insinuating modes of behaviour that complement the practice of baptism. Or, put another way, and to return to the analogy deployed at the beginning of this chapter, we can now see that what appear to be the distracting aspects surrounding baptism are in fact part and parcel of the extended nature of the ritual. The *Punctum*, which for many ministers, apparently take the focus away from the main *Studium* of baptism can be re-read as vital and welcome elements within the ritual. In turn, this allows the ritual of baptism to be re-narrated as a complex set of rituals with overlapping intentions and meanings, in which the provision of the church is, granted, the focal point – but by no means the only element.

Baptismal Performance: Congregational and Ministerial Practice

Studying congregations can appear to be, at one level, a pointless task. Is it not obvious how they are constituted, and what they believe? On the one hand, the adherence to creeds and religious articles can be taken for granted. But then again, many will relate to these, without necessarily fully understanding them or even being in agreement with them. Superficially, it can appear that some congregations talk about God all the time, whilst others never. An outspoken Australian, Caroline Miley, gives a damming description of what constitutes Anglican polity at congregational levels:

> A considerable source of surprise for newcomers to the Church is that Christians do not like talking about Christianity. Not only do they not talk about it willingly and enthusiastically but they have a tendency to become alarmed or resentful if the topic is openly addressed or pursued. This applies to both clergy and laity. This is very odd as in every other interest-based organisation, discussion of the interest is universal, even mandatory. Hang-gliding clubs are full of people who discuss hang-gliding. Rotarians discuss rotary; football fans bore others to death with discussion of their fancy. Christians, however, do not discuss Christianity. To do so after church on Sunday morning is to be made aware that one has committed a frightful faux pas. (Miley, 2002, p. 7)[9]

But this 'analysis' ignores three vital things. First, the deeply coded ways in which people talk and act about God (e.g., 'I'll be thinking of you this week' means 'prayer'; or 'I'll drop by with some scones' means a 'bereavement visit') are not

---

[9]   Caroline Miley (2002) and Kate Fox (2004).

forms of spiritual evasion, but of subtle and intimate religious communication. Second, that religious language is carried in the emotion, timbre and cadence of worship – which for Anglicans is often cool, reflective and apparently detached (when compared to the 'warmer' and more intimate language of, say, charismatics). Third, that deeply coded language is not a strategy for avoiding explicit theological language; rather, it carries and conveys a range of rich *implicit* theological concepts that engage people at a variety of missiological and ecclesiological levels, including intellectually and relationally.

Commenting on this dynamic, Wade Clark Roof notes in *Community and Commitment* (1978/1985), that beliefs of churches cannot be construed entirely in terms of their credal statements:

> Theological doctrines are always filtered through people's social and cultural experiences. What emerges in a given situation is 'operant religion' will differ considerably from the 'formal religion' of the historic creeds, and more concern with the former is essential to understanding how belief systems function in people's daily lives. (Roof, 1978/1985, pp. 178–9)

In this case, 'Operant Religion' is a term that approximates to the use of the expression 'vernacular religion', 'common spirituality' or even 'implicit religion'. Studying congregations, of course, is something that is not taught at theological college. The roots of this absence lie in a profound deficiency in the notion of theological education, and in an impoverished understanding of theology – of how God acts in the world. Disciplines such as practical theology can help the churches here, by rescuing the questions, definitions and shape of theology from the world of the idealized and returning it to the concrete. James Hopewell draws our attention to the agenda, noting how the theological enterprise is something richer and more empathetic than many presume:

> To ponder seriously the finite culture of one's own church, given the promise of God's redemptive presence within it, opens up a vast hermeneutical undertaking. The congregation recedes as primarily a structure to be altered and emerges as a structure of social communication within which God's work in some ways already occurs. The hermeneutical task is not merely the mining of biblical revelation in ways meaningful to individuals. It is more basically the tuning of the complex discourse of a congregation so that the gospel sounds within the message of its many voices. (Hopewell, 1987, p. 197)

Congregational studies can be especially important when considering baptismal practice. For here one can see that such practices are rarely driven by explicit theology or by commonly owned (let alone understood) creedal formulae. For example, in one church there may be considerable suspicion about 'open' baptism policies. The practice of the church will be restrictive, making sure that all who apply for baptism are subjected to appropriate interviews and courses that establish a level of understanding about what the nature of the rite is, and what it confers. Others will be more 'open', but their policy will simply speak (implicitly) of a deeper form of theological praxis. Three brief caricatures can help us gain some further purchase on this.

The first of these posits that a 'low' ecclesial view of baptism sees the rite in somewhat functional terms: this is a movement to God initiated by the person; a confession with a ritual. Typically, congregations and ministers practising like this will reserve baptism for adults: 'God ain't gonna bless til' you does confess.' The rite is, in other words, for believers: faith must be articulated and sins confessed. Baptism is the person's decision and initiation into faith. Behind this praxis, one can see that there is a degree of implicit theology that is normally hidden from the casual observer: God is in people, not in places or 'things' – so a plain building will do for church. Salvation is known in the heart and mind, and invariably individualistic. There may be no need for creeds, as they're not in the Bible. There may be no liturgy or obvious historic 'tradition': the church will normally be led by a Pastor.

The second would suggest that a 'medium' view of baptism identifies the rite as conferring membership of the Church; correspondingly, others can confess on behalf of the child. Baptism, in this sense, is not unlike a form of enrollment. In turn, this places a greater stress on the words and water used in the rite, since these materials become pivotal points of instrumentality through which God meets the child and his or her sponsors, and they meet God. The rite therefore acquires a sacramental and confessional dimension, whereby baptism is seen as a 'sign' of salvation within the church. In terms of implicit theology, the 'medium' view is common to established Protestant churches and Anglicans. The *via media* between symbol and action, words and water, is intended to connote the covenantal dimension of sacraments. God meets us, speaks to us and welcomes us long before we can address God. Baptism is therefore both a response to God's invitation as well as a form of initiation. In such churches, God may be deemed to be 'present' there, where buildings are held to reflect divine glory in spatial structure. The church is therefore a place where you find God in the totality of worship, which will invariably be led by a Minister.

The third position we term to be 'high', whereby baptism is joining the communion of saints. Here, words are important; but it is the water that is holy, taking on a sacramental-salvific character. Baptism makes the child a child of God, redeeming it from the stain of original sin. The 'high' view identifies God's availability in sacramental material. Just as words are vehicles of grace (the Bible), so can water be an instrument of salvation. Correspondingly, the implicit theological emphasis will rest on what God is doing through material to a person: perhaps through bread, wine, or water. Although stress is placed on the condition of the recipient, the high view allows the inarticulate and dumb to receive. God's presence is seen as being available distinctively in sacramental material, holy writ and places (inc. shrines). God's power comes through divinely-instituted Holy Orders, which are imbued in both people and material. Typically, such churches pay attention to aesthetics, with beauty, art and liturgy resonating with the mystical body of Christ, which itself mirrors the worship of the saints in heaven, all of which is normally orchestrated through and by a Priest.

Granted, these baptismal perspectives are caricatures. But each of them corresponds, broadly, to commonly perceived practices which are themselves detectable in a range of implicit and explicit theological expressions. One can also see how each position represents a nascent theory about the identity of the church, and how membership or inclusion is conferred. Noting this dynamic, Stark and Bainbridge use sociological exchange theory to construct their models of church. They balance the *tension* a group desires or tolerates with the *rewards* (sometimes called *compensators*, if rewards cannot be actualized) its members seek. Tension signifies the relationship with the world and the internal structure of the group. Rewards are the spiritual benefits of belonging. The degree of 'exchange' or the 'success' of the congregation is determined, to an extent, by the amount of power that the congregation appears to have, or can call upon, and can exercise. The more powerful a congregation is, the greater the (apparent) rewards on offer.[10]

For example, a 'successful' church may offer a ministry principally concerned with individual salvation. In a 'high-tension' relationship with the world, it assumes sectarian and communitarian properties, and is likely to eschew 'open' baptismal policies. However, a neighbouring congregation with fewer members may well offer a more 'open' baptismal policy, not only for theological reasons, but also because it neither gains nor loses by offering lower thresholds of entry for membership. Put another way, whereas one church can offer a tightly defined type of membership, another may seek a looser form of connectedness that is expressed both in its polity and its baptismal praxis. Both models are valid attempts to construct a theological conversation with the world, which in turn will lead to the conferring of membership. Both models also tend to imply their theological position through praxis, rather than through explicitly stated formulae. Given this, we now turn to considering baptismal practice and theology as a form of modelling cultural conversation.

Theology as Cultural Conversation

One of the most pressing challenges faced by theology and the churches is how to engage with contemporary culture. For many, engagement, it seems, is a contested and risky affair. Some theological and ecclesiological traditions feel so threatened by the prospect of being overwhelmed or consumed by the task of engagement that they retreat before they have advanced; standing apart from key issues and debates in culture is seen to be the only way of protecting the integrity and identity of the Christian tradition. Others prefer a different strategy, namely one of deep

---

[10]   See Stark and Bainbridge (1987).

engagement; but in so doing, can find themselves so transformed that they become alienated from their roots.

There is no dispute that churchgoing has been in decline in most Western countries since the 1960s. Although it is currently the fashion to talk about European exceptionalism here, in truth, it is the USA that is unusual, since declines in churchgoing can be tracked in Australia, New Zealand and many other places. But as we know, and as sociologists reminds us, the statistics we have cannot be read 'simply'; the complex data demands an equally complex interpretation, and if we are to hold our nerve as a church within contemporary culture, it is vital that we have robust cultural understandings of our current situation. Robin Gill suggests that there are four possible theories of churchgoing.[11]

First, there are *secularization* theories – perhaps especially the kinds espoused by Steve Bruce, Callum Brown, the early work of Peter Berger and the offerings of the late Bryan Wilson. However, many sociologists have demonstrated, both from a theoretical and empirical perspective, that crude or blunt secularization theories are inadequate in their interpretation of churchgoing habits.

Second, there are *persistence* theories – those offered by Rodney Stark, David Martin and myself. Here, the argument runs that although there is detachment from the duties and formal obligations of religion, it nonetheless persists as part of public life. Correspondingly, scholars such as Jose Casanova show that religion can both decline and persist at the same time; where religion loses influence in the intensive and specific spheres of public life, it often makes up the loss in extensive attraction: and this movement can flow the other way too.

Third, and perhaps developing theories one and two, there are *separation* theories – perhaps best represented by Grace Davie, Peter Berger's more recent work, but with Anthony Giddens and Reginald Bibby also contributing. Here the key point to acknowledge is the gap that has opened up between believing and belonging, the latter having declined whilst the former mutates and, at the very least, holds its own.

Fourth, and finally, Gill suggests that there is a *cultural* theory to be explored. Here Gill suggests that churches, as moral communities, do hold and foster distinctive beliefs and values that in turn sustain individual and community identity. Correspondingly, a decline in belonging will, inevitably, lead to a decline in beliefs. If belonging collapses, the community and authority that sustains the beliefs cannot continue in the same way. The implications for the future of baptismal practice, and for theology as a mode of practice, are indeed profound.

During the last 50 years, and since Niebuhr's ground-breaking *Christ and Culture* (1951), a significant number of theologians have attempted theological engagements with 'culture'. Broadly speaking, there have been two major modes of engagement in relation to contemporary culture, which have to some extent bifurcated. The first tradition broadly conceives of the engagement as a form of interlocking combative encounter with contemporary culture. The second

---

[11]   Cf. Gill (1999).

broadly sees it as a form of intra-related binding, covenant or commitment. Both lead to the formation of their own distinctive cultures (e.g., characteristic missiological and ecclesiological outlooks), which increasingly do not know how to talk to one other. Whilst the adoption of both strategies delivers a certain degree of poise and reflexivity, their inability to relate to one another leads to an impoverished form of public theology. In effect, both traditions could be said to somewhat culturally dyslexic (the etymology of the word lies in a conflation, from the Greek *lexis*, 'to speak', and the Latin, *legere* 'to read'). Thus, and of culture, it could be said that modern theologians and the churches tend neither to speak properly nor read well.

Niebuhr suggests that there are five theological responses to the complexity of a Christian faith immersed in culture. The first type stresses the opposition between Christ and culture; this is the Christ *against* culture. The second type is diametrically opposed to the first: 'there is a fundamental *agreement* between Christ and culture'. This is the Christ who is *of* or *for* culture. These two basic types represent the two primary faces of engagement that can be identified in the life of the church, and the remaining three types all flow from these two primary typologies. However, there are also four distinct types of religion-culture relationships that can be identified: religion is part of culture; culture is part of religion; culture may be 'religious'; and religion and culture can undertake a variety of serious academic dialogues.

Given the issue of baptism – its social, cultural and religious ambiguity, and following Stark and Bainbridge – we can see why and how the practice of baptism as a form of negotiated ritual between church and world becomes an acute and focal issue for churches. Rather as Troeltsch thought, the bearers of the Christian tradition long to give something to the world, but invariably do not know how. On the one hand, Christians can provide symbolic legitimation for the prevailing society and culture, thereby generating the 'church type' of interaction that theologians such as Barth were so critical of. On the other hand, there can be protest against the prevailing powers and an attempt to set up a counter-society, thereby generating the 'sect type' response that Tillich was so critical of.

So to return to Troeltsch for a moment, baptism is not administered adequately by either the 'church type' or 'sect type' orientation, since the controlling ideology normally restricts the mode and tenor of cultural engagement. Yet if the ministry of the church is to reflect God's self-gift in Jesus Christ, then there will be an element of praxis in the pastoral which will empathetically *shape* the gift that is defined and delimited by the ideological. Baptism (or in more vernacular lingua, 'Christening') will at once be an ambiguous sacrament of welcome at the very *borders* of the church even as it proceeds from its *centre* and speaks of a specific intensity of faith. Thus, rightly conceived, the sacrament invites a church-world 'negotiation' (i.e., between 'culture' and 'religion', or 'orthodoxy' and 'vernacular religion') as a sign of God's grace and inclusivity, but without penalizing the borders of its necessary exclusivity. As one cultural commentator notes:

religion is not effective because it is otherworldly, but because it incarnates this otherworldliness in a practical form of life … a link between absolute values and daily life. (Eagleton, 2000, p. 21)

Such a view might lead us to explore the identity of baptismal culture as a hybrid or relational affair, and to develop a theology and transforming praxis that closely corresponds to that reality, yet without actually mirroring it. Because Christian identity itself is relational, it hinges both on cultural engagement and being open to direction from the free grace of God. This allows us to relate the 'core' values of religious belief to society/culture in a more reflexive manner, which in turn creates new possibilities for theology as a public discourse. Drawing inspiration from writers such as David Tracy, *conversation* can therefore be commended as a major mode of theological engagement. Equally, *collage* can be considered as an analogical and methodological description for how theology is to be constructed in relation to culture – particularly contested cultural practices such as Christening. In so doing, theology is able to attend to whole areas of human experience and understanding that are normally neglected by faith communities. But such a move requires a risk, namely of theology and the churches ceasing to operate as an autonomous discipline ('private grammar of faith'), and to take its place as a distinctive mode of discourse that seeks to operate within a wider nexus of cultural and spiritual contexts.

Conclusion

These observations take us back to some of the points made earlier in this chapter. Churches in Western Europe have, generally speaking, experienced or begun to experience a sharp decline in the numbers of families requesting baptism over the last 50 years. Undoubtedly, part of the reason for this can be located in the responses of the churches to secularization and cultural pluralism. This has led the churches to define the concept and practice of baptism more sharply, over and against those understandings which have persisted within contemporary culture. In some respects this is understandable, given the need for churches – like any other organization – to stand out as being distinctive within a more competitive and consumerist culture. However, in exercising more control over the rite of baptism – and therefore distancing it from established local customs, implicit theology and 'folk religion' – the rite has progressively shifted from being a public ritual offered by the church to being a more privatized ecclesial rite.

Paul Avis, commenting on the rite of baptism in relation to the phenomenon of 'common religion', notes how the rubrics of the *Book of Common Prayer* service for the public baptism of infants urges the clergy and the parents of children not to defer baptism beyond the fifth Sunday after the birth (Avis, 2003, p. 121). Similarly, Richard Hooker warns the clergy against impeding the baptism of infants (Hooker, 1845, vol. 2, p. 373 [Book V, ix. 7]). But the contemporary church, anxious as it is about membership and its meaning, has tended to be seduced by more restrictive baptismal practices. This is a pity, since when new, stricter rubrics are developed by congregations, they frequently fail to read the resonant cultural traditions surrounding birth and ritual that have already been present for many centuries. Carl Jung, writing to a Protestant pastor on infant baptism, states that

> Every event of our biological life has a numinous character: birth, puberty, marriage, illness ... this is a natural fact demanding recognition, a question waiting for an answer. It is a need that should be satisfied with a solemn act, characterising the numinous moment with a combination of words and gestures of an archetypal, symbolic nature. Rites give satisfaction to the collective and numinous aspects of the moment, beyond their purely personal significance ... to unite the present with the historical and mythological past.' (Jung, 1974, p. 208).[12]

Such an insight calls for churches and theologians to recognize the negotiated aspect of sacramental rites; as public rituals with cultural aspects as well as religious meanings.[13] It also suggests that imaginative and reflexive pastoral practice – that deeply reads cultural forms and also understands Christian tradition – is an important key in the 'performance of doctrine'. This is not a state of being that is wholly concerned with establishing the criteria for membership of congregations, but that instead understands that rituals function in an ambivalent hinterland, which brings focus to the collation of perceptions of the numinous that surround the mystery of creation and birth. In turn, this stance perceives that infant baptism is not about 'making' members; it is about drawing near, engaging, affirming and blessing, thereby initiating a process of incorporation, which is itself Christian *initiation*. The ritual, offered openly, is simply a reification of God's complete love and grace. On a purely personal note, this is why I favour an 'open' baptism policy, even to the extent of conducting the majority of rites 'privately' [i.e., not within the context of a normal church service]. [14]

   In this kind of understanding of the practice of baptism, theology itself then begins to emerge as a form of empathetic conversation with contemporary culture, rather than a mode of expression that merely resists it, or perhaps seeks to impose its own different definition upon the world. It is from this kind of position that one can begin to see how much of the nascent cultural practice surrounding birth can be read more generously and creatively. Indeed, such local cultural practices suggest that the timbre, cadences and resonances that are prompted by birth, and stirred in the world by the rumour of God and the sense of the numinous, can be appropriately interpreted as a valid form of 'implicit theology'. If such spiritual sentience can be met empathetically and creatively, churches might once again

---

12   See also Robert Avens (1977).
13   Cf. Avis (2003), p. 193.
14   On this, see Allen (2005) pp. 12–13.

encounter the prospect of the world drawing near at the time of birth. As Jesus said: 'Let the children come to me, and do not hinder them. For to such belongs the kingdom of heaven' (Matthew 19: 13).

Chapter 2

Confirmation and Conversion:
Continuity and Change

The joke goes like this. Three rural Anglican clergy meet up at a local inn for a drink. After a few beers, the conversation naturally enough turns to their respective churches. 'My main problem is bats', says one; 'they're in the belfry wreaking havoc, and I can't get rid of them.' 'Amazing', says the second – 'I have the same problem.' 'Me too' adds the third, 'they are a terrible nuisance.' All agree the bats have to go, and to meet again in one month's time and share solutions to their collective problem. A month later back at the inn, the three clergymen reconvene. The first reports that he used poison; the strategy was initially successful, but the bats soon returned, apparently able to spot the bait. The second had used an air rifle; but his aim had not been good, and the Archdeacon had complained of holes in the roof. The third announced complete success, much to the amazement of the others. 'How did you do it?', they asked. 'Easy', he replied. 'I went up to the ceiling with a bucket of water, baptised and confirmed them all, and I haven't seen them since.'

We know enough about Confirmation and Baptism Rolls within the Church of England during the last 100 years to recognize that the joke contains more than a grain of truth. Yet it is only a grain. The actual 'reading' of these figures is a complex business, as any sociologist knows. And what conclusions are deduced from such statistics can vary widely, usually in accordance with the underlying theological, ecclesiological or sociological presuppositions and interpretations that are brought to bear on the data. This is a commonsensical observation, to be sure; there are no such things as 'plain' statistics – all figures function within a broader narrative that tell a story.

Arguably, it is the job of the sociologist to not only have a good imagination to tell that story, but also to be realistic enough to makes sure that the narrative corresponds with a social reality that is true to its subject. This may sound simple enough, but in the Sociology of Religion, it is often very far from being so. The 'story' that statistics might tell about church decline or growth, or perhaps the rise and fall in the number of baptisms or confirmations, is a field often rich with conjecture, conclusion and counter-argument. The problem, simply stated, is that any reliability attributed to the data can often clash directly with the perceived ecclesial situation, religious imagination or doctrinal outlook. Sociology is an attempt at social realism; religion though, is about idealism. Let me explain a little more.

Some years ago, I chaired a Review of an Anglican Deanery; the area consisted of 18 parishes, a total of 180,000 parishioners, and a mixture of inner city, suburban, and rural-commuter contexts. Each Parish Priest was invited to comment on the attendance patterns of their church in recent times, electoral roll figures, and other ministerial aspects. The Review was not conducted with a view to making savings or cuts, but it was undertaken with a mind to look at areas where new deployment or redeployment might be considered. In order to obtain a long-term view on the parishes concerned, figures were secured from each parish church (but also from the Church of England Records Office, London) that looked at Easter and Christmas Communicants and Electoral Roll figures stretching back 50 years.

The returns from the clergy and the data from the Record Office produced a remarkable polarity. The clergy were characteristically upbeat about the prospects for their churches and the parish ministry; almost all described their situations in terms of 'growth' or 'potential'. The statistics on the other hand, plotted a virtually uniform decline in seasonal church attendance and 'belonging' (Electoral Roll). Which version of reality was true? The answer from this sociologist was neither and both. A more careful reading of the figures available showed that 'popular' piety had transferred its affection for an annual Eucharist from Easter to Christmas. Electoral Roll figures did show an average decline, but there were, in some cases, substantial reasons for this, such as the merging of parishes or the closure of churches. And although baptisms and confirmations were down in number, the quota of adult confirmees had risen sharply. Furthermore, the 'decline' plotted in the statistics was below average for the diocese, such that numbers could be deemed to be holding up relatively well.

The story the clergy offered was – as many things are in the Church of England – based on anecdote, not data or properly commissioned research. The clergy consulted, in telling a story of growth, were not engaging in disingenuous spin. However, the statistics did check, and in some cases critique the narratives offered, and showed a way forward that allowed congregations to look at their mission in a more considered light. The empirical work, hand in hand with the idealism, produced a good foundation for reviewing the present and implementing changes in the future (Percy, 1998).

Confirmation in Culture

The historical 'situation' of Confirmation is a complex affair. In Maria Levitt's *Nice When They're Young* (1996), the author examines the religious beliefs of young people in Cornwall. It is remarkable as a study, not least for its observation that Christianity hasn't so much failed as not been tried. It is almost 'fatal' to be religious in modern Britain (although being spiritual is another matter). Moreover, her work also provides a useful corrective to the stress on individual autonomy rather than communal affiliation. But this is Britain today, where confirmation rates are in single figures as a percentage of the population, and falling. In Denmark, confirmation rates run at around 80 per cent of the population. The disparity is due, in part, to the visibility of the rite of passage that has social resonance. In Denmark, the occasion still marks the passage from childhood to adulthood; something almost entirely eclipsed in Britain by the blurring of these boundaries and the consumerist power and autonomy of 'tweenagers'.

Partly for this reason, many British churches have begun experimenting with Communion before Confirmation, in an attempt to stem the flow of young people leaving before they reach their teens. As an experiment, it is as laudable as it is contentious. Indeed, it must be said that Roman Catholicism, in following this practice, has not found it to be the evangelistic panacea one might suppose. The joke about the three clergy and their problem with bats in the belfry neatly encapsulates this. Whatever churches do, it seems, people who are nurtured in faith will drift off in their pre and early teens. They may well see some of them again in their twenties, and a few more in their thirties. So, one question not to ask is, 'will such initiatives be more effective?' (it might be for a while); but rather, 'who gets to receive communion, and why?'

Confirmation is a neglected area of liturgics and theology. Barely a decent book has been written for more than a quarter of a century: the weight of scholarly literature was written between 1820 and 1950. As a Rite, it has had a chequered history. At its most basic, Confirmation is understood as 'the grace of the Holy Spirit conveyed in a new or fuller way to those who have already received it at baptism'. There appear to be New Testament and early church instances (Acts 8: 14–17, 19: 1–7, 1 Cor. 1: 20, etc) of people being sealed with the spirit in addition to being baptised. The early church fathers symbolized this with water, oil, anointing and ritual.

But by the time of the East-West schism, differences had emerged. In the East, baptism, confirmation and first communion are all done at the same service for an infant, on the basis that the child is now an initiate of the church. In the West, the practice developed of presenting candidates to bishops, as a sign of Episcopal unity and authority. However, reception of communion in either kind was quite rare, and Confirmations very rare, up until the seventeenth century. Elizabeth I was baptised and confirmed together when only three days old. It was not uncommon, in an age of occasional and erratic travel, for Bishops to proclaim a Confirmation from a town square, and then drive on. The Rite has never enjoyed universal acceptance. Aquinas thought it one of the seven sacraments. Others regarded it as indistinguishable from baptism. Others saw it as a rite that enabled a young person to fight evil in their own right.

Since the late Reformation period, there has been a tendency to link Confirmation to adulthood or a particular age. Since 1971, the RC practice has formally been to confirm as soon as possible after the seventh birthday. The BCP, in common with other Reformed traditions, requires a period of instruction. In modern times, theologians such as Lampe and Stone have argued that Confirmation cannot do anything that baptism hasn't already done. Others see Confirmation as a 'completion' of baptism – a view, I think, that is untenable.

The theological views have to be balanced with the practical and ecclesial ones. Christians, if they have any unity, find it located in baptism. George Herbert may be the wisest voice here, who took the view that Confirmation could take place as soon as a child was able to distinguish between ordinary and 'blessed' bread, and could recite the Lord's prayer. He estimated that a child could do this around the age of seven. In general, baptism is admission to the church, and therefore, in principal at least, to its treasures. However, Confirmation provides a valuable ecclesial and social opportunity. It affirms the unity and breadth of the church through the Bishop as President, and it also makes sense of a rite of passage (childhood to adulthood). That said, Confirmation need not be that rite, and first communion need not be tied to an age or another rite. Our views on this are likely to be conditioned by our theological evaluation of sacraments, especially baptism.

With these comments in mind, we now turn briefly to the work of David Martin in order to locate further insight and illumination for the reading of the cultural context of Confirmation. In appreciating David Martin's work, and the contribution it might make to this brief study of Confirmation, one is immediately faced with a problem. Whether it is Pentecostalism, Methodism or Anglicanism, Martin's work has often brought new insights to those communities, as much as his writing has illuminated other scholars. Undoubtedly there are personal reasons why this may be so. Martin is a scholar who is critically engaged with his subjects, but also deeply aware of their own reality and integrity. He is empathetic, kind, and almost generous to the material he works with, mindful that sociology is about people as much as anything else. Yet this does not subvert his skill as a reader and interpreter of the world in which he is immersed. Nor does it obscure the clarity and richness of his method.

Martin was still a Methodist when he wrote 'Interpreting the Figures' for Michael Perry's collection of essays entitled *Crisis for Confirmation* (1967). His fellow contributors included John Robinson, Don Cupitt and Stephen Verney, to name but a few. The book, naturally enough, had arisen out of the perceived crisis that might result from the marked drop in the number of confirmees within the Church of England. Whereas the number of confirmations at the turn of the century was considerable, running at almost 300,000 per year, the number by the late 1960s had dropped to a fraction of that (two thirds, to be precise). In 1999, at the turn of the Millennium, the Church of England confirmed 41,000 people (16,000 men and 25,000 women). Yet the baptised population of the nation (England) is still almost 50 per cent (about 25 million), with around 200,000 people per year being baptised – roughly a quarter of all babies born.

In the late 1960s, as in the late 1990s, these figures show that whilst the Church of England is hardly disappearing, it has nothing to be complacent about either. This was foreseen by many in the Church of England, and Michael Perry's book is one of only a number that called upon the faithful to reconsider their ministry and mission against a background of increasing secularization. Others in this festschrift will have addressed Martin's work on this, but it is perhaps worth noting that even in the late 60s, Martin knew that a decline in confirmation could not be read straight off into a secularization thesis. For example, Confirmation in Denmark still envelopes over 80 per cent of young people there on an annual basis, but no-one could say that Denmark was less secular than England. In Finland the Confirmation rate is 90 per cent; the same applies: As Perry notes, David Martin has commented that our present situation may, in places, be unexpected.

In terms of Confirmation, Martin divides his comments on the recorded decline in numbers into three areas: the demographic, the micro-institutional and the macro-institutional. For reasons that will become apparent, it is the third level that is the most interesting for assessing Martin, for it concerns his feeling and empathy for what he describes as the relation between the English Church and our society. It is in this section that one can begin to see an embryonic Anglicanism forming, in spite of the fact that the comments directed towards the Church of England are mostly captious. What begins to emerge is a kind of critically supportive socio-theology, in which a Methodist layman has obviously begun some kind of pilgrimage.

In examining the demographic context of confirmation, Martin notes that conclusions are far from self-evident. One the one hand, the confirmation figures seem to show that the Anglican church is dying 'millimetre by millimetre'. On the other hand, these figures must be read against other demographic trends in the twentieth century, such as migration, mortality and fertility rates. Furthermore – and here Martin directs a comment to the church – 'the position is even further complicated by those … priests [who] insist on more stringent criteria for both confirmation and baptism and then come [to us] asking why the figures are diminishing' (Martin, 1967, p. 110). His conclusion is that the statistics the Church has are only part of the picture; more study is needed, but it has not been mooted.

At the micro-institutional level, Martin introduces a range of approaches that can help churches begin to 'read' the trends they think they experience. He speaks of the Church of England as an agent of 'occasional conformity', in which people unite at birth, death, marriage and confirmation. The paradox of Confirmation, as he notes, is that 'the process of becoming an adult is roughly collateral with the cessation of religious practice' (Martin, 1967, p. 111), such that Confirmation, even where it is normal, has its meaning inverted, and becomes, in effect, 'the Leaving Certificate'. Martin's response to this is to appeal for more research. For example, one might do some comparative work on youth groups, their genesis and development, and focus on their style of recruitment and approach to faith. This work could lead to reflection on the formal provision of Confirmation. Another approach might be to test causality or efficiency in catachetical methods, which might suggest a 'right' age to confirm. Having said that, Martin is sceptical about the value of this work, believing that it requires too many qualifiers and caveats: 'the Ark of Salvation cannot be run the principles of a motor-works' (Martin, 1967, p. 113).

That final comment in this section is something of an irony for a sociologist. On the one hand, Martin has often stood for preserving the identity of the church, championing for example, the use of the *Book of Common Prayer*. On the other hand, he advocates a rigour in socio-ecclesial research (presumably leading to change) that would rock the very pillars of the church. The resolving of this paradox is not easy or obvious, but it lies in Martin's deep commitment to the value of an innate English spirituality, and a church that can (partly) give this individual, local, national, social and theological shape and colour. Thus, he writes, to my mind amusingly, that 'to me personally the English Church consists of some beautiful sixteenth and seventeenth century bottles cracked by some rather doubtful Evangelical and Catholic wine' (Martin, 1967, p. 115). The point is obvious: the wings of or movements within a church should not be allowed to displace the character of its natural socio-historic centre, which is the broadest place of meeting for the nation.

Correspondingly, the macro-institutional section is Martin's most general, but also his most prescient and persuasive. It is here that Martin – who I normally regard as an embodiment of English genteel liberal-conservatism – turns his attention to class. Martin suggests that the real crisis in Confirmation is actually concealed: it is a class issue, related to the state of the Church of England. He points out that it is illogical to complain about the falling number of ordinands with university degrees *and* of not appealing to the urban working classes. What the Anglican church must grapple with is not falling numbers of confirmees, or Confirmation 'wastage', but rather how to be the church for the nation, and adjusted to the mid-twentieth century. The church, he notes, rather like a university, exists both to adjust and to resist adjustment. And at a time when the population is becoming more mobile and diverse than ever before, the confirmation statistics may indicate not a lack of affection for the rite, but rather a more congregationalist mind-set gaining a grip on the church as a whole.

The Rise of Personal Conversion

In theory, then, the socio-cultural shifts in post-war Britain might also be telling us something quite important about the decline of rites such as Confirmation. Could it be, for example, that the progressive and dispositional in institutional religion (e.g., the movement from baptism to confirmation) is being superseded by a turn to the dramatic and episodic? It would not be surprising. Moreover, it would hardly be a new turn either. The drama of revivalism has, for many centuries, offered immediacy and change; conversion, apparently, without extensive preparation. In effect, one could characterize this as an instant and life-changing epiphany rather than a slow and progressive form of adoption.

This is not a critical observation, mind. It simply serves to draw our attention to the competing ecologies of conversion and confirmation that have existed in mainstream denominations for some time. So in terms of implicit theology, we might say that the rise of individualism and the pursuit of personal fulfilment in contemporary culture – however slow and progressive this development is – favours the valuing of personal conversion more than Confirmation. The latter, here, becomes something that is perceived to be about joining a complex (and perhaps slow and turgid?) institution. Conversion, in contrast, meets the needs of the individual in ways that are personal, episodic and abundant. Such a move would correlate well with our post-institutional age. Moreover, we can see that where Confirmation does flourish, the accent has moved from long-term belonging [to the church] to the event of First Communion. The episodic has, in other words, also edged out the dispositional even within what is left of the ritual in contemporary socio-religious life.

To some extent, I think I can chart something of this profound cultural shift in my own life. When I was in my early teens, I went forward at a Christian rally and gave my life to God. I forget the precise date and venue. But I remember it being a marquee somewhere near Watford, a bus load of us having travelled from our local church youth group. There were hymns, a choir, a rousing sermon, and an 'altar call', in which the preacher invited any who 'had not given their life to the Lord' to get up out of your seats, come to the front, meet a counsellor, pray a prayer and receive some free literature. Of course, initially, nobody moves: this is England, after all. And the English are a quintessentially reserved people, who like being at the back of orderly queues that move rather slowly.

Eventually I did pluck up courage to go forward, with my mate Jim – I think we had figured out that we were as likely to be guilty of sin as any other folk. We prayed our prayer of commitment, received our literature, and went home on the bus rejoicing – changed people. Changed, that is, until the next time there was a rally or crusade. Growing up evangelical, as I did, mostly, it was not unusual to give your life to Christ several times, and I was no exception to that statistic. 'Dedication', 're-dedication', 'affirmation', 'commitment', 're-commitment', 'assurance' ... and in the maelstrom of teenage years, with guilt bursting into your psyche with as much frequency as the spots on your face, you could be forgiven for feeling as though your were drowning in a cauldron of your own hormones. Quite simply, you are not sure of very much in those 'wonder years'; religion, for me at least, gave an important anchor.

I do not regret a single one of my responses to an altar call. But of course, I now see them in a different perspective. I now see that my baptism, even as an infant, was a fundamental adoption into the life of Christ – into which I slowly grew, and continue to gradually come to own. Archbishop Michael Ramsay, when once asked what was the 'best day of his life' replied that he knew what it was and when it was, but had no memory of it: it was his baptism. It was Confirmation for me, at the age of 14, by Robert Runcie, that stopped me 're-committing' myself virtually every time an altar call came along. I realized that what I affirmed, God had confirmed in me: it would take a lifetime to respond. The Christian life is a marathon, not a sprint. It is not possible to hand over 'the whole of our lives' to God at once, because we live, and as we live, we change – hopefully though, from glory to glory. To be a Christian is to be a 'becoming person'.

Today, few people come to faith because they have been convinced by a powerful preacher, or by the sight of a miracle. What brings people to lasting faith is the quality of help, friendship and life offered by the church, and the relationships made in and beyond its boundaries. This is how the resurrection is lived – by ordinary day to day Christian living. From this flows the 'abundant life' that Jesus speaks about – a fullness of being that makes sense of joy and suffering, bound up in Jesus' resurrected body. This is what the church is to become: a holding together of celebration and consolation, life and death, birth and decay, pain and joy.

So what exactly is conversion? The term itself is part of everyday language, and simply means 'to turn' – either one currency into another, electricity into light or heat, or ingredients into a meal. The widespread use of the word carries over into the field of religious studies and theology. A 'convert' is someone who has turned away from something and embraced a faith; but this faith need not be new, for conversion can be 're-turning'. Studies and narratives of conversion have a long history within religions, including Christianity. Augustine's *Confessions*, or Newman's *Apologia Pro Vita Sua*, function as an ideal 'template' for conversion in the ancient world as much as David Wilkerson's *The Cross and the Switchblade* (1977) has done for some in the modern world. And yet in spite of much study of the phenomena, some of which is exemplary (e.g., William James, Lewis Rambo, etc), scholars have barely scratched the surface of the subject. Theologians are often squeamish about prying too far into the realms of religious experience. Those engaged in the social scientific study of religion (e.g., sociology, anthropology, psychology, etc) have often been guilty of reductive studies, which have done less than justice to the richness of the experiences. Yet it is here that the question of implicit theology is at its sharpest.

For example, to what extent do rallies and crusades really 'work'? Is a course like *Alpha* mainly a 'refresher' for like-minded Christians, or something that appeals to non-religious people? What are the strengths and weaknesses of a 'join-the-dots' approach to Christianity? Do people who join 'cults' do so freely? Is it true that Roman Catholicism is losing ground to Pentecostalism in South America? Why do people join New Religious Movements? How can you convert to Islam (using the world wide web)? Why do some people change from one faith to another – and at what cost?

According to the American scholar, Lewis Rambo (1993) one of the best guides to the territory, the concept of conversion, although used primarily in Christianity, Judaism and Islam to refer to the process of joining a religion, is associated with various forms of personal and communal change. Throughout religious history one can observe a great variety of transformations of individuals and groups which vary in intensity and duration. Nearly all religions or religious groups have identifiable rites of passage and initiation, many of which involve ways of either converting outsiders to 'insider' status, or of reallocating roles to those who were once insiders but have lost their status or role within the group. Rambo considers that conversion should be understood as having three dimensions: Tradition, Transformation and Transcendence. In practice these dimensions interact and are not discrete but to distinguish between them is useful for a better understanding of conversion.

'Tradition' refers to the historical and contextual aspects of both the convert and the religious group, taking into account such aspects of the conversion process as relationships with groups members and non-groups members, previous life of the convert, institutional aspect of the religion, its symbols, rituals and so on and the social situation in which conversion takes place. From a more anthropological stance, ideological and cultural aspects of tradition may be considered and the way in which culture impacts on conversion and *vice versa*.

'Transformation' encompasses personal aspects of change in thoughts, beliefs, and actions through a study of experience, selfhood and consciousness. This may be done through the discipline of psychology, an example being studies such as William James's *The Varieties of Religious Experience* (1902), which focus upon factors which may predispose individuals towards conversion such as anguish, conflict or guilt. Various schools of thought in psychology may focus on different aspects of the experience of conversion and interpret them in different ways, for example psychoanalytic psychologists may focus on the relationship between the convert and his or her parents, while the behaviourist may address aspects of conditioning and behavioural reinforcement.

'Transcendence' refers to the encounter with the sacred, that which is for many religions, the goal of conversion. From the perspective of the theologian, the perceived relationship with the divine inherent in religious experience is central to an analysis of conversion. Again, according to Rambo, these three dimensions to conversion – tradition, transformation and transcendence – lead to at least five different types of conversion:

1. *Tradition transition* refers to conversion from one major or traditional religion to another. This may occur on a large scale through exposure to different cultures, an example of which is the expansion of conversion to Christianity in other cultures following European colonialization in the eighteenth, nineteenth and twentieth centuries.
2. *Institutional transition* involves changing allegiance from one sub-group within a major religion to another, for example switching between denominations of Christianity either for convenience of location or because of a religious experience or shift in belief.
3. *Affiliation* is the process of a group or individual without previous religious commitment becoming involved with a religious community. This has been regarded as problematic in analysis because of allegations of brainwashing among New Religious Movements.
4. *Intensification* is used to refer to renewed commitment within an existing previous religious affiliation, a deepening of commitment or a making central to life that which was previously peripheral.
5. *Apostasy* refers to a rejection and defection from a previous religious group or orientation which does not involve a commitment to a new religious

system but leads to the adoption of a new or prior system of non-religious beliefs or values. The processes involved in leaving a group are important in the study of personal change, in particular study has focus on the forced 'deprogramming' and defection from New Religious Movements.

Each of these types involves a different degree of change and a different process of conversion from the next. Some require a major reconstitution of belief system and dislocation on a cultural level, whereas others only require a minimal degree of social or institutional movement. It is therefore possible, argues Rambo, to present a model of the process involved in conversion which can be broken down into a number of stages. This is not put forward as a universal, but rather as a way of organizing the diverse literature which exists on the subject. For example, the relevant contexts of conversion can be addressed, which might include the social, cultural, religious and personal circumstances of the individual. In turn, those contexts can be usefully broken down into macro and micro elements.

An example of macro-context might be a consideration of the social, cultural and institutional circumstances of the society in which conversion takes place. Secularization and the pluralist culture which exists in contemporary British society may be seen as something which promotes uncertainty and the choice of a new religious orientation in order to find meaning and grounding in life. An example of a micro-context could be more concerned with the immediate interactions of the individual convert. This involves their family situation, religious life, and peer group and reference to the way in which they impact upon the identity of the individual. The micro-context interacts with the macro-context and can promote criticism of it or counteract its influence in the life of the individual. For instance some religious groups seek to separate themselves from wider society or change it in some way in seeking religious goals.

Another stage of conversion which can be drawn from the literature is that of encounter with the particular religious group. Many factors are analysed surrounding the encounter such as setting, demographic characteristics of, and congruence between the convert and group, the role and background of the advocate of the religion, and the interaction between them and the potential convert. In the analysis of the encounter, the role of charisma is often important. The way in which the charismatic leader advocates and legitimates the belief system may be considered along with the relationship between the leader and other members of the group. It has been suggested that charisma can have a large effect on an individual's decision to convert. Groups can be seen to provide solutions to a variety of needs which the individual has, from the need for community in the face of the erosion of the social networks in wider society, through to religious needs which the individual may experience. Evidence suggests that, in large part, converts may use religious belief systems or ways of life creatively, modifying them to fit their own particular set of needs or aspirations.

Following the initial encounter with the group, continued interaction is important, and is the next stage which can be identified. This allows the potential convert to learn more about the belief systems of the group and its way of life. The length of this period of interaction and its intensity varies between groups. Some advocate a long period of learning and socialization, whilst others may demand a quicker decision from the potential convert and interaction may be more intensive. This is influenced by the degree of contact the group has with the outside world and the views they have towards it. Groups in which boundaries with the outside world are flexible may be less controlling of the individual and interaction may be less intense and *vice versa* for those who separate themselves from the world. A quick decision may be required from a group regarded as deviant by the outside world, for fear that the potential convert may be put off by the stigma attached to the group.

During the phase of interaction, personal relationships are particularly important. Acceptance and affirmation by those in the group may help to promote conversion and overcome crises. The nature of this interaction and the degree and type of persuasion which operates between groups and converts is a much debated area. Some theorists have cast converts in the role of victims of the irresistible brainwashing techniques of religious groups asserting, that such groups pick out vulnerable people and manipulate them through reference to their deepest needs and desires.

The final element of the interaction phase is the need for a public declaration of the decision to convert in many groups. Often anguish and confusion surrounding the adoption of a whole new set of values and ways of living may be alleviated by the public declaration of a decision to convert by the experience of divine and group affirmation.

The last stage to be delineated is that of commitment. Religious traditions, through commitment to the new perspective, tend to require a radical rejection of old ways of life and of the world and its 'evil'. Symbols of death and rebirth may be used in the commitment stage, which is characterized by a clear distinction between the 'right' and the 'wrong' way, the inadequacy of past life and the superiority of the religious way of life. Previous life becomes reinterpreted through new frames of reference often assisted by the giving of public testimony. Life experience is gradually rearranged and modified using the discourse of the group. The giving of testimony has been perceived variously as a precondition for conversion, a result of conversion and a way of adopting the ideology, roles and vocabulary of the group. At the least, testimony is likely to consolidate belief and at the same time it reminds the group of the validity and continued relevance of its world view.

Correspondingly, many scholars believe that conversion is merely the first step of an ongoing process. Conversion may be moral, intellectual or emotional in the first instance but it must then come to pervade all aspects of life for the convert to be totally transformed. It is not just a personal change but a reorientation to the world in general. Nature, intensity and duration of conversion affect the consequences in individual cases and it is difficult to make judgements as to the exact degree of change which occurs in each convert.

Conclusion: Confirmation and Conversion

In view of this brief discussion, it is possible to characterize Confirmation as belonging to the realm of the institutional: belonging to a complex body through a set of processes that identify the life of an individual with something more corporate. As one can now perhaps see, this is less 'fit' (in Darwinian terms) for the new Millennium than a culture than encourages personal conversion, which allows the individual to experience something more spiritually bespoke, and is less inured within established ecclesial and institutional life. This indicates, in turn, that a focus on implicit theology could and should pay proper attention to the cultural 'tectonic plates' that support ecclesial and religious fads and fashions. It might also suggest that the elative decline in the observation of Confirmation, and its narrowing and individualizing in the environs where it still flourishes, needs to be situated within a larger cultural picture that confessional theology may be able to do little to control.

Within this field, of course, conversion may be analysed from a variety of different viewpoints, from a consideration of the religious tradition involved, and the developmental process of the convert within it, to a more social perspective regarding, for example, the extent to which the convert remains within or is alienated from their immediate and wider society. Conversion is not a unitary phenomenon, but a multi-faceted process of change. Conversion cannot be analysed from any one 'objective' standpoint; it is always to be seen from a particular viewpoint, in which specific ways of theorizing obtain insights, which in turn must be made explicit.

The variety of definitions of conversion extant in both religious and academic writing is an attempt to cover the excess of the phenomena. Within Judaism and Christianity, conversion can signify the rejection of evil and the coming into a relationship with God. This can occur between denominations, converting, for example (in one scenario) from 'Godless and idolatrous' Roman Catholicism to 'true' Christianity – as some Irish Free Presbyterians might believe. Academic definitions of conversion vary as to the degree of change which takes place in a person, and the amount of time over which it takes place. Some regard it as a sudden change involving radical alterations in belief, behaviour and group membership. Others see it as more gradual and developmental, and not as all-encompassing of a person's life.

Equally, the subject of conversion – as an area for theology and religious studies – has often presupposed that 'conversion' is an individualistic narrative of change. However, it has taken a century or more of missiology to show that conversion is more complex. Vincent Donovan's moving account of the baptism of the Masai (1982) explores the more subtle phenomenon of communities in conversion. Donovan, working within an individualistic (and Western?) paradigm of conversion, attempts to baptise only those members of the tribe that have played a full part in his instruction courses. But Ndangoya, a tribal elder, will have none of it:

> Padri, why are you trying to break us up and separate us? … there have been lazy
> ones in this community. But they have been helped by those with much energy.
> There are stupid ones in the community, but they have been helped by those who
> are intelligent. Yes, there are ones with little faith in this village, but they have
> been helped by those with much faith … I can declare for them and for all this
> community, that we have reached the step in our lives where we can say 'We
> believe'. (Donovan, 1982, p. 91)

Donovan agrees to baptise the whole tribe: 'conversion' is a communal
phenomenon, no longer individuals responding in their 'own' time.

Missiology still has much to render to the study of conversion; increasingly,
so does sociology. Grace Davie has recently characterized the story of religious
affiliation in post-war Britain as 'believing without belonging' (1994). The
thesis itself raises further questions for the study of conversion. How do church
members define themselves? What is the difference between being religious and
spiritual? If there is an apparent decline in the number of converts – perhaps
perceived because there are less large-scale Christian rallies (e.g., Billy Graham,
Luis Palau, etc), does that make Britain a less religious place? If millions attend
Alpha courses, does that mean there are, in fact, now more converts? The answers
are far from clear.

If the study of conversion is the study of change; then arguably, the study
of Confirmation is the study of continuity. Yet even here, and from our brief
discussion, we can only begin to guess at the contexts ('religious' and 'social') in
which change is constant. The claim to be 'born again', for example, now carries
a different weight and significance in British evangelical churches, compared to a
quarter of a century ago. Not so long ago, this claim and its meanings, were largely
uncontested within evangelical circles. But successive revolutions – Charismatic
Renewal, Post-evangelicalism and neo-Conservative evangelicalism, to name but
a few movements – would all now claim to or wish to qualify such a statement.
Suffice to say, much of the concern would centre on the significance of religious
experience in relation to 'basic' doctrine.

Confirmation, I would suggest, is no different. Rather like personal conversion,
it is a phenomenon with an identity and value that is more fluid than many
would suppose. The explicit meanings are invariably clear in each generation.
But I would argue that the implicitness of these rites of passage and rituals also
carry important theological and cultural codes that merit careful and considered
attention. In attending to the style and structure of contemporary ecclesial practice,
we also start to uncover some deep truths about the transient-yet-resilient nature
of religious rituals. This suggests, in all likelihood, that Confirmation can re-
emerge as an important socio-religious rite, even within late modernity, once post-
institutionalism is eclipsed, and belonging and believing, for so long bifurcating
in the post-war era, begin to come together. Of course, this involves nothing less
than a deep form of conversion – but not here, of individuals seeking meaning,
fulfilment and value. But rather the conversion of society, who may yet come to

see that rituals which mark the movement from childhood to adulthood, and from dependency to interdependency, are aided through the practice of Confirmation. Implicitly.

Chapter 3
Tripping Down the Aisle:
Churchgoing, Culture and Contemporary Eucharistic Practice

Introduction

The Dutch missiologist Herbert Kramer once commented that the church is always in a state of crisis, but that 'its greatest shortcoming is that it is only occasionally aware of it' (Bosch, 1991, p. 2). There is, of course, no shortage of neuralgia and anxiety when it comes to the subject of statistics pointing to a decline in church attendance, coupled more generally to a waning of Christian knowledge and observation. There is almost no need to narrate the apparent erosion of visible Christian signs, symbols and practices that appear to point to an ascendant secular society. One could begin such a mapping exercise almost anywhere.

Church attendance statistics appear to suggest a declining number of churchgoers. There are fewer festivals and holy days that command obligatory observation, even from the most faithful. Thus, whilst Easter many be observed and continues to be popular, there is no guarantee that Good Friday will fare as well; as with Christmas, so with Advent. Whitsun and Ascensiontide are long-forgotten public holidays in Britain and other European countries. Hymns are seldom sung in state schools, and the reservoir of Christian knowledge amongst society seems to have reached dangerously low levels.

Such a sweeping narrative is, however, far from fair, let alone accurate. Yet there is something in this trajectory (of decline) that feels as though it is real. Churches have, for the most part, responded to these changes by turning inwards. Even though many have resisted this turn, the movement is, in truth, traceable to at least the Victorian era, and specifically the response to perceived and emerging secularization and industrialization of the age. The secularization of the Victorian era was, in effect, a double move. On the one hand, it was the emergence of the state to take control of institutions and works that had previously been the provenance of the church. And on the other, it was the acknowledgement of other Christian denominations, and a slow ending to the monopoly and privilege of Anglicanism in England.

The Church of England responded to their loss of extensity with a renewed intensity. The emergence, in the nineteenth century, of strong wings in the church (evangelical and Anglo-catholic) arguably points to an inward turn: an absorption with nuanced theological and ecclesial identity, at odds with other church parties, and caught up in an interiority of intensity that compensated for the loss of extensity in public life. Indeed, the story of the Church of England over the last two centuries is, arguably, its compression and slow marginalization within public life. This explains why, on the one hand, church attendance figures now appear to matter to Anglicans, when once they seldom registered as significant indices of anything in particular. And why, on the other hand, rites and rituals have become more specialized, and therefore remoter from the public.

This is ironic, of course. The relatively recent emergence of the Parish Communion as the weekly rite for the locality (parish) represents a rather more exclusive form of worship for the community than previous generations have known. Matins, for example, used to be an inclusive and participative form of worship that did not require attendees to engage in a corporate act of communion in the way that a Eucharist requires. Matins offered canticles, psalms, readings, a choir and usually a sermon – all of which could be engaged within a characteristically English way –allowing space for reticence, reticulation and rumination, but without requiring a specified level of commitment. Matins was, in other words, a confident expression of faith at a time when Christian belief and knowledge was extensive. The erosion of this extensity has led to forms of religious and liturgical observance that are more intensive, and therefore reflect the gradual marginality of faith, rather than its restoration to a more central mode. Thus, the rise of the Parish Communion movement – leading to the phenomenon of 'tripping down the aisle', as it were – reflects an inward turn for the church, even as it proclaims, of course, the very opposite.

Another way of expressing the inherent tension between intensity and extensity is to see this in Anglican approaches sacraments. There are two main modes of engagement. The first tradition broadly conceives of the engagement as a form of interlocking combative encounter. The second broadly sees it as a form of intra-related binding, covenant or commitment. Both lead to the formation of their own distinctive cultures (e.g., characteristic missiological and ecclesiological outlooks), which increasingly do not know how to talk to one other.[1] These two tensions in Anglican polity are usually fruitful, but sometimes frustrating. For example, there is a tension between what I would call 'concrete' or 'earthed' ecclesiology and 'blueprint' ecclesiologies or theological ideologies. Put more simply, whatever may be said about the Eucharist, the faithful – especially in a public church – are free to make up their own mind. Another classic tension is that between scripture, tradition and reason. Again, this can be used to 'balance' and weigh fine theological debates, but the tension also exists at virtually every area of parish life and public ministry. In short, to ask 'what is the Anglican view of sacraments' is to ask a wide range of questions amidst a wider set of cultural

---

[1]   I.e., resonant with Snow (1959). See also Becher (1981) on academic disciplines as sectarian 'cultures'. Interestingly, few theologians read David Martin's theology, whilst few social scientists acknowledge Milbank's critiques.

questions and considerations. So in this chapter, there are two areas to consider here. First, there is a brief consideration of how the habit of church-going and sacramental devotion is contentious in its extensity. Second, an exploration is offered on the framing of doctrine – the intensity of tradition within the wide extensity of practice – through a consideration of the work of Richard Hooker. Finally, a brief conclusion argues that the tension between extensity and intensity need not be inimical for churches. Indeed, implicitness and explicitness in faith are to some extent predicated on the inherent tension between the two.

Extensity Revisited: Churchgoing and Communion in English Culture

I suppose if I had to pick out one phrase or sentence that summed up the ambivalent nature of English religion, it would be these words from Paul Vallely: 'He had the gift of being able to talk to the English about God without making them wish they were somewhere else.'[2] Vallely, writing of the late Basil Hume, captures the English attitude to religion perfectly: a mixture of embarrassment and respect, coupled to a yearning for presence and yet a fear of excess.

It was Bede Frost who once quipped that English people have often been obsessed with the idea that the spiritual life consists in going to church, which is 'a fond thing vainly invented by the Puritans in seventeenth century' (Moorman, 1955, p. 222). This contrasts with the view of Martin Thornton, who contrasts *continuity* of Christian life with *regularity* of church attendance as competitive embodiments within English spirituality. Thornton's work provides an excellent if eclectic introduction to English spirituality, reflecting an unconscious kind of Anglican imperialism: Anselm, Hilton, Rolle, Kempe, Julian of Norwich and the Caroline Divines are all discussed – but there is little space for Thomas More or the Wesley brothers (Thornton, 1963).

England has never been an outwardly religious country, if church attendance is anything to go by. Adrian Hastings describes the Church of England in the eighteenth century as being 'profoundly secularised'.[3] When Edward Stanley took up his family living in 1805 (at Alderley, Cheshire), the custom was that the Verger waited on the path leading to the church, the Vicar only being called if anyone actually turned up. It remains the case that for much of English history, vast numbers of people have stayed away from church.[4] Religious enthusiasm and revivals have occasionally held sway in the tenth, thirteenth, seventeenth, eighteenth and nineteenth centuries. Otherwise, the English seem to have been

---

[2] Paul Vallely, writing of Cardinal Basil Hume, *The Independent*, 31/12/99, Review, p. 3.

[3] Cf. Chadwick (1975), p. 265.

[4] See Russell (1998), pp. 11ff. Cf., R. Harries, 'Christianity Soldiers Onward', *The Observer*, 26/12/99, p. 17.

rather lukewarm about religion – the Reformation is, arguably, the very settlement of that.[5]

Yet although the English may be said to prefer their religion tepid (like their beer: flat, and without much froth), their spirituality deserves closer attention. Opinion polls and surveys consistently show that anything from two-thirds to over three-quarters of the population believe in God. In recent history, this has comforted many clergy, who have understood the English to be, in the words of Grace Davie 'believing without belonging', and worked their parish ministry within that paradigm. Davie points out, as others have done in the past, that the decline in church attendance is nothing like as steep as, for example, Trade Union membership or membership of political parties: nearly all traditional institutions and many associations have experienced a marked decline in numbers, power and prestige since World War II. Furthermore, the apparent success of recreational or leisure activities should be seen in perspective: cinema attendance is a fraction of what it was 50 years ago. Football, although attracting significant media coverage, can only muster one sixth of the number of people on a Saturday who attend church on an average Sunday (Hastings, 1986, p. 669ff.).[6]

Of course, it is not quite as simple as that. Davie's 'believing without belonging' paradigm is, in my view, *not* quite right. I prefer to describe the contours of English belief and its connection to institutions and associations as a matter of 'relating and mutating'. Very few people choose to have absolutely no relationship with a religious body of belief or institution whatsoever. They may be close to such things or very distant from them, but they nonetheless continue to relate to them, even if only through the media or the most casual contact. Furthermore, that relating is constantly mutating, as social and religious memory is transformed through new insights and experiences.[7]

Correspondingly, contemporary cultural commentators are at least partly right when they talk (excitedly) of 'pastiche spirituality', academics (coldly) of 'religious pluralism', church leaders (critically) of 'syncretism'. It is true that many mainstream Christian denominations no longer enjoy the coherence of a homogeneous culture: movements *within* them are trying to transform them. The 'New Age', growing exposure to other religions, globalization and privatization have driven many to interrogate their faith, and then adapt it. In spite of the numbers of people who claim to believe in God, the undeniable reality of our time is that England is shifting from being a 'Christian nation' to a spiritually diverse society.[8] Moreover, there is evidence to suggest that individuals are now

---

[5]   See Marsh (1998). This book, in the Macmillan 'Social History in Perspective' Series, will be mentioned later.

[6]   Cf. Davie (1994); cf. Russell (1998), p. 16.

[7]   The elasticity of the 'relating and mutating' paradigm makes more sense of Davie's more recent book, *Religion in Europe: A Memory Mutates* (2000), which in turn draws on Hervieu-Leger (2000).

[8]   See Creedon (1998). Cf. Barna (1996) and Brown (1998).

beginning to be more inventive with their spiritual lives, assembling private faiths from religious bits and pieces; what is created has meaning and coherence for its creator.[9] Many commentators also agree that there is now a sharp difference between the transmission and reception of spirituality in previous generations to that of our own.[10]

For many observers and commentators, it is therefore a 'given' that society is becoming more secularized. Furthermore, there is some degree of collusion between those who regard this as a welcome development, and those who, to quote Eliot, identify the moment as 'an age which advances progressively backwards'.[11]

Yet it is a fact that there have been very few periods in English history when everyone went to Church or Sunday School, knew right from wrong, and absolutely believed everything their parish priest said. As Keith Thomas notes: '… what is clear is that the hold of organised religion upon the people [of England] was never so complete as to leave no room for rival systems of belief …'.[12] As further evidence, Thomas cites an extract from one of Oliver Heywood's *Diaries*:

> One Nov 4 1681 as I travl'd towards Wakefield about Hardger moor I met with a boy who would needs be talking. I begun to ask him some questions about the principles of religion: he could not tell me how many gods there be, nor persons in the godhead, nor who made the world nor anything about Jesus Christ, nor heaven nor hell, or eternity after this life, nor for what ends he came into the world, nor for what condition he was born in – I ask't him whether he was a sinner; he told me he hop't not; yet this was a witty boy and could talk of any worldly things skillfully enough … he is 10 years of age, cannot reade and scarce ever goes to churche … (Thomas, p. 206).[13]

Granted, the Yorkshire region could be argued for as a special case. Ever since records began for the area, church attendance figures have been consistently poor, and always below any national average.[14] Ted Wickham's masterly study of Sheffield religion confirms the apparently bleak prognosis, when he notes that

---

[9] See Roof (1994) and Collins (2000)

[10] See Ammerman and Roof eds (1995), and Mead (1970). Mead's book, far ahead of its time, distinguished between post-figurative (elders are paramount, and answer life's questions), co-figurative (elders set and define boundaries, but expect the younger generation to eventually make their own way in life) and pre-figurative societies (the younger generation establish the primacy and uniqueness of their experience of the world over and against those of the elders).

[11] Eliot (1963), 'Choruses from the Rock', p. 178 and 161–2.

[12] Thomas (1971), p. 178. This quotation is resonant with David Edwards' quip (echoing Ted Wickham's work – see below) that the Church of England 'have not lost the inner cities – they never had them'.

[13] Cf. Heywood (2007), iv, p. 24.

[14] See Gay (1971).

From the emergence of the industrial towns in the eighteenth century, the working class, the labouring poor, the common people, as a class, substantially as adults, have been outside the churches. The industrial working class culture pattern has evolved lacking a tradition of practice of religion. (Wickham, 1957, p. 14)

Wickham also cites a clergyman, one Mark Docker, writing in 1817, who observes that 'Sheffield is not the most irreligious town in the Kingdom', but that out of one community of residents 'you perhaps see a solitary instance where a whole household of several persons are regular attendants' (Wickham, 1957).

That said, detailed readings of parochial records from almost any age can illustrate the pragmatic, amateurish nature of 'official' English religion, and how ordinary people chose to relate to it:

Clophill We present William Spellinge the 23 of Marche beinge then called Palme Sondaye in the churche & tyme of eveninge prayer, before suche maydes as then had receaved the communion, dyd in theyre seate lye upon his backe verye unreverentlye till the ende of the fyrste lesson, and also other tymes dothe seem to forgette to yeilde dewe reverence in the tyme of dyvyne service.

Langford Our chancell is owte of repayre in tymber & wyndowes, at the parsons defaute. Our churche wyndowes are in decaye by reason of fowle that cometh in at the chancell wyndowes which hathe broken them.

Bedford Sancti Petri [sic] There is no pulpitte in the littel churche. The x commandments are not on the walles. The chancell & churche are not paved in some places.

Colmworth We have had no service on the weeke dayes not from Maye daye last tyll September & no service on Sancte Peters Eve nor Sancte Bartholemewe Eve nor Michaelmas daye at nyghte & they had iiij children christened iiij wayes, & he woold not let the parishe see his licence & one syr Brian Hayward dyd in the like case. Umphrey Austyne churche warden last yere wold not present the lead that was missing oute of the steeple. Item Nicholas Dicons, Thomas Jud, William Quarrell & his wyfe have not receaved this xij monthes. Item the Quenes Iniunctions or the bisshoppes were not made thes iij yeres nor the catechisme taughte.

Tylsworth We have had but one sermone since Michaelmas, which was the Sondaye after New yers daye.

Farandiche The chancell & parsonage are in decaye by the parson's defalt. They have but one sermon this year.

Bidham We doe present that we had no Communion but once this yeare, and that our last churchwardens dyd not make there accompt for the yere.

Patnum [Pavenham] Our chansell is in decaye and redye to faule dwone, at the defaute of Trynitye College in Cambridge.[15]

The picture painted of religion in sixteenth-century Bedfordshire is probably enough to raise Bunyan from his grave. Yet it is interesting to note how little has changed. The Churchwardens are really only concerned about two things: the state of their church building, and where they are going to get their next priest from. There is no mention of the Mass or its absence, no mention of the *Book of Common Prayer*, and no indication that the laity care for their diocese or for their bishop. In other words, the cares and concerns of the laity in 1578 are very similar to those of today's churches.

The Medieval and Reformation periods are often characterized as ages of great faith. Certainly, individuals and communities did die for their faith. Equally, however, the scale of apathy and antipathy should not be underestimated. The eleventh century monk, William of Malmesbury complained that the aristocracy rarely attended mass, and even the more pious heard it at home, 'but in their bedchambers, lying in the arms of their wives' (Fletcher, 1997, p. 476; cf., Starke and Finke, 2000, p. 63). At least they heard mass though; according to Murray, 'substantial sections of thirteenth century society hardly attended church at all' (1972, pp. 92–4; cf., Stark and Finke, 2000, p. 63). Were the clergy any better? Hardly. William Tyndale complained that, in 1530, few priests could recite the Lord's Prayer or translate it into English. When the Bishop of Gloucester tested his clergy in 1551, of 311 priests, 171 could not repeat the Ten Commandments – but this is hardly surprising, as there were few seminaries (Thomas, 1971, p. 164; cf., Starke and Finke, p. 66). Did any of this matter? Hardly. It would seem that the impact of the clergy on their congregations was very slight. As Keith Thomas notes, 'members of the population jostled for pews, nudged their neighbours, hawked and spat, knitted, made coarse remarks, told jokes, fell asleep and even let off guns', with other behaviour including 'loathsome farting, striking, and scoffing speeches', which resulted in 'the great offence of the good and the great rejoicing of the bad' (Thomas, 1971, pp.161–2; cf., Stark and Finke, 2000, p. 66).

This haphazard, semi-secular, quiet (but occasionally rowdy and irreverent) English Christianity, continues well into successive centuries (Spurrell, 1998). James Woodforde's *Diary of a Country Parson* provides an invaluable window into the life of the clergy and the state of English Christianity in the eighteenth century. Again, a close reading of the text suggests that whatever secularization is, it is not obviously a product of the Industrial Revolution. Woodforde is writing just before the social and economic changes; his parish is ten miles from Norwich

---

[15]   *Archdiaconal Visitations in 1578* [Bedfordshire Historical Records Society, no. 69, Bedford, 1990].

Cathedral, yet he clearly thinks it is reasonably good to have 'two rails' (or thirty communicants) at Christmas or Easter, from 360 parishioners. His church is only ever full when there is either a war on, or a member of the royal family is gravely ill. (Again, not so different from today, except the Royal Family are in better health, and England doesn't go to war as much as it used to.) In this respect, Woodforde is typical of his time: few people went to church. Indeed, rates of attendance then are comparable to those of the late twentieth century: the Oxford Diocesan Visitations for 1738 record that 30 parishes drew a combined total of 911 communicants for Easter, Ascension, Whitsun and Christmas – less than 5 per cent of the total population.[16] He carries out sundry services (especially christenings) in the warmth of his parlour and not in church, and we learn more from his *Diaries* about the food he eats and the company he keeps than we ever do about the Christian year.[17]

Overall, his attitude to his own profession is mild, relaxed, rather lacking in zeal, and certainly exhibiting no anxiety about the small numbers of people attending his church on an ordinary Sunday. For example, his diary entry for Sunday 17 October 1758 states that 'Mr Dade read and preached this morning.' – it would seem that only four attended. On 5 October 1766, he tells us that 'I entirely forgot about St Luke's Day, and therefore did not read prayers at Castle Cary which I should have done otherwise. As it was not done wilfully, I hope God will forgive it'. On 5 September 1759 – another Sunday – he takes the afternoon off to go 'to the Bear-baiting in Ansford'.

Perhaps we forget that in the eighteenth and much of the nineteenth century, clergy did not have 'vocations' and 'professions' in the ways that we take for granted today. Clergy did not wear dog collars until about 1860 – before then, they were undifferentiated in dress and status from other gentry and their professions. The age of the 'serious clergyman' who spent all his time ministering – instead of writing essays, being a naturalist, geologist, astronomer, hunting, theatre lover or engaged in general social hobnobbing – did not arrive until the mid-Victorian period. To be sure, serious clergy who spent all their time consumed in parochial and liturgical tasks did yield results – for a while, more people went to church, and more churches were built. But the downside was that the Church of England lost the more gentle, mellow form of pastoral life that Herbert or Donne knew, or that Coleridge called 'clerisy' – the social communion of the educated classes. Consider, for example, this description of a father's hope for his second son, and a career in the church, during the eighteenth century:

> Dr Darwin, a confirmed freethinker, was sensible and shrewd. He had only to look around him, recall the vicarages he had visited, and ponder the country parsons he entertained at home. One did not have to be a believer to see that an aimless son with a penchant for field sports would fit in nicely. Was the Church

---

[16]   See Stark and R. Finke (2000), p. 67.

[17]   See Woodforde (1999); Introduction by Ronald Blythe, p. vii.

not a haven for dullards and dawdlers, the last resort of spendthrifts? What calling but the highest for those whose sense of calling was nil? And in what other profession were the risks of failure so low and the rewards so high? The Anglican Church, fat, complacent, and corrupt, lived luxuriously on its tithes and endowments, as it had for a century. Desirable parishes were routinely auctioned off to the highest bidder. A fine rural 'living' with a commodious rectory, a few acres to rent or farm, and perhaps a tithe barn to hold the local levy worth hundreds of pounds a year could easily be bought as an investment by a gentleman … (Desmond and Moore, 1991, p. 47).

Even in epochs of revival and religious fervour, such as the Reformation period, it is not possible to show that church-attendance was high. Historians agree that there is a 'general lack of statistically reliable evidence' (Marsh, 1998, p. 41). Part of the burden of Keith Thomas's work is to show that 'a substantial proportion' of the population remained hostile to organized religion, resulting in paltry church attendance. On the other hand, Eamon Duffy asserts that certain Masses were *very* well attended in some places – but there is little evidence supplied to support this contention. Scarisbrick argues that most late medieval people seldom went to church, and when they did, probably only arrived for the elevation of the host (Marsh, 1998, p. 46)[18]

Intensity Reconsidered

One of the great architects of Anglicanism was Richard Hooker,[19] and like so many Anglican theologians, he allowed his theology, both in tone and content, to be partly formed by his context. For example, in March 1585 Hooker was appointed as Master of the Temple for the Inns of Court in London. It was a fraught appointment (following the death of Dr Richard Alvey, a noted Puritan), with the leading candidate for the post being Walter Travers. Elizabeth's Chancellor, Lord Burghley, strongly supported the candidature of Travers; but it was sunk by a sharp missive fired by Whitgift, Archbishop of Canterbury, who wrote to the Queen describing Travers as 'an earnest seeker after innovation'. Whitgift's own first choice was too sick to take the post. Hooker was Whitgift's second, and the Queen appointed him.

The description applied to Travers was a code for indicating him to be a Puritan. A continental reformation based on Luther's prescription that the church should not perpetuate any practice to which scripture was demonstrably opposed was now fused to a new conviction that nothing at all should be done unless provable from scripture. It was a tide of opinion which swept through the Elizabethan Church,

---

[18] See also Duffy (1992), p. 465; Scarisbrick (1984), p. 163; Thomas (1971), pp. 190, 204.

[19] For a fuller discussion of this section, see my *Richard Hooker* (2000) and Rowell, Williams and Stevenson (2001).

making the borders with continental Protestantism indistinct, questioning the identity of the church.

It was this form of Puritanism that Hooker was to set his face against. Yet Hooker was to encounter considerable opposition. Travers was a radical reformer. Worse, for Hooker, he was also a lecturer and preacher at the Temple. After a sermon by Hooker, Travers appealed to the Privy Council (sometime in 1590), accusing Hooker of claiming God to be merciful to Romanists, who might place more emphasis on works rather than justification by faith.

It was to escape the worst exertions of such controversy that Hooker sought to leave the Mastership for a return to parish ministry. Yet he also wished to devote a great proportion of his time in the parish to take part in that controversy by writing *The Laws of Ecclesiastical Polity* (1845). From 1591–95 he was Rector of Boscombe, Subdean of Salisbury and a Prebend of Netheravon. From there, Books 1 to 4 were published in 1593. In 1595 he moved to Bishopsbourne, near Canterbury, where Book 5 was published in 1597. Books 6–8 were completed before Hooker's death – on 2 November 1600. But manuscripts were lost, and the books as we now have them are later constructions based on some notes and earlier drafts. Books 6 and 8 were not published until 1648, and Book 7 until 1662, the year of the Restoration.

Hooker understood that a genuinely catholic church would be innovative. He had little time for Puritans who would not countenance anything that was not enshrined in scripture. Equally, he was set against a kind of traditionalism that prevented the church adapting. Substantial parts of Book 5 are taken up with apparently trivial matters – the attire of ministers, music in church, architecture and the manner for administering sacraments. Yet for Hooker, these concerns arise directly out of his conviction that the church, in its doctrine, preaching, practice and teaching, has some degree of leeway for adapting culturally and temporally. It was obvious to Hooker that church polity need not be *in* scripture, as much as it was obvious to him that it must not be *against* it. Thus, he writes that:

> Seeing therefore those canons do bind as they are edicts of nature, which the Jews observing as yet unwritten, and thereby framing such church orders as in their law were not prescribed, are not withstanding in that respect unculpable: it followeth that sundry things may be lawfully done in the Church, so as they be not done against the Scripture, although no Scripture do command them, but the Church only following the light of reason, judge them to be in discretion meet. (Hooker, 1845, Book 3. VII. 2)

The authority given to reason here is not the elevation of rationality so much as the recognition of the place of common sense. It may well be that certain aspects of the life of the church do not occur in the New Testament. But their absence does not invalidate their efficacy, since the laws of God (which are for goodness) are part of an ongoing organic church that is imbued with the presence of God.

In Book 5, the vision of God – which has underpinned all laws – begins to mature in the various descriptions of the sacraments and the general conduct of ecclesial life:

> Sacraments are the powerful instruments of God to eternal life. For as our natural life consisteth in the union of the body with the soul; so our life supernatural in the union of the soul with God. And forasmuch as there is no union of God with man without that mean between both which is both, it seemeth requiste that we first consider how God is in Christ, then how Christ is in us, and how the sacraments do serve to make us partakers of Christ. (Hooker, 1845, Book 5. L. 3)

In the specific case of the Eucharist:

> The bread and cup are his body and blood because they are causes instrumental upon the receipt whereof the participation of his body and blood ensueth. For that which produceth any certain effect is not vainly nor improperly said to be that very effect whereunto it tendeth. Every cause is in the effect which groweth from it. Our souls and bodies quickened to eternal life are effects the cause whereof is the Person of Christ, his body and his blood are the true well-spring out of which this life floweth. (Hooker, 1845, Book 5. LXVII. 5)

For Hooker, the ultimate location of the presence of Christ's body and blood is not to be sought in the sacrament, but rather 'in the worthy receiver ... only in the very heart and soul of him which receiveth him'. This might appear to be rather bland at first sight, but it is far from that. The key to Hooker's sacramental theology lies not in the minutiae of the Reformation debates about the real presence, but rather in the essence of 'participation', which he calls 'the fruit of the Eucharist'. This participation flows from his dynamic and organic ecclesiology. For Hooker, participation is not over-prescribed or narrow, but is rather public and corporate, and is the key to individual and social life intricately wrapped within the life of God.

Correspondingly, he is wonderfully diplomatic in his treatment of competing doctrines of the Eucharist that dominated the debates of his day. In Chapter 67 (LXVII) of Book 5, he gives space to air the three main theories on Christ's presence in the bread and wine. But Hooker has the last word, using a phrase that resonates with his warning in the Preface that 'our safest eloquence concerning him is our silence':

> He which hath said of the one sacrament (i.e., baptism), 'wash and clean', hath said concerning the other likewise (i.e., the Eucharist), 'eat and live'. If therefore without any such particular and solemn warrant as this is that poor distressed woman coming unto Christ for health could so constantly resolve herself, 'may I but touch the skirt of his garment I shall be made whole,' what moveth us to argue the manner of how life should by bread, our duty being here to take what is

offered, and most surely to rest persuaded of this ?…Let it therefore be sufficient for me presenting myself at the Lord's table to know that what there I receive from him, without searching or inquiring of the manner how Christ performeth his promise; let disputes and questions, enemies to piety … let them take their rest …' (Hooker, 1845, Book 5. LXVII. 12)

Here, Hooker reveals himself as an explicit conciliator, only demolishing arguments in order to make peace and bring about a wider form of ecclesial participation. As a form of apologetics, it is a model for all those who seek to hold together competing convictions, and seek to promote unity in the face of polarization.

The sentiments of Hooker on the Eucharist echo those of Cranmer: 'Christ ordained this sacrament of our spiritual feeding … because the bread and wine do represent unto us the spiritual union and knot of all faithful people, as well as unto Christ … .' Note the language: 'represent', yet real, and 'knot' to each other and to Christ. Moreover, they – the bread and wine – are for our 'real nourishment and regeneration'. For Andrewes, the sacrament is 'like Christ in the cratch (crib)'; the outward husk contains the inward spiritual grace, and so he likens the altar to a cradle. For Ridley, the sacraments are 'seals and confirmations of God's promises' … not bare and naked signs, but 'heavenly tokens … signs of grace and mercy imputed upon us'.

The characteristic view of Anglican sacraments does, I venture, two things. First, they are more pastoral than mystical or 'magical'; typically, Anglican writers stress their efficacy in terms of refreshment, renewal, regeneration, nourishment, feeding and relationality, rather than as a miracle or happenstance around which to build a shrine. Second, the sacraments are public in character; signs of God's grace for all; the outward signs of a spiritual and inward grace. And broadly, this is how the sacraments have been offered for several centuries or more. The sacraments have a social nature; they are offered within a context that is pastoral and temporal rather than a construct that is ideal.

Sacraments in Culture

Statistical surveys continually support the thesis that Britain is a place where the vast majority of the population continue to affirm their belief in God, but then proceed to do little about it. So, church attendance figures remain stubbornly low. Moreover, Christian practices in relation to sacramental life are also variable. Only two centuries ago, a weekly celebration of the Eucharist in an average Anglican parish church in England would have been very unusual. Many congregations only experienced the rite a few times a year, with Easter being the most important one to prepare for. In the Presbyterian Church of Scotland, so infrequent was Communion, that the Elders could visit each person on the roll and assess their readiness and worthiness to receive. Matins and services of the word were far more frequent and popular than sacramental rites. Thus, variable church attendance figures are not a modern malaise, but rather a typical feature of western societies down the ages. Granted, there have been periods of revival when church attendance has peaked. But the basic and innate disposition is one of believing without belonging; of relating to the church, and valuing its presence and beliefs – yet without necessarily sharing them. Or, as one wit puts it, 'I cannot consider myself to be a pillar of the church, for I never go. But I am a buttress – insofar as I support it from the outside'.

So what are the churches to do about the statistics that apparently point to the imminent funeral of organized religion? Is the future really so bleak? It seems unlikely, given all that the churches have already lived through. In view if of this, I am inclined to make modest observations at this point, namely to consider three new 'R's' of religion, which might help churches and religious communities deal with the apparently multiple movements of modernity with some more composure and confidence.

First, *relax*. Even in the most modern societies, there is still demand for religion that is public, performative and pastoral. Furthermore, there are thousands and thousands of private spiritualities and beliefs that flourish in modernity, demonstrating that faith does not wither and die in our culture. Rather, religion mutates and lives on; churches, to take advantage of this, must be open to the world, and not closed to it. They must engage empathetically with their cultures, and try and shape public ministry and a public theology for a wider world that respects its boundaries, and yet yearns for their porosity. In this regard, the sacraments must be offered as publicly and freely as possible; the answer to indifference is not restriction.

Second, religion is remarkably *resilient* in the modern age. Resilience has two faces to it: resistance and accommodation. And the Church of England, like any national church, combines both in its missiological engagement with society, since it has the wisdom to recognize that some of its most sacred practices and their religious value have cultural rather than revelatory origins – although these are not easily separated. Correspondingly, religion is still in demand, and where it is absent, it is more often than not created, or the gap filled with new forms of spirituality. In the absence of religion, people tend to believe anything rather than nothing, and the task of the church must be to continue to engage empathetically with culture and society, offering shape, colour and articulation to the voices of innate and implicit religion. Again, we note that with a sacrament such as baptism, the church itself has to behave sacramentally to offer the ministry faithfully. People bring children to baptism for all sorts of reasons; but it is the point of entry for the church, not the culmination of an education.

Third, the churches can *respond* to the challenge of an apparently faithless age with a confidence founded on society, which refuses to leave religion alone. Often, the best that churches can do is to recover their poise within their social and cultural situations, and continue to offer a ministry – including a sacramental one – and a faith to a public that wish to relate to religion, without necessarily belonging to it. With rare exceptions in history, this is what all clergy have had to work with most of the time: it is both an opportunity and a challenge. So the recipe is this: relax; have faith in the resilience of God and the church; but also respond to the many tests of faith that dominate every age.

In short, the statistics for church attendance, if read crudely, relate one of the great lies of the modern age. For the statistics tell us little about the faith of the nation; believing and belonging should not be confused. Very few people choose not to relate at all to the church, or to mainstream religion. In any secular age, there is space and demand for religion, faith and spirituality. So, rather than cursing the alleged darkness of secularization, churches should perhaps ponder the virtues of striking the odd match, and begin to start pointing to the discreet, contestable and ambiguous signs of religious life – millions of them – that thrive beyond the tightly controlled margins of the church. These signs are not competition for organized religion, but are rather an indication that the hunger for spiritual illumination will never really disappear. And in the midst of these disparate signs, the sacraments are amongst the brightest lights the church offers – yet how often they are hidden.

Three points need making here by way of concluding. First, the social, pastoral and cultural hunger for religion should not be underestimated. The phenomenon of 'vicarious' religion has long been acknowledged, the mechanism whereby an institution and its representatives are needed to believe in things that others are not quite so certain of.[20] At times of death, birth, love and loss, the church is often there to provide focus, articulation, meaning and interpretation. It is there for the liminal moments in life, where transition and change often demand a transcendent point of reference. It remains the case that few leave church because of intellectual doubts; and few join out of conviction. *Relating* to the church remains a very English thing (Russell, 1998, p. 20). Most people come to church through friendships, relationships or life-changing events; considered choices seldom play a significant part.

Second, religion continues to provide enchantment within the modern world; people know there is more to life than the explainable and visible. Moreover, religion is also part of the chain of social memory that enables society to cohere. Whether or not churches are well-attended at Christmas, the popularity of nativity plays at school and carol singing remains significant and pervasive, as Elaine Graham is currently researching.[21] Small wonder that church buildings – even apparently empty ones – continue to say something to the English, and something about England; that faith is not dead, and is woven into English culture, history, fabric, and identity.[22] As Simon Jenkins points out, 'an English church is more than a place of denominational worship. It is the stage on which the pageant of the

---

[20]   See for example the treatment of English religion in Carr (1992).

[21]   See Graham (2000), pp. 89–100.

[22]   Witness the discussion on the importance of church buildings in rural communities in *Faith in the Countryside, The Report of the Archbishops Commission on Rural Areas*, London, Church House Publishing, 1990.

community has been played out for a millennium' Jenkins (1999).[23] In other words, the church itself is a sacrament – stone, glass and other materials, not to mention people – ordinary profane materials that God nevertheless blesses, imbues with his grace, beauty and holiness, and allows to be an outward sign that points to a spiritual and inward grace. The local church, just like the bread and the wine, can be God's chosen broken material that reveals just something of his love for all.

Third, and for all the tension between extensive and intensive expressions of religion, and the implicit and explicit, the pairings need each other. Belief and practice need to respond to the God who is revealed both implicitly and explicitly, in the extensity of life and in the intensities of faith. God is in all of these, and mature faith seeks understanding and comprehension rather than clarity and coherence. It is, perhaps, about recognizing where God is in the moment, and knowing that sometimes the presence of God is in the opaqueness of the cloud; and sometimes in the clarity of the pillar of fire. God, it seems, will not be tied by our preferences and proclivities. We need open minds, open eyes and open hearts to the places where God will be found. And even when he is not discerned, he is nonetheless present. Elizabeth Barrett Browning's poem puts it well:

> Earth's crammed with heaven,
> And every common bush afire with God;
> But only he who sees, takes off his shoes –
> The rest sit round it and pluck blackberries.[24]

---

[23] See also Howes (2000), pp. 30–31.

[24] Elizabeth Barrett Browning, *Aurora Leigh*, 1857 (2007 edition), p. 32.

PART II
Church – The Nature of the Body

The second part of our study continues with a grounded ecclesiological approach, and explores the relatively modern preoccupation with church growth. Chapter 4 delves into the world of Fresh Expressions, revealing how it is possible to read the 'text' of the explicit manifestations of the movement, in order to reveal the complex theological, social and political influences that lie beneath. Chapters 5 and 6 reflect on the popular myth that conservative churches have a monopoly on growth. Spending time immersed in the stories that congregations tell of themselves, in different understandings of growth, and the complex ways in which statistics are used and misused, Chapter 5 reveals the implicit forces that lie behind the way in which congregational identity is constructed in relation to notions of growth and decline. Building on this analysis, Chapter 6 offers an alternative analysis of the rich text of the church, in order to expose the multiple and hidden ways in which church growth can be identified across the Christian spectrum.

Chapter 4
Fresh Expressions:
A Critique of Consumerism

The Fresh Expressions movement has come to prominence since the publication of *Mission-Shaped Church*, a groundbreaking report from the Church of England (2004) that argued for new and complementary forms of evangelism that would work alongside parishes in their ministries. Also adopted by the Methodist church, this movement has spawned 'Pioneer Ministers' and new patterns for selecting and training (so-called) missiological entrepreneurs. The movement has also generated substantial numbers of publications and consultations, resulting in some dioceses and Methodist districts promoting and resourcing their own brands of Fresh Expressions. A Fresh Expression (of church) is:

> … a form of church for our changing culture established primarily for the benefit of people who are not yet members of any church. It will come into being through principles of listening, service, incarnational mission and making disciples. It will have the potential to become a mature expression of church shaped by the gospel and the enduring marks of the church and for its cultural context …[1]

Fresh Expressions abound. No self-respecting diocese is without one, and in most cases, each will have several. Resources have been poured into the movement, with many dioceses and Methodist districts having dedicated officers. In some Anglican dioceses, individual deaneries have set aside income and resources to cultivate distinctively local Fresh Expressions. Thus, there are Fresh Expressions for clubbers, Goths, Mums n' Tots, silver surfers, post-Evangelicals, pre- and post-Christian folk, generation X and Y, and more besides.

Indeed, the very idea of targeted or niche church seems to have captured the attention of most denominations: a 'shape' of church that reaches out to those who lack a specific 'connection' to church is the primary driver for a plethora of rhetoric that appears to respond sensitively and resourcefully to a range of neuralgic concerns about the place of faith in public life. Thus, a phrase such as 'mission-shaped church' will often accompany a theological construction of reality such as 'being church'; and 'staying fresh' will be a spiritual and missiological imperative. Cultural relevance – and by implication, something that 'ordinary' churches can no longer truly accomplish – is elevated as the primary mode of engaging with contemporary society. The movement is not without its critics. For example John

---

[1]   Source: Church of England Fresh Expressions website.

Hull (2006) points out that he can legitimately register his anti-nuclear Christian protest group as a Fresh Expression of church. His case is supported by a glance at some of the literature emerging from within Fresh Expressions groups.

At a recent visit to the Greenbelt Festival in Cheltenham, a large and wide range of Fresh Expressions were offering sample services and hospitality, or actively recruiting new Christians who might fall within their locality. Proponents of Fresh Expressions are very open to conversation, and throughout the Festival it was possible to meet members and savour something of the experience and ethos that one might encounter in each group. That said, and as with most ethnography, the diversity of experiences available is best described by the organizations themselves:

- *Park* – Officially nameless, but we are a Christian community living in Park, Sheffield, so that will do. The name's been given to the area because it doesn't seem to actually have a name. So it's quite fitting. It'll probably stick and we'll be called this forever … Natal Faith … You'll never understand the mystery of life forming in a mother's womb or the mystery at work in all that God does. Meditation on feminine images of God and the mystery of birth within ourselves and our communities.

- *Foundation* is an alternative worship community based in Bristol, whose goal is to bring the experience of Christian community into a healthy relationship with contemporary culture … Unknowing God … A service exploring how experience of ordinary life erodes our fixed ideas about God. How can faith be reborn on the other side of weariness and doubt?

- *mayBe* is an emerging church community in Oxford, attempting to follow in the way of Christ by prayer and action for a better world now … Beautiful Day … A sacramental journey into the earthly holiness of the present moment. Breathe in and find the unexpected in the ordinary.

- *Journey* is a group of spiritual explorers in the Christian tradition who meet in Birmingham … Stations of the Cross … Join Journey as we take you through a guided meditation of art and music based on the ancient practice of the stations of the cross.

- *Moot Community* is a developing spiritual community who seek to find a means of living a life that is honest to God and honest to now. A Divine Sense of Place. Buses, cars, platforms, trains, desks, beds, coffee shops. Meditations for daily life; the divine in the everyday; come, taste and see.

- *Sanctuary* (Birmingham) – The focus of Sanctuary is unconditional love, acceptance and forgiveness to people of other or no faith. In order to help people feel safe and secure, lighting is low and there is space for private meditation and prayer. Sanctuary meets in a suburb of Birmingham outside the main Asian areas in order to be safe for people to come without being seen by their community … a safe place for British Asians or anyone interested in exploring eastern and western spiritualities in Christ. It is a place of space, peace, meditation, grace and friendship.

- *Sanctuary* (Bath) ... meeting in Bath seeking to explore and build Christian community. This takes the shape of meeting together regularly for worship, bible study, discussion, art events and food ... An All-age communion service, particularly appropriate for primary age children.
- *Dream* – a network of seven groups in the Merseyside area of Bolton. Our focus is on building community that values openness, honesty and freedom in the exploration and pursuit of spirituality centred on Jesus ... A Life More Ordinary ... An invitation to fishermen, shepherds, vicars and tarts, and all other extraordinary people with ordinary lives to explore the presence of God and reality of heaven in your story ...

These descriptions – all drawn directly from the *Greenbelt* brochure of 2007 – draw one's attention almost immediately to the sense of identity that each group appears to have constructed for itself. The groups clearly see themselves as groundbreaking, original, novel, cutting-edge and alternative. That said, a slightly closer inspection of some texts could cause some to wonder whether or not the authors are either being naive, or merely trying to be ironic. What, after all, is original about a church group that meets regularly for 'worship, bible study, discussion, art events and food'? There cannot be many ordinary churches that do not engage in most of these activities. It is something of puzzle, then, to really get underneath the rhetoric, codes and ciphers that are being presented, since they appear to be somewhat bland, and in some senses, quite superficial.

The self-narration of the groups though, does reveal a fascination – even obsession – with being new and alternative. That is, ironically, not an especially fresh development within the sub-culture of 'soft' or open' British evangelicalism, which has an established tradition of continually re-inventing modish associational models of the church.[2] That same tradition has been gently experimental with a variety of dense and intense forms of congregationalism in the post-war era. It has also tended to derive its ecclesiology from biblical roots (usually accessed in a hermeneutically direct rather than nuanced manner) that focus on either the (alleged) pre-institutional state of the church (e.g., Book of Acts, Jesus and his disciples, etc). Or, the configuration, organization and ethos of the Fresh Expression has been derived from an apparently obvious biblical grammar and theological construction of reality, which assumes that the shape and identity of the New Testament church could be easily agreed and was somehow its ideal and complete (or even revealed). Ergo, the more *like* a New Testament church a group can appear to be, the better, purer or more original it is held to be.

---

[2]   See Weston (2006). Newbigin (2006) contrasts 'associational' (or congregationalist) models of the church with the parish system. Whilst recognizing the power of the associational, Newbigin remains firmly committed to the parish model (p. 141). See also Dulles (1974), who develops five models of the church: institution, mystical communion, herald, servant and sacrament. And Hopewell (1987), who offers four models: mechanistic, organic, contextual and symbolic.

This, in part, accounts for why many fresh Expressions resemble small church 'home groups' or early versions of House Churches – but with a slightly enhanced ethos and sense of identity. The groups are trying to return to a kind of (mythic) primitive and intimate fellowship that, it is held, the New Testament primarily advocates as the 'model' for the church. Here, the size of the group will not matter especially. What binds the members of such groups together is the sense that they are participating in something that is simultaneously fresh, new, original and culturally relevant on the one hand; and on the other, securely located in the past (i.e., the scriptures or the New Testament Church).

What follows from this is that 'church' – as an institution – emerges as the problem, rather in the same way that the early House Church Restorationists used to read and interpret scripture and the complex sweep of church history. As Andrew Walker pointed out in *Restoring the Kingdom* (1985), early Restorationist leaders believed that church history had rarely witnessed a 'pure' version of the church. The first four centuries up until Constantine, and the reformation period (significantly, both anti-establishment eras) were deemed to be times when the Holy Spirit was 'active', and unencumbered by the established nature of an institutional church. Early Pentecostalism (i.e., pre-denominational) was affirmed, as was Restorationism itself, which of course did not regard itself as an expression of denominational identity, but rather a restoring of the kind of Christian fellowship that is allegedly narrated in the New Testament. For it is the church, with all its trappings, miscibility, complex structures and organizational baggage, that is held to have masked or corrupted an arrangement of people and ideas that should be fairly simple, and in some ways quite virginal. For this reason, I note with interest that very few participating within the Fresh Expressions movement add the rider 'of church'. The second part of the phrase has been quietly, innocently and unconsciously parked by most adherents, leaving only the proponents (who need the resources and income of the church to sustain the movement) as the ones using the full phrase.

But what evidence might there be that the Fresh Expressions movement is a form of collusion with a contemporary cultural obsession with newness, alternatives and novelty, rather than the recovery of a lost theological, missiological or ecclesiological priority? We are on tricky ground here, to be sure. Yet a sketch of recent 'open' evangelical history in England might lend some gentle support to this hypothesis. To help us here, I wish to introduce two fictional friends, whom we shall call Geoff and Anne, and who have been leaders within English charismatic renewal and related evangelistic movements for around 40 years. Geoff and Anne are 'into Fresh Expressions in a big way right now'. They speak for the movement, and are closely aligned with its agenda.

We first meet Geoff and Anne in the early 1970's, and are immediately aware of their interest in the Fisherfolk and other experimental Christian communities. The Fountain Trust, Michael Harper, Colin Urquhart and other pioneers of early charismatic renewal also feature in their interests and conversations during this time. During the 1970's and 1980's these foci develop apace: the church growth movement (Donald McGavran, Eddie Gibbs, etc), as well as a number of individuals who are beginning Christian healing ministries such as Jean Darnell, Jackie Pullinger, Doreen Irvine and David Pawson. The work of John Wimber then emerges as something of a breakthrough, following a close interest in David Watson's ministry and 'conversion' to charismatic renewal. First Geoff and Anne sign up for 'power evangelism'; then 'power healing'; closely followed by the third and fourth waves of the Holy Spirit, before the Kansas City prophets and the Toronto blessing. There were other interests too: Disciple a Whole Nation (DAWN), Alpha Courses, 'Jesus in Me' (JIM), Minus to Plus, church planting, cell churches, a wide variety of healing and therapeutic ministries, and many more movements and initiatives besides. As the millennium approaches, their interest with Wimber fades, and they begin to follow the revival at Pensacola, and also become more absorbed with neo-Pentecostal figures such as Benny Hinn and Reinhard Bonnke. The early years of the twenty-first century see Geoff and Anne being drawn into the new alternative of the cell church movement, and then Fresh Expressions.

I do not mean to offer a cynical or critical perspective. But Geoff and Anne's spiritual trajectory here prompts several questions. Is it the case that Geoff and Anne have been on the cusp of every micro and major wave of the Holy Spirit over the last 40 years? Or, that they are simply part of an associational church or congregationalist culture that is almost instantly absorbed and captivated by whatever seems to be new, fresh and alternative? Or that, in the late-modern elevation of the individual in relation to God, religion and faith have become consumable commodities, that constantly require updating, some discarding and regular (novel) replenishment?

In other words, the very character of believing and belonging follows the traces of all other 'fashions'? And what does all of this tell us about the missiological drivers that might be underneath the surface of an apparently innocent movement, such as Fresh Expressions? In the commentary that follows, we shall seek to flesh out some of these concerns in a little more depth, in order to try and engage in some empathetic yet critical decoding of the Fresh Expressions movement.

Commentary

Contemporary English church-going habits correlate with the two main religious economies that can be observed in Europe. The first is a 'market model', which assumes voluntary membership will soon become the norm. The second model is 'utility', where membership is ascribed rather than chosen. In the first model, individuals opt in to become 'members'. In the second model, all in some sense are deemed to 'belong', unless they opt out. The two models are in partial tension, and arguably depend upon each other. One may further characterize these differences as 'intensive' and 'extensive' forms of ecclesial polity. Some sociologists of religion think the 'extensive' will not be able to survive without the intensive.

Some ecclesiologists think that the intensive is fundamentally dependent upon the extensive.

If one accepts this hypothesis, one becomes immediately aware of a tension and ambiguity around the identity of the Fresh Expressions movement. It uses all the rhetoric of extensity, outreach and engagement. Yet it is largely composed through intensity and in-reach; apart from some notable exceptions, it would seem that many individual Fresh Expressions are made up of Christians who are weary of the church as an institution, but still desire fellowship and individual spiritual sustenance. This suggests that the Fresh Expressions movement, despite its claims to the contrary, is a form of collusion with the post-institutionalism that is so endemic in contemporary culture. Some exponents openly admit this, and point out that this is 'church' for people who no longer join bodies or associations. But this risk here is clear. Belonging together in a body with higher purposes places demands on individuals and groups, including those of duty and service: this is discipleship. Demand-led groups, in contrast, may just service people's desires for more meaning and fulfilment, whilst vesting this in the language of purpose, connection, and even sacrifice. As Peter Schmiechen puts it, 'While Jesus Christ does in fact meet our heartfelt and deepest needs, in America the gospel too often has become a technique for self-improvement and personal happiness' (Schmiechan, 2005, p. 247).

On a recent visit to a church that has spawned a large number of 'cell churches' and Fresh Expressions, a map on the wall in the foyer illustrated the problem more starkly. Maps, of course, as any anthropologist knows, are representations of reality. They require the reader to collude with scales, symbols and other codes to develop a sense of what is on the ground. But the map is not reality; the same applies to any description of anything – it must also be interpretative. This particular map placed itself at the centre of the city it was ministering to, and from the centre, ribbons flowed out far and wide to the suburbs, which were then pinned in a significant number of peripheral locations. It was kind of web-like image, if you will. The message of the map was clear: we have the city covered.

Yet I was well aware that a number of the identified locations were far from obvious. To be sure, there could be no question that groups of Christians, who attended this church, were meeting in these neighbourhoods, week in, week out. They were praying for these localities too: 'naming and claiming' the streets in passionate and concentrated extemporary prayer meetings. But I also knew where these gatherings were held, and that, with one or two rare exceptions, the vast majority of the inhabitants of these neighbourhoods (including those that attended their own ordinary local or parish churches) were ignorant of these gatherings. In other words, for the church in the city centre, there was a map and a story that spoke of widespread engagement with all these different neighbourhoods. Yet on the ground, there was little evidence to support this. Thus, the city centre church continued to feed off and promote its rhetoric of *extensity*. Whereas the actuality – in missiological terms – was one of *dispersed intensity*. The two are not, of course, the same. Dispersed intensity lacks the complex social engagement that can really only come about through dense and reticulate institutional structures that emerge out of churches that are committed to deep local extensity. Further, it could be argued that this form of Fresh Expression is merely a mere imitation of a much older established mode of church. The genius of the Deanery system – a legal collation of parishes in the Church of England – is that it consists of a range of extensive and intensive models, and an assortment of hybrids. This ensures that a relatively small area offers different types of parish ministry. The mixed ecclesial economy arguably offers a far stronger missiological foundation than the modern innovations.

So, based on what we currently know about the Fresh Expressions movement the following brief comments may be salutary for the majority of examples under consideration. First, the local church is under severe pressure from both outside and inside the church. Ironically, the proliferation of the Fresh Expressions movement may threaten the relationship between religious and social capital. But if Fresh Expressions movement turns out to be an expression of post-associational-ism, there may be serious trouble ahead.[3] The lack of 'thick' connection between a Fresh Expression and local commitment (i.e., duty, obligation, etc) may diminish social capital, despite many claims to the contrary.

Second, as Robert Bellah notes, multiple-choice ('niche spirituality') 'suggests the possibility of million[s of] American religions – one for each of us'. So does the Fresh Expressions movement collude with pluralism and individualism – whilst cloaked in the rhetoric of 'alternative', 'new' and 'fresh' forms of church? If it does, then the survival of the 'community of memory' is at risk – replaced by 'empathetic sharing' by loosely associated individuals. Faith is privatized; it becomes the property of a sect that sees itself as engaged with but apart from society.

Third, faith in the Fresh Expressions movement may lead to 'over-specialization' in the 'faith sector'. 'Quasi-therapeutic blandness' sets in, which cannot resist 'the competition [with] more vigorous forms of radical religious individualism, with their dramatic claims of self-realization, or the resurgent religious conservatism that spells out clear if simple, answers in an increasingly bewildering world' (Bellah, 1986, pp. 113ff). Put another way, the Fresh Expressions movement may represent a conservative, therapeutic and individualist *retreat* from the world, whilst cloaked in a rhetoric that emphasizes the very opposite of this: namely 'cutting edge', 'radical', and so forth.[4]

Fourth, it would seem that the insights of Putnam concur here. He notes how the [apparent] 'community building efforts of the new denominations have been directed inward[s] rather than outward[s]' (Putnam, 2000, p. 123). Thus, members of the Fresh Expressions movement may well join important (and of the moment)

---

[3]   On this, see Bellah (1985), esp. Chapter 6, and Putnam (2000).

[4]   On this, see Woodhead and Heelas (2005). The authors argue that formal religious organizations are giving way to individualistic and relational forms of spirituality and sacralized therapeutic insights.

politically active or campaigning groups to achieve certain ends, at local, national and international levels. But the investment in the complex relationship between spiritual and social capital will often be lacking (e.g., paying church quotas that support a vast and complex ecclesial infrastructure – parish coverage, sector ministry, education, prison ministry, etc).

Fifth, 'the primary objective of 'brandscaping' is not to sell the product but to generate a fascination with the brand; to get the customer to identify with the world of the brand, creating a brand awareness and providing it with a deep emotional core' (Riewoldt, 2002, p. 2). One can conceive of the Fresh Expressions movement as a 'brand', but not a product – in fact, it is not clear what is being sold. But the brand creates the sense of 'fresh' starts, horizons and newness: just one 'expression' of something existential and grounded. It is a kind 'commodity fetish', as Marx would arguably have concurred: an obsession with reified and recent – a sort of postmodern product that confirms the virility of the producer. Almost anything can be a fresh expression – a Book of Common Prayer service; a drop-in centre; a toddler group with some prayer and choruses. None of these are 'church', *per se*; but they have a new 'brand' that offers hope, newness and the simulation that in-dwelling the novel will somehow take us somewhere different, and better – it is a pure but subtle form of consumerism. The websites seem to confirm this, offering an array of soft, subtle and toned spiritual choices.

Sixth, the rhetoric of 'alternative' is also problematic, because it is overly dependent on (a mostly) docile but larger 'host' body to support the implied contrast. But there are dangers here for the Fresh Expressions movement. After innovation and charismatic authority has waned, bureaucratization inevitably emerges as a strategy to cope with potential disenchantment. One also questions the cultural relativity of modish quasi-ecclesial rhetoric. For example, the attention to 'steps' and 'programmes' in health, wealth and prosperity movements (deeply rooted in American pragmatism, but only thinly and derivatively connected to gospel values). Or take the emphasis on 'power', 'expansion' and 'growth' in more mainstream Protestant churches in the 1980's – precisely correlating with capitalist culture, producing congregations obsessed with the latest [apparent] biblical, experiential or ecclesial steroids: how to get maximum growth with minimum effort; how to be bigger and better than your neighbour.

Seventh, the Fresh Expressions movement is a curiously bourgeois phenomenon.[5] One website advertises prayer mats inspired by 'our [leaders'] visit to Tuscan', and a 'souk' that sells/exchanges home-made bags, purses, broaches, belts and other items that 'express [our] creativity'. There are meals, walks in the park, holidays, days out, art galleries, exploration and journeys. The imagery is telling – stones, rivers, sunsets, sky; children, young people and families. No old people, death, images of decay or hardship. The language is born of a middle-class 30–40-something age-group beholden to 'fresh' and 'organic' concepts (including nutritional advice); a God of the *Gap* or *Habitat* consumer. One idea

---

[5]   See Cobb's (2005) discussion of commodity and Cavanagh (2008).

for prayer suggests 'it's the holiday season – and if you can, go for a swim. If that's not possible take time to enjoy the sensation of water on your body as you shower ...'.[6]

Eighth, the Fresh Expressions movement is somewhat Janus-like in its missiological outlook. Is this movement the new highway to mission, or rather a series of new intricate cul-de-sacs? For example, what is a Fresh Expression doing when it designates their leader 'Abbot', and key or core members as 'Guardians'? Can it really be much more than hubris that such a dense and traditioned concept as 'Abbot' is appropriated for what is still a new, thin and rather un-tested group? The danger is that we are all too easily immersed in a semi-detached and sacred meaning-making enclave within consumerist culture. Left to its own devices, the Fresh Expressions movement may actually be deeply collusive with consumerism, offering alternatives and affirmations simultaneously (but note, not critiques); a kind of 'commodity fetish', as Marx might say. As Jackson Lears notes, 'under certain circumstances [the marketplace holds] out a vision of transcendence, however fleeting' (Lears, 1994, p. 9).

Conclusion – Ecclesiological Reflections

The purpose of this short reflection has been to challenge the relationship between contemporary culture and apparently new forms of Christianity such as the Fresh Expressions movement. The theological analysis of the implicitness of the movement that emerges from this brief discussion suggests that many examples of Fresh Expressions are symptomatic of contemporary culture, which has typically adopted the rhetoric of 'new', 'alternative' and 'fresh', which in turn is rooted in increasing individualism, and the inward turn to fulfillment and personal enhancement. This, in turn, represents an uncritical absorption of post-institutionalism within the movement, that is further vested in a rhetorical cluster of tropes – 'local', 'cell', 'fresh' come to mind – which legitimize the retreat from the duties (and occasionally drudgery) of supporting and sustaining larger organizations that seek to offer something to society through utility-extensive models of service. The work of Susanna Freidberg (2009) lends weight to this. She explores the contemporary consumerist absorption with 'fresh', which connects consumers to nature, community and health – but also as a cheap, convenient and immediate form of sating consumer appetites. The paradox here is that the hunger for that which is fresh is the outcome of mass consumption: simultaneously proof of and the antidote to progress.

The plethora of Fresh Expressions – dispersed forms of intensity – masks the retreat from the drudgery of engaging with older organizations, and in so doing critically undermines the very host body that sustains it. The core body appears to be too weak to resists the onslaught of 'alternatives'; yet the alternatives can only

---

[6] Source: mayBe website.

survive if the core body is sustained.[7] This is indeed ironic. Fresh Expressions appears to be a form of faith that exists for those who don't like religion: spiritual, but not religious. Forms of faith that are sufficiently fluid and light to catch the attention of individuals, but at the same time ensure no-one is overly burdened with commitments they may not wish to ultimately entertain.[8]

Of course, it may be possible to counter the current momentum of the Fresh Expressions movement with a number of commonplace observations. For example, new is not necessarily better than old; fresh is not necessarily superior to established; and effervescence is not a substitute for substance. One might also add that in theological terms, innovation should be judged by tradition. (However, this is a complex argument to mount in both Anglican and Methodist ecclesiology.) Perhaps a better way of putting this would be to underline that 'emerging church' is not likely to be superior to the emerged church; infancy is not better than maturity; that innocence (and its assumed accompanying purity) is a starting point, not a goal. Moreover, that simplicity is not better than the demanding and dense complexity of wisdom.

Defining the turn of phrase 'fresh expressions' on its own terms of reference can also be illuminating. Definitions of 'fresh', from just about any dictionary, include the following: not salted; untainted; pure; new, novel, additional; recent, newly made; not stale; lively; not faded or fatigued. 'Fresh': implies 'consume immediately' and/or 'discard after sell by date'. The question, therefore, is how long before we speak of 'traditional fresh expressions'? And then what? Similarly, the definitions of 'expression' include: the action of pressing or squeezing out; character or feeling; an act representing something in a word or symbol; an appearance; sentiment; a sign or token. The question here is, I suppose, does this have sufficient density to be church?

Part of the puzzle of the Fresh Expressions movement is that its newness and lack of settled identity allow it to point in several directions. There is a clearly an enormous amount of energy and vision to admire and commend. The diversity of projects, encounters and ideas seems to be almost limitless, suggesting that the identity of the movement is very much caught up in the sense of this being centred on evangelism for a generation that is post-institutional, and perhaps post-ecclesial; but not post-spiritual or post-Christian. This must partly account for why the official Fresh Expressions website is rather coy about ecclesiology. It acknowledges that definitions of the church are 'difficult', and that Fresh Expressions are therefore not easy to define.

But underneath a rather playful ambivalence about what may or may not be 'church', there lurk some potentially serious dangers. Some of these are rooted in the constituency that Fresh Expressions has primarily drawn upon, namely individuals who have been weaned on associational patterns of the church, but are now expressing their spirituality in what they perceive to be a post-institutional

---

[7]   For further discussion, see Milbank (2008), pp. 117–28.

[8]   Or to follow the Clintonesque edict, smoking, but not inhaling.

culture. One consequence of this is that individual Fresh Expressions may be able to demonstrate a thick surface commitment to social and political engagement (e.g., Jubilee, a variety of ecological concerns, etc, will feature as organization supported by individual groups). Yet this is all a matter of conscious choice – the selection of issues and projects that further galvanize the identity of the Fresh Expression in question. But these same groups will not usually be engaged in helping to sustain the institutional church in all its miscibility and complexity. Put more sharply, how does a Fresh expression or one of its members *invest* in ordinary, serious, extensive ministry, whether that is in prison ministry, church schools, or simply ministry in an unremarkable place that needs sustenance and engagement? The danger for the Fresh Expressions movement is of colluding with post-institutionalism: legitimizing support for preferred causes with the promise of immediacy, and a clear return on a focused investment; whilst undermining the organizations that sustain our social and spiritual capital.

A further question can be put here: can this new type of post-institutional associational model really Christianize and convert society? Some advocates of Fresh Expressions would see the movement as engaging with the 'spiritual, not religious' generation. Laudable though this may be, a potential hazard here is that the movement may collude with contemporary culture in a potentially perilous way. Is there not a danger of weaning a generation of spiritual consumers who are resistant to religious demands? This would be directly counter to gospel teachings. As Woodhead and Heelas note, when asked by a lawyer what he had to do to inherit eternal life, Jesus did not reply 'well, what works for you?' (Luke 10: 25–8).

Where, for example, is the self-examination or deep intra-accountability of the Methodist Class systems? People bringing concerns and interests to a group composed through 'shared values' bears no real relation to prayer and discipleship groups of previous generations. Moreover, I have this nagging sense that the line between sacralized narcissism and some contemporary worship is wafer thin. Too much of the spirituality in Fresh Expressions seems to celebrate the self (e.g., 'beautiful me') in a kind of spiritual aspic.

More generally on the subject of ecclesiology, there seems to be little in the Fresh Expressions movement that has evolved beyond the cultivation of the kind of (bourgeois?) niche groups that could potentially be advocated through Donald McGavran's homogenous unity principle (church growth). (1970) McGavran argues that differences in economic, social and caste positions (e.g., in India) inhibit church growth. Ergo, by developing 'homogenous units' in which such differences need not be presented or surface, 'like attracts like'. Thus, a church simply for Hispanics, blacks or whites will tend to fare numerically better than attempting one large inter-racial church. For McGavran, the most effective way to numerically grow groups of Christians was to adopt his Homogenous Unit Principle – a section of society (or subculture) in which all members have something in common. There is no deep difference between the missiology that McGavran advocates and that of the Fresh Expressions movement. Indeed, the lack of reference to McGavran's work in the Fresh Expressions movement is a puzzle, since it is clear that his missiological DNA has deeply influenced the movement.

Fresh Expressions are, primarily, contemporary versions of the homogenous unit principle for church growth that were promoted over 40 years ago, but were subsequently widely discredited by theologians, and also condemned by missiologists for their focus on pragmatism, and their willingness to sanction narrowly-constituted groups (on the basis of age, gender, race, class, wealth, etc) as 'church', which of course then legitimizes ageism, sexism, racism, classism and economic divisiveness.

In one sense, then, we can say that Fresh Expressions is a case of 'old tricks for new dogs'. Or to paraphrase and adapt G.K. Chesterton's quip, it is not that church has been weighed and found wanting by many in the Fresh Expressions movement. It is, rather, that, it has been found too difficult and not really tried. Many Fresh Expressions therefore constitute a perfect fit for a post-institutional culture that does not want to invest in complex organizations and infrastructure for the common good.

That said, I do think that the Fresh Expressions can make a modest and positive contribution to the mixed economy of church life. At worst, the movement is a distraction – another way of keeping energetic folk occupied. On one level, this is not a problem. Why not have lots of epochs that enhance energy? I can only think of one reason. And that is that many of these movements have one thing in common – they avoid the 'C' word, with a relentless appeal to another 'C' word. It is fine to talk about Christianity: but Church is boring, cumbersome, institutional, messy and difficult. But I think Church is also *deep*. And I am wondering – with all the emerging post-evangelical rhetoric about religion-less Christianity – when it will be realized that Church is actually it. That parish ministry is still the cutting edge. And that without the institution of the church, all we'll have left is multi-choice spirituality, individualism and innovation. And that this simply won't be enough to sustain faith in future generations.

In terms of implicit theology, the Fresh Expressions movement can be seen as a form of faith that expresses contemporary 'secular' preoccupations: with pragmatism, growth, freshness, alternatives and newness. The movement reflects its post-millennial context, as well as post-institutional culture. The spirituality is individualistic, controllable, meaning-centred and inward-looking; and even when it is outward-looking and collective, it is fundamentally shaped by eclectic and individualistic concerns. In this sense, the implicit theology described here is the contemporary ecclesiological underside of what Edward Bailey suggests might constitute implicit religion (Bailey, 1997). In the kind of implicit theology I have been outlining, secular values have been consumed by associational patterns of the church and gently sacralized. Whereas in implicit religion, the secular expresses the sacred in ways it has yet to come to terms with.

Then again, the Fresh Expressions movement represents a serious attempt to engage with contemporary culture, and the fact that it can be identified as an enculturated version of contemporary faith should not necessarily lead it to be judged harsh. The emerging pragmatic missiology that the movement is producing will help to shape future entrepreneurial leaders: risk-takers who may indeed help to reframe our ecclesial paradigms.

The challenge for the church will, I suspect, lie in maintaining the extensive, utility and parochial forms of mission that go on each day, and are often unsung; yet also allowing the effervescence of new movements (usually associational in outlook, market-driven, intensive, etc) that will continue to both challenge and feed the institution. The church will need to avoid falling in to the trap of imagining that spiritual forms of post-institutionalism hold out any long-term hope for the future. I am sure they do not. What is now deemed to be fresh will probably not last. Indeed this is already happening: At the time of writing, two 'local fresh expressions' have announced that they have been unable to become self-funding ecclesial propositions within the five year time frame offered by their parent denomination. Indeed, the hope that these 'emerging churches' would become fiscal net-contributors to their denominations is not within reach.

The task of the church, sometimes, is just to wait, and hope, pray and work for better times. It is one of the major themes of the Old Testament, after all: waiting. We know that the period of exile may indeed be very long. But the answer is not to be found in turning our gaze to the new gods of a very different kind of Babylonian captivity.

Chapter 5
Alternative Perspectives:
Can there be 'Liberal' Church Growth?

Apparently, conservatism works. The 'Silver Ring Thing' (SRT), created in 1996 by Denny Pattyn (an evangelical Christian youth minister from Arizona), has been promoted as a means of combating sexual promiscuity and sexually transmitted diseases (STD's) amongst American teenagers. It has also provided a platform for the explicit promotion of 'biblical' outlooks on sexuality over and against mdern 'liberal' sexual values and behaviour. SRT has claimed to have won pledges of chastity amongst more than 25,000 young adults since its inception, and the movement has stated that they aim to have silver rings – signs and symbols of chastity – on the fingers of more than two million American teenagers by 2010. The movement has won praise and courted controversy. It was endorsed and funded by the government of George Bush (2000–2008) as a 'faith-based initiative'. This partly accounts for why the 'Silver Ring Thing' received over $700,000 of aid from President Bush, as part of a $270 million programme in 'virginity training' to combat teenage pregnancy and sexual diseases amongst the young. But the movement proved less successful when exported to Europe. Moreover, critics claim that the professions of abstinence do not last, and in any case, appear not to tackle the root and branch problem of an over-sexualized society – one that is utterly inured in sensuality.

That said, the conservative argument appears, more generally, to be playing a winning hand in social and moral public discourse, and in churches. The USA and Great Britain have high levels of teenage pregnancy, despite a great deal of investment in sex education. Ergo, the solution is to cut back on ('liberal') tried and tested forms of sex education, and invest public money in programmes that advocate abstention. Is this right? Well wrong, actually. The logic of the argument is deeply flawed, even on its own terms. If one accepted the diagnosis and prognosis asserted by the conservative viewpoint, one would naturally expect that countries where access to 'liberal' sex education and contraceptives were more widely available, it would lead to greater levels of teenage pregnancy and sexually transmitted diseases amongst the young.

But the truth is, at least in Europe, quite the opposite. America and Britain are two countries where Puritanical and Conservative sexual attitudes flourish, and where sex education amongst the young is comparatively weak. The figures tell an alternative story that rather undermines the Conservative narrative. In the USA, there are 53 teenage pregnancies per 1000 of the population – a record, incidentally, that is marginally worse than India, Rwanda or the Philippines. In the UK, the figure is 20 per 1000, in contrast to Germany and Norway (11 per 1000), Finland (8 per 1000), Sweden and Denmark (7 per 1000) and Holland (5 per 1000).

In contrast to the message of the 'Silver Ring Thing', these figures suggest that explicit sex education is more effective than the advocacy of ('Victorian'?) restraint and implicit moral values, focused on abstinence. The latter only leads to secrecy and guilt; it keeps important social, moral and personal issues locked away. But it fails to stifle desires and urges, the consequences of which are all too plain to see. To put it bluntly, abstinence programmes probably do more harm than good. Or perhaps to press the point more forcefully, 'conservative' agendas tend to breed the very 'liberal' cultures that they seek to check. 'Liberal' cultures, in contrast, can lead to the establishment of more conservative cultural values, where in this case, teenage pregnancy becomes less socially normative.

These points may seem tangential to a discussion of church growth, but my purpose in beginning this way is to highlight just how unhelpful the labels 'conservative' and 'liberal' can be in describing not only ethos, but also outcomes. To be sure, there are plenty of complex cultural and demographic reasons why explicit and widely available sex education in one country leads to enhanced moral and social responsibility, and in another, leads to embarrassment and prurience. We are all, I suppose, studies in contradictions. Take Japan: is it a conservative or liberal society? Many cultural commentators would be quick to assess it as conservative and progressive. But then what does one make of that same country that has one of the lowest ages of consent (13) in the G8 economies, and thinks nothing of selling rather 'childish' sex toys in almost any corner store?

Labels such as 'conservative' and 'liberal' are notoriously unreliable as guides to church growth. Too many exceptions suggest that Dean Kelley's rules for success have been broken long ago. There are theologically conservative churches, which are at the same time organizationally progressive and liberal, at least insofar as they sit light to their parent denominational structures. There are theologically liberal churches (the rise of 'mega' gay and lesbian Metropolitan Churches comes to mind) that unashamedly borrow growth strategies from Evangelicalism. There are burgeoning numbers of post-Evangelical churches, Cell Churches and new church movements, which are neither conservative nor liberal, theologically or otherwise. There are substantial Christian Unions at universities and colleges, but much evidence to suggest that the conservative religion that is espoused by such groups fails to captivate and equip most individuals beyond the thrall of years as students. Quite simply, the map of 'growing' churches does not show an easy delineation between the profits brought about by conservatism and the deficits allegedly created by liberalism. The economy is much more complex than this.

In this essay, therefore, I want to look at two specific areas that enable us to look below the surface of superficial analysis that all too readily identifies conservative growth and liberal decline. I want to suggest that, first, stories of growth and decline are often stubbornly rooted in particular cultures (that make space for both 'liberal' and 'conservative' worldviews), which unless understood and deconstructed, can paint a rather distorted interpretation of the ecclesial landscape. Second, I consider some of the recent theorists and strategists in 'mainline' or 'liberal' church growth, and how their contributions might alter prevailing ecclesial horizons. A brief conclusion looks at the possibility of empowering mainline churches for growth and mission in a way that is spiritually consonant with their tradition.

Conservative Culture and the Narrative of Decline

To tackle the first of these sections, we turn to James Hopewell's fine book *Congregation: Stories and Structures* (1987), and will use his insights to 'read' a fictional Anglican diocese. In Hopewell's narrative analysis of local congregations or churches, he identifies four genres of story that characterize ecclesial life and worldviews. These genres closely correspond to Northrop Frye's analytical categorization of literature: *Irony*, *Comedy*, *Romance* and *Tragedy*. Hopewell holds that irony relates to 'empiric', comedy to 'gnostic', romance to 'charismatic' and tragedy to 'canonic' (see Northrop Frye (1957), *The Anatomy of Criticism*). Now there is not enough time here to discuss these genres in detail, and, suffice to say, they can all be found in virtually every congregation and diocese, irrespective of its theological commitments. But my purpose in introducing the notion of genre at this point is to identify the diocese of Northfield. The diocese of Northfield is a northern Church of England diocese that comprises about 200 or so stipendiary clergy and parishes, in an area that is largely post-industrial. Its churches are primarily (but not exclusively) 'tragic' or 'canonic' in their storytelling. In turn, this identifies the diocese, at least in Hopewellian terms, as 'conservative'. But it is a form of cultural conservatism that is in fact wedded to a traditional understanding of Socialism, rather than being a particular form of theological conservatism. (There is a paradox here, about which more later.) The 'tragic' genre 'fits' with the prevailing 'low-church', post-industrial and working-class culture that dominates the diocese. But there are also deeper reasons why Northfield's narrativity is primarily 'tragic' in outlook.

In listening to congregational stories around the diocese, one is immediately struck by how deprivation and struggle are identified as 'true' and 'authentic'. Correspondingly, stories of 'success' or 'growth' are often seen as deviant, 'unreal' or 'inauthentic'. The clergy, particularly those who are native to the region, seem to share and cultivate these perceptions with the laity. The self-perception of the diocese is that it has the lowest church-going population in Europe – a mantra often repeated by senior clergy of the diocese. But the claim (ironically several other dioceses in the region also believe it of themselves) is used as a way to *validate* the story of struggle. In other words, it is a kind of trope; it *sounds* like a complaint, but actually, it is more of a boast.

Further attention to congregational and clerical narrativity also reveals some interesting binary paradoxes. Sacrifice is valued; but positive transformation is seen as illusory, and perhaps false. Suffering solidarity is a dominant and valued motif; but stories of 'slow resurrection' are essentially mistrusted by clergy and laity alike. It is not unfair to say that numerically growing churches are almost uniformly resented by the wider church culture within the diocese. It is almost as though 'growth' were somehow a betrayal of the gospel; the pathology of the diocese is that it anticipates a tragic worldview, in which its destiny is already settled, and the future ('faithful struggle in the midst of decline') already predetermined.

Thus, the 'mission statement' of the diocese places a stress on empathy with 'the pain of the world', but is reticent when it comes to articulating the role of the church as an agent change or transformation, except in the most general of terms. At a clergy conference (based on the theme of resurrection), senior staff chose the theological input for the residential gathering. It was not a lecture or a seminar led by a theologian (this was deemed to be potentially 'too contentious'), but the film *Regeneration*, from the novel of the same name by Pat Barker. In the story – a good fit for the tragic genre – shell-shocked officers during the First World War are rehabilitated at a special centre in the Highlands of Scotland, but only to be sent out to the front line once again to face further injury or death. Of course, *Regeneration* is not a story of resurrection or transformation at all, but one of ultimately hopeless and wasteful recycling. But as a story, it would speak (subconsciously) to many in the diocese, especially clergy, and would frame their sense of calling and destiny.

Arguably, the choice of such a film to convey a theological message could be seen as an odd, even ironic selection. But in actual fact, its emergence at the conference (and the absence of any challenge to the story-line) shows that the 'tragic' worldview is part of the established semi-conscious life (or identity) of the diocese. So it is not the case that any one person or group *consciously* articulates the necessity of tragic actors and plots. Rather, the tragic worldview emerges out of a long, multi-layered oral history in which expectations are already shaped. Semi-consciously, in the very act of local ministerial engagement, ministers find themselves colluding with the tragic worldview and ethos. So for many congregations and dioceses, there is a close match between *ethos* (the way things actually are) and *worldview* (the way things could or should be), since the church seeks to embody kingdom values.

In the case of Northfield diocese, the 'sacrificed hero' (either a minister or congregation) often emerges (in individual and congregational narratives) as the ikon of suffering in the midst of adversity; triumph lies in the ability of ministers or congregations to *indwell* tragedy, not in overcoming it. And, rather as in *Regeneration*, the task for younger ministers is to simply follow in the footsteps of their fallen or wounded comrades, who can only prove their worth to their peers by further acts of sacrifice. In other words, demonstrative suffering (but not necessarily acute failure) is actually *valued*. Correspondingly, those clergy that need rehabilitation are often regarded as those that have been *truly* engaged in the struggle (and are therefore heroic). Those who have no need of such help can therefore find themselves being characterized as being less engaged in the sacrificial struggle – not really working on the 'front line'. But the 'war' is never won or lost by such ministerial tactics and tropes. It is only lives that are sacrificed (which is, strangely, what counts). In the world of the tragic genre, Christ and his ministers are perpetually called to crucifixion.

Thus, and typically, many of the illustrative stories that are told by senior staff in sermons or at large diocesan occasions are ones where consolation, affirmation and 'making do' emerge as major motifs. Theologically, their sermons often place a stress on 'sacrifice' – either that of the laity or the priest – and then resource this from a catholic perspective or through evangelical doctrine. Consistently, oblation is offered alongside consolation. Where this does not happen, the tragic outlook quickly shifts into a romantic worldview, but reifying the visions and dreams is inevitably 'just out of reach'. The most frequently prescribed opiate to take away the pain of tragedy is a dose of romance – of what could be, if only ... . Stories or strategies of transformation or radical revision are rare. Sacrificial self-expenditure frequently emerges as the key value that shapes the horizon of possibility.

Furthermore, the culture of clerical obeisance in a primarily working-class diocese ensures that there is little self-critical awareness at any level that might lead to revision or transformation. This, coupled to an abundance of pride and paternalism that regards malfunction as confirmation of the authentic nature of the 'gritty' ministerial struggle, ensures that the diocese lives under a pervasive cloud of 'low-grade' depression, which is then, oddly, celebrated. The narrative of pride in suffering becomes sanctimonious. One is reminded of Monty Python's famous 'Four Yorkshiremen' sketch, which satirizes glorying in poverty and the lack of resources, in one of many famous tropes: 'We were happy in those days, though we were poor ... ay, *because* we were poor!' In effect, then, it is the Christ *of* or *under* culture that constantly emerges in diocesan narrativity. Pain is shared, and spread around as much as possible; but it is seldom challenged. The Christ who is against culture – who would resist struggle, pain and sacrifice – is conspicuously absent in the canonical litany of socio-ecclesial stories that shape the life of Northfield.

In a diocese where a tragic worldview dominates, outcomes are accepted as they are predictable: 'Christ lays aside his prior glory and accepts the tragedy of his life' (Hopewell, 1987, p. 81). Or, as Northhrop Frye puts it, 'tragedy seems to lead up to an epiphany of law, of that which is and must be' (Frye, 1957, p. 207). So the diocese consoles, comforts and affirms its clergy and parishes as they fulfil their destiny in the arena of tragic sacrifice. But little changes in a diocese that has a primary tragic or canonic worldview, because obedience to the plot is ultimately the path to fulfilment: 'the pattern for life in the present land is that of Christ, who was willing to take the cross and, in the words of the famous evangelistic hymn, willing to suffer all of life's misery' (Hopewell, 1987, p. 81).

To be sure, I am conscious that such remarks can only be generalizations. Any diocese will be bigger than the theory applied to it; churches will invariably exceed any analytical interpretation. And in sketching the narrativity of one diocese and its congregations, it is important to remember that other dioceses will have different emphases in their narrative structures and outlooks (or worldviews), and that these will frame quite different attitudes to organization and expectation. Certainly, historic patterns of church attendance will have a bearing on congregational expectations and the shaping of local narratives of growth and decline. However, the paradox of this particular conservative working-class is that it seems to fundamentally mistrust concepts of growth, whether 'organic' or 'engineered'. Interestingly, this means that virtually all initiatives that foster growth, whether or not they hail from radical-liberal or theologically conservative quarters, are more often than not placed at the periphery of the life of the diocese. Put another way, one can identify a form of conservatism, alive in churches, that is suspicious of growth. This, in turn, undermines at least part of the thrust of Kelley's thesis. As we shall now see, there are further complications when considering patterns of growth and decline in mainline church situations.

Mead and Mann on Mainline Church Growth

Amongst those who have reflected theologically and sociologically on the subject of growth in mainline denominations, Loren B. Mead is, by any standards, a name to be reckoned with. His ground breaking *The Once and the Future Church* was first published in 1991, and has gained a steady following amongst the mainline denominations within the United States of America, and indeed beyond. Mead is very conscious that the paradigms of being Church and local congregations in any given community have been rapidly eroded during the latter part of the twentieth century. He makes a remark that has an eerie resonance with some of Callum Brown's thinking (2002) that secularization began suddenly, in 1963, with the advent of popular culture. Mead notes:

> When and how did we change? Although it may sound trivial, one of us is tempted to take the shift sometime on a Sunday evening in 1963. Then, in Greenville, South Carolina, in defiance of the State's time honoured blue laws, the Fox Theatre opened on Sunday. Seven of us – regular attenders of the Methodist Youth Fellowship at a Buncombe Street Church – made a pact to enter the front door of the church, be seen, then quietly slip out of the back door and join John Wayne at The Fox. (1991, p. 42)

That said, Mead's *The Once and the Future Church* identifies three core ecclesial paradigms. The first, the Apostolic, can be understood as the initial Church, which followed in the wake of the death and resurrection of Jesus. These were the churches that sent people out, and their period of expansiveness fundamentally altered a variant of Jewish spirituality into a full-blown faith that embodied a myriad of cultures, creating pluralities of churches and congregations. This, secondly, led to the formation of the Christendom paradigm, in which sacred and secular combined to legitimize Christianity across the Mediterranean world, and in time beyond Europe to other continents. The third paradigm is Mead's identification of the gap between the first two paradigms, namely the church between the apostolic and the

Christendom models. Mead sees this as a set of conditions that have already been present in Christian history, but are arguably returning again in late modernity, albeit with some important cultural differences. He argues that:

> The third way of being Church has begun to be born, but its birth is not complete. Once again the Church and the individual person of faith are beginning to discover a sense of a new mission frontier. That frontier has not yet become clear or compelling enough; we see the horizon, but the path that we must follow remains obscure. (Mead, 1991, p. 20)

Mead then goes on to explore the tension between these paradigms that typically find their expression in churches today. For example, there is a tension between being a church of the parish as against being the Church of the congregation (1991, p. 44). Similarly, there is a tension between an emphasis on servant-hood, and conversion (1991, p. 46). The stress on servant-hood might well lead to the notion of the Church being actively engaged in a form of social service and cultural renewal, which may, in order to achieve its ends, downplay the differences it has between itself and its community, and in so doing place little emphasis on the conversion. On the other hand, churches that are actively engaged in 'saving souls' may be inclined to emphasis conversion, even if that risks the alienation of the very community in which the church finds itself situated. Mead contends that all churches have a tension between being exclusive and inclusive which can also have a profound impact on their sense of mission and identity.

Although one may dispute the sweeping diagnostic tendencies in Mead's work, the freshness with which he addresses the situation of churches in late modernity is nonetheless appealing and challenging. Specifically, Mead is interested in challenging those impediments to change that prevent numerical growth in mainline churches, especially those where atrophy and indolence has set in. For example, Mead identifies different kinds of resistances that are built into the systems of success that were developed by the Christian paradigm (1991, p. 60). These include strong, conservative institutional frameworks, leadership patterns, dependency-affirming relationships, and financial systems. Mead also shows that inadequate leadership can be an obstacle to growth, partly because many leaders have a poor theology of institutions, which in turn allow personal resistances to change to flourish. In an intriguing turn, Mead uses the work of behaviourist Elizabeth Kubler-Ross and her work on bereavement. Kubler-Ross, you may recall, identifies several key stages in the bereavement process: beginning with denial, working through to depression, coming through to bargaining, arriving at anger, and finally resting in acceptance. Mead suggests that the anatomy of change (including change directed at growth) within many congregations and denominations is essentially a form of bereavement process, albeit masquerading (in the bargaining and anger phases) as passion and innovation. To be sure, this is challenging material, but what does Mead have to say about future church and the particular ways in which mainline denominations might extricate themselves from their gradual disintegration?

Mead, wisely perhaps, offers general principles that can be applied to specific congregations and denominations. Mead begins his prescription by identifying the four dimensions of congregational life that are normally accepted by those within the discipline of congregational studies. These are:

1. Programme – the sum total of the things a congregation does, including what is on its calendar.
2. Process – the way in which the congregation does what it does: How its leadership works, and how its people and groups make choices and relate to one another.
3. Context – the setting of the community and the denomination, the external forces that constrain or influence what the congregation and its members are and do.
4. Identity – that rich mix of memory and meaning that grounds the congregation defining who it really is in its heart.

Mead obviously argues that the field of applied congregational studies needs to address each of these areas, and their inter-relationship. He suggests that working experimentally with congregations is a key to finding a way forward, which in turn means that congregations have to be willing to be patient with new initiatives. Tellingly, Mead also suggests that congregations need to pay attention to boundaries: The boundary one crosses in choosing to go to church; the boundary a pastor crosses in moving from one congregation to another; the boundary a person crosses in moving from one town to another, life boundaries; and the like. In all of this, Mead says that paying attention to margins, congregations can begin to understand how easy and how difficult it is for the churches to become open and closed, welcoming and unwelcoming and open or resistant to change. Steadiness and accountability also play their part, as congregations learn to trust those processes and begin to develop responses to spiritual needs, not only in the congregation, but also for those beyond them.

In *More than Numbers* (1993), Mead develops his earlier thinking, exploring the different kinds of growth that occur within congregations. He begins by acknowledging that many congregations will never grow in numbers, but, and this is crucial, this does not render those churches pointless. On the contrary, the varieties of growth that occur in congregations are to be identified and encouraged if the church is to have a future. Mead understands that some communities will benefit by churches deepening their spiritual growth, but that this in itself may not lead to numerical growth in the congregation. Similarly, the growth in the congregation that occurs because of a charismatic new leader might well be extensive, but it is not necessarily intensive and rooted, and may leave the congregation in a worse position (ultimately) than when there was no apparent or obvious growth before.

Mead illustrates the polarities in perceptions of growth by examining a case study. A small bequest is left to a congregation, but the question is what to do with it. There are several ideas, which include preparing the church, increasing the amount of time that the pastor can be available, setting up a feeding programme for the hungry, and revamping the education programme. But as Mead describes the debate, he points out that one fact seems to capture people's imaginations more than anything else: there were simply no resources in the area to help people to figure out how to get a job. So the bequest is used to rent some space in a shopping centre, which brokers services from public agencies, and also solicits the help of a nearby university, to help neighbourhood people analyse their skills, locate training opportunities and get some help seeking work. As Mead points out:

> The congregation's decision was not primarily shaped by jobs and money, but by a concern that people discover their gifts and learn how to use these gifts in service to the community. So while the community sees a Job Centre, the congregation sees it as a place for people to discover their ministries in the world. So far there has been no impact on membership of the congregation, although a number of neighbourhood groups and agencies now relate to the congregation. (1993, p. 40)

With a vignette like this, Mead suggests that there are four different categories of church growth:

1. Numerical Growth – that is growth in the ways we ordinarily describe it. Sunday attendance, size of budget, number of activities and growth in numbers of active members.
2. Maturational Growth – this is growth in the stature and maturity of each member and congregation; spiritual development, etc.
3. Organic Growth – this is the growth of the congregation as a functioning community, able to maintain itself as a living organism and one which engages with other institutions within its context.
4. Incarnational Growth – this is growth in the ability to take on the meanings and values of the faith story and make them real in the world outside the congregation. The congregation grows in its ability to enflesh in the community, which is what the faith is all about.

The kind of growth that very often applies to mainline denominations is organic and incarnational. Mead states that

> organic growth is about the task of building the community, fashioning the organisational structures, developing the practices and processes that result in a dependable, stable network of human relationships in which we can grow and from which we can make a difference. Organic growth is about interaction; between frustration and hope in all congregations. Many people find the

structures of their congregation are an obstacle to their ministries, draining energy away rather than generating it to spark mission. Organic growth is the call to shape congregations themselves to become communities that generate life and energy. Organic growth helps the organisational structures of the congregation, becoming a launching pad for the ministry rather than an institutional albatross around the collective neck of its members. (1993, p. 60)

Here I can offer two local examples of incarnational growth where the signs of the kingdom are present, but not immediately obvious. In one case, a businessman takes on a disused factory in a run-down part of town, where the economy is depressed. Through the development of an innovative product, the company grows from a tiny outfit into a sizeable organization. However, each of the workers is given a share in the management of the company, its future development, and a share of its profits. Jobs bring hope; workers are empowered; the local area begins to experience regeneration.

In a similar but different vein, another company structures its business so that all the workers subscribe to a core ethos, and affirm a common set of workplace values. The company is placed in 'common ownership' by its founders, so that all those engaged in its employ can share in its profitability. The Directors agree to be paid no more than ten times the amount that the lowest paid worker receives. The company creates a climate of opportunity, empowerment and responsibility.

Intriguingly, the founding directors of both companies attend the same church, and whilst they know each other slightly, have quite independently developed patterns of incarnational growth that marry their Christian commitment to their everyday commercial life. The strength of Mead's work lies in his recognition of the multiple ways in which, within a single congregation, growth can be happening unnoticed.

Alice Mann, another writer in the field of applied congregational studies, offers a slightly different take on the nuances of church growth. In her groundbreaking fieldwork, she has been concerned with explorations of size transition that puzzle many clergy and lay leaders of congregations. Mann provides analytical tools, stories from real situations, research and practical hints that are helpful in looking at expansion and decline in congregational contexts. In her *The In-between Church* (1998), she suggests that there are optimum sizes of Christian gatherings, which to some extent dictate both the style and process of leadership. In each of the four 'models' she identifies, the numbers refer to average worship attendance on any given Sunday.

First, there is the *family sized church* (1–50 members). Mann points out that this is a kind of single cell organism, a social system resembling an extended biological family in which everyone knows each other. Second, the *pastoral sized church* (50–150 members), is a multi-cell organism with a coalition of several overlapping family friendship networks, which are unified around the person and the pastor. When a congregation is portrayed in literature, films or in television, it is often made in this pastoral image: a church on the green with a single resident parson. Third, the *programme size church* (150–350 members) is known, as the name suggests, for the quality and the variety of its programmes. Its larger and more diverse membership will contain a critical mass of people from several different interest and age groups. Typically, the church will have part- and full-time staff, and lay leadership that is concerned with pastoral care, new member incorporation, community outreach and education. Fourth, the *corporate size church* (350–500+ members) is usually a significant institutional presence in the community. It may even have a cathedral-like building in a prominent location, plus associated institutions like a day school or a community centre, and a sizeable staff of highly skilled professionals.

Mann places no particular value judgement on each of these four models, but the distinction between single cell bodies, multi-cellular bodies, coalitions and conglomerates is intriguing. Mann understands that the negotiation between sizes, whilst not exactly a science, is nonetheless part of a complex nexus of social interactions, which includes the evaluation of the church by the community and its own sense of belonging. Critically, Mann's analysis raises a question about the suitability of the size of the congregation in relation to its environment. Should the congregation be growing? Should the congregation be attempting to try something different that engages the community? What is the relationship between spiritual and numerical growth? What is the relationship between resourcing and staffing and outreach? To be sure, it does not follow that the more congregations do, try and spend, the more likely they are to succeed. What Mann's research shows is that congregations need to centre on themselves, their core spiritual values, and what kind of community they belong to, in order to identify new prospects for growth and mission.

Building on this work, Mann suggests that there are real factors that may inhibit growth that need addressing. In her *Can Our Church Live?* (1999) she suggests that certain demographic realities are factors. People can move away, and new incomers may have different tastes that do not relate to what is already available within a given community. She also suggests that a more powerful factor in church decline is 'the loss of our first love'. She suggests that many churches have forgotten that God is primarily in the business of *redemption* rather than being engaged in the (undoubtedly wholesome) enterprise of *maintenance* – an immaculately tidy building, tidy records, ordered worship, and regular fellowship.

To be sure, she acknowledges that these are all fine, but she argues that unless the church can re-enter the redemption business, it will soon be out of business. Mann also understands that a factor in church decline is the difference between form and content. By this, she simply means that many churches implicitly assume that they must first convert individuals and groups to a style of life, values and preferences and it is only then and through those things, that they can be introduced to the gospel. Finally, Mann suggests a further factor in church decline: brittleness, the lack of flexibility and intransigence that bedevils many mainline denominations can make individual congregations unappealing and inhospitable.

So, what of redevelopment? Interestingly, Mann champions 'organic church growth'. Granted, social organisms are different from biological ones but nevertheless, they often manifest similar patterns of emergence and decline, and key stages in the life cycle of the congregation therefore need identifying if the church is to engage in or maintain its growth. This includes an understanding of the birth of the church, its formation, its stability and maturity, as well as what leads to its decline and death. The temptation in this organic life cycle of the congregation is to attempt to pivot the church on an axis between stability and formation. But the danger of this, in attempting to stave off death, is that no new birth can happen either. Correspondingly, the congregation becomes fixed in its sights, on efficiency and maintenance. Mann suggests that regaining flexibility, renewing identity of purpose and being willing to entertain dramatic transformation are key principles for mainline denominations as they seek to grow.

Again, Mann develops these ideas in *Raising the Roof* by suggesting that congregations that seek to actively grow must move from implicit and indirect assumptions about mission and spirituality to explicit and direct activism in relationality. This is important, because it allows the congregation as a whole to own afresh the spiritual charisms and core values that make up the life of the congregation. Instead of the congregation being allowed to become comfortable by investing time and energy in institutional maintenance, Mann suggests that congregations need to actively own the spiritual and religious reasons they have for being there together. Typically, this will involve engaging in steep learning processes that centre on Christian education, and exploring the ways in which power flows in and out of the church, as well as individual and corporate faith formation frameworks that account for how and why people belong to local congregations. It is only at this point, congregations can begin to truly explore the barriers to growth (which may well be within them). By placing the emphasis on spiritual growth, Mann understands that it is from that perspective that numerical and organic growth can be truly addressed. Here, Mann's work complements the early work of Loren Mead by calling congregations to pay attention to the barriers and boundaries that are within them, and that may inhibit growth. This is the case across the spectrum, whether congregations espouse 'liberal' or 'conservative' identities.

Conclusion

Concurring with these insights, Roozen and Hadaway (1994) suggest that there are now four types of growing liberal church. First, there are those that are market driven, and barely differ from those evangelical churches, except in their content and style. Second, there are growing mainstream churches in many denominational settings where the demographics make organic church growth relatively easy. These might include particular kinds of rural or suburban areas, or occasionally certain kinds of inner city areas that are undergoing regeneration or renewal. A third group of growing mainstream churches could be identified as 'niche'. These are churches that reach for gay and lesbian congregations, death congregations, churches for small racial or ethnic groups of various kinds, or may be radical and *avant garde*. The fourth and final group of growing mainstream churches, which arguably provide a greater source of hope for denominations but which are struggling with the loss of identity and apparently experiencing decline in members, are those churches that are spiritually orientated and liberal. Such churches are often involved in community ministry, with a clear focus on social justice. Yet at the same time, their work is rooted in deep and powerful worship experiences, which in many cases have transcended the established patterns set by their parent denomination.

Roozen and Hadaway recognize that Peter Berger's analysis (namely that there has been turn from the authority of tradition to experience as the focus of religious thought) does mean that liberal mainstream denominations are arguably particularly well suited to provide a reflexive and engaging spirituality that would lead to numerical church growth in the twentieth century. Roozen and Hadaway suggest that churches that are spiritually alive, radically inclusive and justice orientated have a real future, provided that those churches are clear about their identity and purpose, and willing to take risks. Moreover, they avoid the fear of revitalization if they are to become a spiritually orientated liberal church.

But what lessons can the diocese of Northfield, together with its congregations and parishes, learn from Mead and Mann? What would it mean to speak of 'church growth' in these situations? Several points need making here, which suggest that there are plenty of challenges, but also that much has already been quietly achieved. Arguably, the strategy as a whole turns on making the implicit far more explicit, and learning to celebrate varieties of growth and transformation rather than colluding with a conservative culture that is suspicious of change.

First, Mead and Mann both suggest that congregations and churches need to rediscover their core spiritual message. This is not merely an exercise in cognition, let alone 'adopting' an agreed mission statement or motto. It is, rather, a task that is centred on the passion and energy that gave life to the church in the first place. Leaving aside all issues of maintenance, what are the core spiritual values that enable this congregation to cohere? What is its good news for the neighbourhood? What does it want to proclaim in word, deed and ethos? What bad news is the congregation currently holding, that hinders growth? Only when this has been discerned can the congregation engage in collective outreach that is energetic and explicit.

Second, congregations need to identify and celebrate the different types of growth that occur within its life. Maturational, organic and transfer growth may be implicitly assumed to be commonplace. But can congregations learn to share stories of such growth in ways that are empowering and affective? Are there opportunities for congregations to offer feedback on how their spirituality has developed in recent years? Can such conversations be turned to engage the community, so that they see the church as a place of transformation and energy, rather than merely maintenance?

Third, mainline congregations must constantly confront the myth that only certain types of conservative church can grow. As we saw earlier, there are forms of conservativism that inhibit growth by curtailing questions and prematurely ceasing in exploration. Conservative cultures, ironically, attract large numbers of people who are effectively engaged in the business of maintenance, and seek transformation to that end. Liberalism, in contrast, has much to offer in terms of openness, questioning, freedom and fellowship that is no less attractive. Mainline churches need to continually discover new ways in which this can be celebrated, and remind the rest of Christendom that, whilst liberal churches can grow too. The growth can occur in their depth of discipleship, in their connectedness to the community, in their spirituality, and also in numbers.

As if one needed reminding, some of the most effective forms of ecclesial witness in the world are actually quite small, numerically. Numbers are something, to be sure. But they were never everything. The God of small things continues to smile on the marginalized and the overlooked. Mainline churches need to worry about size a little less, and concentrate on worship, discipleship and outreach just a little more. Whoever planted, and no matter who watered, it is only God who gives the growth.

Chapter 6
Organic Church Growth: Some Possibilities

Introduction

In his thesis, *Why Conservative Churches are Growing* (1986) Dean Kelley contends that in order for a church to grow numerically, there has to be some kind of clarity about its purpose. Religion, claims Kelley, is about providing ultimate meaning for people: making sense out of existence; and also answering the question 'why do bad things happen?' So Kelley argues that in order for a strong sustainable community to develop, there needs to be a sense that the community itself is so important that it demands commitment, and that this same commitment needs to be at some cost to the members. Correspondingly, for a church to grow numerically, there needs to be a sense that it has something to offer in making sense of life; and that it demands a commitment by return. If it costs nothing to belong to such a community, it can hardly be worth joining

There is a good deal of implicit assertiveness in Kelley's thesis, which bears analysis. He discusses the importance of strictness in upholding the values and boundaries of such a community, and reflects on Kierkegaard's call for 'serious religion'. Here Kelley asserts that liberal and mainstream churches have lost the sense of 'defined boundaries', with the principle of religious tolerance and individual freedom being embraced to such an extent that the churches no longer espouse a faith that people deeply and sacrificially commit to. Such churches are 'lukewarm', and though they may be engaged in much good work, they do not have clarity in their religious expression. Correspondingly, energy is expended into espousing a good cause or practical service, which though implicitly connected to the understanding of faith, is not about the churches main purpose of drawing people in to a community of salvation. Kelley therefore argues that the more conservative churches have a better record in turning round the lives of the socially excluded, by converting them to a new meaning in life which demands a changed lifestyle.

To be sure, Kelley's ideas constitute a simple, compacted and logically coherent thesis. But the question contemporary ecclesiologists, missiologists, practical theologians and sociologists of religion might ask is also simple: does it make sense? The answer here must at least be in some doubt, for we know that even in measuring numerical strength, there are multiple ambiguities. How does one account for the large rise in numbers attending cathedral services in the Church of England, where there is patently no relationship between strictness and strength? Equally, how would one explain the burgeoning number of metropolitan churches that attract niche neo-liberal groups? Even a preliminary survey of churchgoing habits in the twenty-first century suggests that there are more exceptions to Kelley's 'rules' for growth, which therefore renders the thesis somewhat unsafe.

That said, there can be no denying of the importance of meaning in churches. But defining the purpose of the church need not be strict or exclusive; it can also be inclusive and open (and no less attractive for this). The complex struggle for mainstream and liberal churches remains, stubbornly, centred on how to continue to encourage commitment, and how to communicate the seriousness of the gospel and teach people about the cost of discipleship. Or put another way, the task might be to discover ways of being unapologetic about faith, which do not inhibit those same churches from being tolerant. Is it possible to be religiously tolerant, and yet truly communicate a faith that is life changing? Can liberal and mainstream churches teach about lifestyle, but without interfering with individual liberty?

It might be said (and perhaps this is something of a caricature), that mainstream churches do not expect too much from their members. They tend not to worry about members who miss three or four Sundays. Anxious to avoid inducing guilt, and equally concerned to under-communicate a sense of urgency, mainstream churches typically adopt a mellow attitude to belonging, and tend to tolerate a variety of inchoate expressions of belief. In one sense, mainstream churches are reconciled to understanding their congregational composition: a mixture of loyalists and consumers. Yet this attitude should be contrasted with more evangelical churches, where the 'non attendance' of a member is interpreted rather than tolerated. Perhaps the person is 'backsliding'? Maybe they are struggling with their faith and need support? Where Kelley is correct is in understanding that evangelical and conservative churches grow first and foremost by engaging their members in deep bonds of commitment; and then again through evangelism. Such churches readily accept that people want to make seriously informed choices about church attendance.

Yet church growth has never been such a simple matter. There is a multiplicity of institutional and contextual factors that can account for the numerical growth of a church. In England, a popular junior Church of England school can lead to extensive community involvement in the church. Other demographic factors may also have a bearing, such as class, ethnicity and wealth. If action flows from identity, then a community with a close-knit sense of itself may find its religious expression more 'productive' than a more disparate community. In general, effective evangelism flows out of a sense of purpose, excitement and mission. Correspondingly, strictness and strength may not be, as Kelley suggests, such decisive factors.

That said, the most fundamental problem for the ebbing mainstream churches is often the lack of compelling reasons for people to participate. Mainstream churches can be embarrassed about talking about God, and their fear of intolerance can then lead to a chronic lack of religious conversations and overt religious output in the local community. All too frequently, mainstream and liberal churches can lose their core public identity in asserting their breadth and diversity (i.e., tolerance), rather than communicating they do, in fact, believe in God.

How Do Churches Grow?

One of the more interesting questions any Vicar of a parish might have to ponder is, 'why do people come to this church?' Granted, the answers that one is likely to get will reflect, to a certain extent, what the laity thinks they should say. Posing this question in a small group recently, we were offered two very different answers. The first person replied that he came to church 'to worship Jesus Christ as his Lord and saviour'. The second stated that 'she came out of habit'. Yet in encouraging people to come to church there is a sense in which both these answers become important. People need to know what it means to be a Christian; and that this involves worshipping the God who is known and encountered through Jesus Christ. They also need to develop a lifestyle in which Church attendance becomes habitual (as well as desirable), and a normal part of their daily existence. More conservative churches then need to work hard on both communicating a neatly defined definition of faith (with a strong sense of obligation in personal lifestyle), which will in turn include regular attendance. This combination – of a strong message and a demanding commitment – is given as one of the reasons for the growth of conservative churches.

In agreement with Kelley, we would also wish to affirm that a healthy church is likely to be a numerically growing church (or at least 'self-replenishing'). Central to the Christian faith is the belief that Christ's message is for all, and that people can find their lives enriched and blessed if they turn to Christ. Therefore, all churches, whatever their theological position, should rejoice when new members join them, and indeed anticipate this. Yet numbers are very far from being the main rationale for being a church. Some of the most powerful forms of witness come from the smallest Christian communities, whose numbers do not obviously grow, but whose impact is extensive far beyond its slight membership. Equally, some (apparently) successful and large churches can turn out to have only slight and marginal impact upon a wider community. As the old adage goes, it's quality that counts, not quantity.

That said, we agree that a declining attendance will have a debilitating effect on a congregation at lots of levels. In practical terms, falling numbers impact on volunteers and on finance; and they also alter the feel of worship. A church which sees new members is invariably stimulated and encouraged. It usually benefits from new gifts and skills as well as better finances. Some traditions in the church are strongly driven by a missionary zeal to make disciples for Christ. This zeal is usually underpinned by a belief that those who do not profess faith in Jesus Christ will not attain the (eternal) rewards of belonging to God. Sharing one's faith is an obligation, and the concern for the eternal destiny of others can provide a clear motivation. Then again, if the theology of the church takes a more liberal view of salvation, then clearly the task of recruiting can become less urgent, as less depends on belonging and believing. If this is also coupled with a sense that the tradition is hesitant about articulating ultimate truths, and must also allow for individual freedom, then the missionary task becomes more complex. Yet we would also wish to argue that churches which hold a liberal position can do so with passion and commitment, and can still believe that the message of the gospel is life-enhancing, and well worth sharing. How do they put this message across, and how do they draw others from interest into commitment?

Our own experience is in working within this theological tradition, and whilst we cannot claim rapid numerical growth, we have observed that the liberal or mainstream Anglican tradition of which we are part can consistently and regularly welcome new members. Reflecting on Kelley's assertion – that religion needs to give people a means of making sense of life – it is clear that people join churches across the traditions, because of specific life experiences that they need to make sense of. What is perhaps especially interesting has been to observe that people have been attracted to ordinary, broad and mainstream churches precisely because they do *not* provide simplistic explanations of theology or life.

To earth this contextually, we note that over the seven-year period when my wife Emma was Vicar of Holy Trinity Millhouses (a parish of some 4000 in a northern English city, with an electoral roll of about 160, and a weekly attendance of about 100), new members included a mother whose first child was born severely handicapped and died, a couple whose 30-year-old son died of a heart attack, two couples with mentally ill sons, two mothers of adopted children, and many others who have had to cope with complex bereavements. In different ways, each of these people was looking for a place, which could give meaning to their life – but without trying to explain away their suffering. A theology that provides hope, knit together with the sustaining love of God, and at the same time without tidying up loose ends, seemed to provide for these people something they cannot find either in the world, or in a more conservative church. Some of the new members had in fact moved from more conservative churches, whilst others became involved for the first time or after a long break.

Another group who joined the church were mothers of children, and occasionally their fathers as well. The experience of becoming a mother leads some to want to return to church, having been taken as children themselves. They are often all too aware of the complexity and fragility of life, and sense a need for God to be watching over their child or children. They also find that children ask big questions about life and death, purpose and meaning. Interestingly we encountered a number of parents brought to church by their children, who had expressed a strong desire to be part of our church without being drawn in by friends. They were attracted to a Church that was not over proscriptive, and that valued children encouraging their involvement in the life of the church.

Others who joined are much harder to categorize; individuals who had encountered the church through occasional offices; or people who had been drawn in by friends because it provided a sacred space, an experience of worship and an encounter with others that is somehow deeply transcendent and satisfying. The church also grew through simple transfer, as people who are already regular church worshippers, moved into the area and came looking to be involved in the community, for which the church continued to provide a focus.

These simple observations lead us to reflect on the fact that one of the primary ways in which churches grow numerically is through ordinary pastoral, maternal and paternal ministry. In her recent *What Mothers Do* (2004), Naomi Stadlen intriguingly subtitles her thesis: 'especially when it looks like nothing'. She argues for a focus on 'being' rather than 'task-orientation' in motherhood, and her observations translate well into the field of contemporary missiology and ecclesiology, by setting a fresh agenda for growth and development.

What Mothers Do: Especially When it Looks Like Nothing offers a beautifully simple argument. Stadlen says that contemporary culture is gripped, almost mesmerizingly, by formulae and recipes that seldom correspond to reality. So-called 'Mother and Baby' books are a good example: they offer step-by-step advice, which appears to be simple and effective. But, argues Stadlen, most of these kinds of books actually tend to infantilize the mother. What happens if I have a baby that doesn't do what the book says? Guilt, frustration and anger can quickly set in. Or try another book: but then, what happens if that also fails to mould the child in the image of the author? The 'how to' books, says Stadlen, reduce motherhood to a series of tasks, instead of concentrating on the relationship between mother and child. She argues that mothers rarely need to be told how to care; it is learned and developed in relationships, not through advice-lines and programmatic books.

The heart of the book suggests that mothers are always doing something with their offspring, and most especially when it looks like *nothing*. They are *engaged* with their child. They are relating. They are being with and being for the child. So the question 'what have you done today' – often asked of a young mother – needs no obvious reply, even though it often prompts guilt and embarrassment. To simply have been with the child is enough; to have discovered a song or a sound that comforts him; or something visual that simply amuses and stimulates her. This is enough.

We have opened up the argument in this way, because it seems to us that one of the most pressing problems that besets the church today is that it too is gripped by a culture of formulae. Many ecclesial recipe books have appeared in recent times: *How to Grow your Church*; *How to Manage your Congregation* (surely a work of satire?); *Ten Steps to Growth*; *Mission Shaped Church*; *The Purpose-Driven Church*; or Alpha Courses; and who can forget 'the decade of evangelism' (RIP)? Each of these initiatives is well-meaning, but also deeply formulaic; a kind of panacea for panickers. And clergy (and sometimes congregations) are easily seduced by such things. Many wince at Christmas when someone sidles up to them at a drinks party and says: 'So Vicar, your busy time then.' Because the flip side of the question often asked of clergy is also implied by this remark: 'what exactly do you do all day, Vicar?'

Clergy are often stumped for an answer. Communion in a residential or nursing home for five senior citizens, a couple of visits, some paperwork, morning and evening prayer, one meeting, and some thinking doesn't sound like a very productive day. But here clergy are at one with mothers. They have been doing a lot; it just seems like nothing. They have formed, deepened and kindled relationships.

They have related to lots of people for whom dependency is a fact of life, and concentrated deeply on being, not just doing. They have made somebody's day, simply by dropping by, or by smiling.

Formulas, like recipes, anticipate success: and churches are usually too tempted to worship both the rubric and the outcome. But unlike recipe books, those courses and books that address the apparent malaise of the church forget that just as every child is different, so is every congregation: a uniquely constituted set of ingredients. What works in one place probably won't in another. So, the moral of this analogy is simple. Don't impose formulae for growth on children or churches; and don't try and cook up congregations in the same way that you might try and cook up some food. Respect what has come naturally, and work with that. Even if that simply means just being, and apparently doing nothing.

We are struck by how many of the metaphors that Jesus uses to describe the numerical increase of the kingdom are organic, and require a slow patience in husbanding growth. The parable of the sower, for one, hardly anticipates a packed schedule for the sower. After her work is finished for the day, what does she do? She will need to wait, water and wait. Similarly, the parable of the mustard seed reminds us that although there is an extensive outcome to be enjoyed, the process of moving from seed to tree is 'natural' rather than 'driven'. We do not, of course, think that the organic parables on kingdom growth that Jesus tells give licence to clergy to sit back and do nothing. But we do think that they suggest that the true growth worth striving for is more likely to be crafted through patient tending, working empathetically with natural ingredients, rather than with 'instant' formulae that produces growth for its own sake. We have consistently levelled a criticism at Donald McGravran's work on church growth in this respect, namely that his relentless push for growth was not unlike introducing steroids into the body of Christ. The results were fast and looked spectacular (judged from one perspective); but the long-term health implications were less than convincing. Building up the mass of the body can be a form of idolatory. There is no real substitute for healthy, natural and sustained growth.

Growth in Rural Ministry

Having made some preliminary remarks based on an experience of ministry in a suburban experience, we now turn to reflect on a rural context. Not so long ago, the village of Elmdon could justly claim to be one of the most studied rural communities in England. Two anthropologists – Marilyn Strathern and Jean Robin (1980 and 1981) – published their ground-breaking studies that explored the changing face of village life in rural Essex, and how these communities were evolving. Robin's study charted continuity and change in village identity from the mid-nineteenth century through to the 1960's. Covering the ownership of land, labour, farming, marriage and social mobility, it is one of the first analyses that points to the present context of a typical rural village today. Namely, profound shifts in the composition of such communities; yet at the same time a sense of continuity with the past that seemed to be remarkably resilient.

Similarly, Strathern was able to map the underlying value-systems that seemed to shape community identity. This included the persistent notion of a 'Real Elmdon' (used to distinguish it from anything apparently alien or new), which she maintained was held through tightly formed patterns of kinship. Indeed, Strathern argued that the concept of kinship provided a vital key to understanding the delicate way in which the community was arranged. Kinship cuts across employment, class, gender and other apparent divisions, and identifies who 'really belongs' and who has yet to be integrated. To 'outsiders', the question as to who is a 'real' villager may seem unnecessarily parochial and quirky. Strathern showed, however, that kinship played a vital role in identifying Elmdon.

Both Robin and Strathern were able to foresee something of what the future might hold for villages such as Elmdon towards the end of the twentieth century and the beginning of the twenty-first. Factors included increasing numbers of commuters, who would slowly turn the community into a predominantly dormitory village. Less work would be available for local people, as rural industries changed or disappeared. Rising house prices would force some settled and established forms of kinship to become more attenuated, as the economic pressures caused greater degrees of familial dispersal. The effect of this, ironically, is often to intensify a sense of community identity. Resilience is manifested in both resistance and accommodation. And indeed, this kind of outlook can powerfully influence the whole approach to rural ministry, especially in the occasional offices.[1]

Yet despite the depth of their ethnography and anthropological analysis, Robin and Strathern devoted little time to the church itself. This omission is comprehensible, in some sense. The blindness to the presence of the church arises directly out of a collation of social sciences that colluded with the classic secularization theses from the 1960's. These tended to stress the increasing impotency of 'established' religion, and assumed that its residual power lay merely in rituals that affirmed kinship, ties to the land, the capacity to engage folk religion and the rites of passage that marked generational continuity and change. The authors therefore might be surprised to see that many rural churches are surviving in the twenty-first century, or even flourishing, occupying a pivotal position in their respective communities. In some cases, the church will be the sole public community building remaining; not only a spiritual amenity, but also a place for the whole village to gather. In other cases, the church will have a key role in supporting or hosting a Post Office or small shop, and acting as a conduit for a range of voluntary and care services.

As David Martin has noted, churches are markers and anchors in many rural communities; the primary or sole repository of all-embracing meanings pointing beyond the immediate to the ultimate. Rural churches are institutions that deal in

---

[1]   For further discussion, see Clark (1982). For an account of the development of ministry in a small rural town, see Lunn (2009).

tears and concern themselves with the breaking points of human existence. They provide frames of reference, narratives and signs to live by. And they continue to offer persistent points of reference that are beyond consumerism, fashion or other forms of transitory existence. This is why burial places can be so important – the availability of a public space that still enables a real relationship between the living and the dead to be appropriately maintained. Moreover, this is not mere maintenance. Rather, it is mission – providing the space in which people can live and move and have their being, within a context of bereavement and its attendant ministry.

The nature of contemporary rural life places some interesting demands and challenges upon the ministry of the church. These include the recognition that the [somewhat dubious] distinction between mission and maintenance – so easily assumed in urban and suburban contexts – is a false dichotomy in the majority of rural contexts. Good maintenance is likely to be, *de facto*, good mission. It involves and affirms the wider community, thereby nourishing social and spiritual capital. The relationship between a church and its people in many rural village contexts is essentially perichoretic – the 'mutual indwelling' of various cultural and religious currents that blend and inter-penetrate, yet also maintain their distinctive identities.

This is especially suggestive for ministerial formation and education. Quality may need to be valued more than quantity. Affirming the resonance of the past may have a higher spiritual value than the apparent obviousness of the need for relevance and progress. Presence and deep relational engagement may have a greater missiological impact than overt evangelistic schema and initiatives. The ministerial 'blend' of being and doing (i.e., the clergyperson as both contemplative and activist) may need to be adjusted in any transition from urban or suburban contexts to rural ministry. Because rural ministry may only have one 'professional' clergyperson for several parishes, she or he will normally fare better as a generalist than as a specialist; as a person of breadth and accommodation rather than being overly particular in theological outlook; of accepting the prioritization of extensity (partly brought about by there being less choice) instead of the comfort of distinctive intensity.

One fertile notion that comes from the vocabulary of sommeliers might be helpful here. 'Terroir', as we have noted before, is a Gallic word for which there is no English equivalent. The term refers to the combination of factors that make one wine slightly different from another, even when they are geographically proximate. Sunshine and temperature; north or south facing, and the amount of rainfall; the height of the land (and the drainage, the type and acidity of the soil, the types and subtypes of grape, and their progeny; local know-how and human skill; the amount of time permitted for a wine to mature, and the types of barrels chosen: all combine to make wines taste different.

This accounts for why one Burgundy tastes quite different from another, even though they might be from the same village. And this analogy has something to teach theologians as they reflect on the composition of local ecclesial identity.

On one level, church is church, just as wine is wine. Yet to the refined palate, the differences are detectable and telling. The ecclesial history and ethos of one rural church might be composed through all manner of stories, buildings, forms of organization, ecclesial and theological accents; and in adjacent church, yet in a similar context, turn out to be entirely different. And arguably, it is only through deep and patient immersion and reflection – the refining of the palate, in effect – that good mission can be undertaken.

The 'ecclesial terroir', in other words, is something that a minister needs to be able to read sensitively and deeply if they are to cultivate congregational life and offer connected parochial ministry. Moreover, if a minister is overseeing several rural churches, their clustering together, for organizational purposes will seldom disguise the fact that although roughly proximate, each congregation will have a slightly different feel, flavour, history and dialect. (Rather as in anthropological terms, as neighbouring tribes in a given place can be very different. Indeed, the surfacing and expression of difference is what makes identity possible). So ministerial formation and training will, at this point, need to find ways of providing deeper forms of discernment that enable ministers to move beyond the surface or presenting task of demand-led organization, and make time and space to read each congregation and parish as a semi-discrete but related locally distinctive expression of Christian faith.

Arguably, Karl Barth understood something of the necessary patience required in rural ministry, and from his Swiss canton penned these words:

> The true growth which is the secret of the upbuilding of the community is not extensive but intensive; its vertical growth in height and depth ... It is not the case that its intensive increase necessarily involves an extensive. We cannot, therefore, strive for vertical renewal merely to produce greater horizontal extension and a wider audience ... If it [the Church and its mission] is used only as a means of extensive renewal, the internal will at once lose its meaning and power. It can be fulfilled only for its own sake, and then – unplanned and unarranged – it will bear its own fruits. (Barth, 1958, p. 684)

But what might Barth mean by this? He has several things in mind, I suspect, but for the purposes of this brief chapter, three merit noting. First, that rural churches and ministries may need to be genuinely patient and resilient. They have vested interests in continuity and perpetuity. This means that a (quick) results-orientated immediacy often has to be set aside in favour of something more natural, organic and slower. Sustaining and maintaining is as important as changing. Second, there is a sense in which Barth clearly understands our earlier reference to utility-extensity and market-intensity models of the church. And theologically, Barth graciously points out that that intensity cannot be adopted in order to produce extensity. Third, Barth goes some way to redeeming the notion of intensity, by suggesting that a more concentrated focus on God is at the heart of all good ministry, but that this does not necessarily lead to the kind of extensive growth one might witness in a city or suburban context. Quality of discipleship, in other words – the sheer faithfulness of ministries – may not necessarily lead to quantifiable results.

So what of a vision for formation and training for ministry in rural contexts? Jesus, interestingly, offers quite a range of powerful organic or natural metaphors that may be of some help to us here. But I want to focus on just two for the moment – yeast and salt:

> He told them still another parable: 'The kingdom of heaven is like yeast that a woman took and mixed into a large amount of flour until it worked all through the dough.' (Matthew 13: 33)

Here, Jesus tells us most of what we probably need to know about ministry. He suggests that the kingdom of heaven is like yeast that is mixed in with dough. Yeast? That microbe fungi? That discard-able and forgettable material that is, oddly, the key to so much of our lives? It would seem so. For yeast is what ferments the wine and beer; and it makes the dough rise to make the bread. It is the tiny, insignificant catalyst for our basic commodities and the formation of our communities. The leaven in the lump; the difference between bread and dough; juice and wine; refreshment and celebration.

Yeast is, of course, small. Moreover, it is lost and dispersed into the higher purposes to which it is given. And when Jesus talks about the kingdom of God as yeast – and our ministries too – he is not advocating the concentrate of *Marmite* in jar: yeast for the sake of yeast. Rather, in Jesus' imagination, we are invited to purposely disperse. To lose ourselves in something much bigger. But not pointlessly. Rather, in 'dying' to our context, we activate it. We become the catalyst that brings flavour, strength, depth, potency and growth. Without yeast, there is no loaf; just dough. Literally, we die to ourselves for growth. We are the ingredient that makes bread for the world.

But this is not a call to dying or dissolving. God wants his people alive, not dead. So the notion of our ministry is not that we are the yeast, *per se*; but rather that we offer a yeast-like-type ministry. It is about being the agent of transformation that is often small, or even unseen. It is about being immersed so deeply in the world and the parish that the depth of growth is often unquantifiable. As Einstein once said, that which truly counts in life can seldom be counted. The work of yeast is one of deep fission.

John Paul Lederach, in his *Moral Imagination* (2005) offers a rich meditation on our calling to be yeast. Consider this. The most common ingredients for making bread are water, flour, salt, sugar and yeast. Of these, yeast is the smallest in quantity, but the only one that makes a substantial change to all the other ingredients. Lederach says you only need a few people to change a lot of things. So yeast, to be useful, needs to be moved from its incubation and mixed into the process – out of the seminary and into the parish. Clergy (like the proverbial manure), do the most good when they are spread around. But yeast also needs to grow – it requires the right mix of moisture, warmth and sugar. And it initially needs covering and cultivating before it is ready to do its work. Only then should the yeast mix with the greater mass. In bread, it is kneaded into the dough; it requires a bit of muscle. And it also requires someone else to light the fire to make the oven. Bread, in other words, is not just about the yeast, but about a context – one of feeding, desire, need, and the skills of others.

So in talking about small fungi that produce change and growth, Jesus is asking us to imagine his kingdom – one in which tiny spores mixed in to the social mass can make a massive difference. Similarly, Jesus also invokes his disciples to be the 'salt of the earth'. Matthew 5: 13 reads:

> You are the salt of the earth; but if salt has lost its taste, how can its saltiness be restored? It is no longer good for anything, but is thrown out and trampled under foot.

In interpreting this text, most preachers and many bible commentaries work with a false assumption: that the 'salt' in this text is the white granular chemical we know as sodium chloride, normally found in a condiment set or kitchen cupboard, where its purpose is to add flavour to foods, or occasionally to act as a purifier or preservative.

Yet the fact that Jesus refers to 'the salt *of the earth*' ought to immediately alert us to another meaning for the text. The 'salt' (*halas*) mentioned in the text is hardly likely to be table salt, since it is a chemical and culinary improbability that sodium chloride will lose its flavour. Any salt that is extracted from food, water or any other substance remains 'salty'; even if it loses its form; it retains its essence, as many a spoilt meal and frustrated chef can bear witness.

The substance of Jesus' words are, in Greek, *to halas tes ges*, 'the salt *of the earth*', with the word for 'earth' here not referring to the world at all, but rather to soil. In other words, the 'salt' that Jesus is referring to here is probably a kind of salt-like material or mineral such as potash or phosphate. These *halas* elements were available in abundance in and around the Dead Sea area of Palestine, and were used for fertilizing the land and enriching the manure pile, which was then spread on the land.

There are further clues as to why our usual understanding of this text is in some respects flawed. The word 'taste' that features in most English versions of this passage is actually a poor translation of the Greek word 'moranthe', which literally means 'to become foolish'. (The English word 'moron' is derived from the term.) A number of translators render the word as 'tainted', but 'loses its strength' is probably the best way to translate the word: loss of strength and foolishness would have been synonymous in Jesus' age. Moreover, and ironically, although paved paths also have their uses; Jesus' salt is arguably never 'useless'.[2]

---

[2] For a fuller discussion of this passage see Shillington (2001). Cf. Luke 14: 39. Interestingly, *The New Jerusalem Bible* (1985) is the only modern translation that renders the Greek correctly with 'you are the salt *for* the earth'.

The soil, of course, contains many different elements, all of which are intertwined. 'Soil', then, is a kind of cipher for the particular cultural contexts (i.e., religion, culture, ideology, etc), in which Christians are to 'be salt'. The many soils of the world carry, in various degrees, qualities of empowerment and disempowerment within cultures. Moreover, in a post-modern world, we can now see that culture is being increasingly homogenized through globalization, which has brought with it materialism, individualism, consumerism and hedonism, with the undesirable result of suffocating the life-giving force of the earth.

The empowering mission of the Church, like the salt of Jesus' parable, has a consistency of power. However, that power, enculturated into contexts, does not lead to uniformity. Rather, it leads to considerable diversity of expression, growth and human flourishing. The salt has always to respect the type of earth in which it is situated. Diverse cultural sensibilities have to be taken into account in the mission of the Church. The soil can also be inhospitable: it may be rocky, thorny, and adversely affected by climatic conditions. Under these circumstances, the task of being the salt of the earth is more demanding.

A key to understanding the relationship between Church and culture rests on a tension. On the one hand, Christians are to be engaged in the world and influence it, perhaps in ways that are not easily identified as specifically 'Christian'. The power of salt is that it is pervasive, and nourishing. Here, the church accommodates culture; Christ is therefore, in some sense, *for* culture. On the other hand, Christianity also proclaims God's Kingdom – a radically 'other' culture that will sweep away the present order. This is the beacon of light set on hill: it illuminates the present, but points to a new order. This is the Christ who is above or against culture. The church seeks a kingdom that is to come, and it therefore resists the standards of the world.

Accommodation and resistance are, of course, closely related. What they share, in character, is resilience. We might say that accommodation is a 'soft' form of resilience: flexible, pliable, adaptable and so forth. Whilst resistance is a 'hard' form of resilience: concrete, unyielding and defiant. The true character of ecclesial resilience – construed in almost any local church context – will show that most congregations will simultaneously resist and accommodate culture. The church, albeit unconsciously for the most part, understands that it lives between two cultures.

This way of understanding the *halas* (salt) of Jesus' metaphor changes the sense of the text significantly. In fact, it completely undermines the most conventional translations and expositions. The 'salt' is not to be kept apart from society, and neither is it to be used as a purifier or as an additive stabilizer. Ministers are not to be simply preservers of the good society, and neither are they merely agreeable folk adding flavour to either an amoral or immoral society. More powerfully and positively, true religion, as salt, is a life-bringing force giving itself to an otherwise sterile culture.

Thus, the 'salt' of Jesus' metaphor is a mutating but coherent agent that is both distinct yet diffusive in its self-expenditure. As a result of individuals, communities, values, witness and presence – the *halas* – being literally dug into society, the earth or soil will benefit, and many forms of life can then flourish. Correspondingly, salt that loses its strength (rather than its 'flavour' – the more usual translation) is only suitable for making paths, as the biblical text confirms. Thus, the salt of Jesus' metaphor is not only counter-cultural; it enriches 'the earth' and many more things besides, by being spread around and within it.

So there is an irony here. The 'task' of the salt is not necessarily to maintain its own distinctiveness, but rather to enrich society through diffusiveness. There is a temporal dimension here: what must begin as distinct to be useful ends up being absorbed and lost. Of course, this reading of the metaphor makes sense of Jesus' own self-understanding, which in turn is reflected in his parables, teachings and other activities. So, if the church or the disciples of Jesus are the salt of the earth, they will begin by being a distinct yet essential component within society, but will ultimately fulfil their vocation by engaging in self-expenditure.

What, then, are the practical implications for training and formation in rural ministry arising from these two organic metaphors? Three brief points can be made by way of conclusion. First, the yeast is suggestive insofar as it reminds churches and ministers that Christianity is about change and conversion. But that such transformation is often natural and organic, rather than traumatically disruptive. Nonetheless, the church is to be a catalyst, not just a catacomb. Second, the salt suggests that a patient vocation of nourishing lies at the heart of many rural ministries. To actively engage in the nourishment of the soil is to be committed to a time-consuming and costly process that will *not* yield instant results.

Moreover, the 'salting' of the soil is about broad coverage – a deep and extensive parochial exercise rather than something solely concentrated in congregations or in confessional particularity. So third, ministers need to develop a wisdom that can both resist and accommodate culture, but set within a broader understanding of how the church (and its tradition, the gospel, etc) remains fundamentally resilient.

Training in colleges, courses and in post-ordination schemes therefore needs to continually develop forms of theological reflection that help ministers surface the tensions and changes that are part and parcel of rural life. It also needs to equip ordinands to be animators and mobilizers in mission, as well as providing pastoral enablement and consistency. The call for clergy is, in other words, to be agents of change as well as continuity. For both change and continuity are at the heart of the gospel, just as they are the very centre of good, balanced rural mission and ministry.

It is ironic that it is this new breadth and emergent diversity in Elmdon – seen by 'real villagers' as the apparent fragmentation of its true identity – that now presents the church with a fresh opportunity. To be the gathering place in a community that needs to find new and old purpose in being knit together. To bring 'locals' and 'strangers' together; to foster relations between established families and newcomers; to create a genuine community of worship that expresses the complexity and richness of the parish, in its emerging composition. Kinship is indeed at the core of this, to be sure. But it is the kind of kinship of the kingdom that Jesus speaks of that is to be fostered; something in the world, but not exactly of it.

Conclusion

The question naturally arises from these reflections, what would ministry to a developing congregation look like? From one perspective as an Anglican priest, we suggest that there are several ways of being in a congregation that shape the task of ministry, but are fundamentally centred on role and identity rather than any particular outcomes. We recognize, to begin with, that the church as the body of Christ – as a metaphor – is imperfect, since the church is never complete, and cannot complete or delimit itself. In one sense, the church has an open definition because its boundaries and identity are, at a fundamental level, contested and open. Who belongs, who attends occasionally but not frequently, who believes this or that, will be a feature of even the most conservative congregation. Tight definitions of a church will seldom correspond to its grounded context; there is always a gap between ideology and reality.

What then, is the minister or priest to be or do in such an ambiguous situation? Clearly, it is tempting to be seduced by recipes and formulae that deliver clarity. But we would suggest that a focus on the role and identity of the minister (and minister) is a more fruitful path towards encouraging super, natural, organic church growth. We offer four hallmarks of priesthood and a priestly church by way of conclusion.

First, ministry is Sacramental-Transformative. To be a priest or a priestly church is to have an understanding that ordinary material (such as bread, wine, water, etc) can be transformed by prayer and worship into something through which God speaks to us and spiritually nourishes us. But we do not confine this axis to the standard tokens of the sacramental life of the church. We observe that congregations and ministers find that casual conversations, pastoral encounters, acts of service and other activities are also sacramental and transformative; they become 'places' where the life of God meets the life of the world. The more alert a congregation is to how God feeds and sustains his people, the more likely it is that this food will be shared, and more people transformed.

Second, ministry is Reciprocal-Representative. That is to say, that whilst the minister or priest may undoubtedly represent Christ to the people, the congregation continually looks for the ways in which Christ is present within them and outside itself. This is an important dimension in mission, for it affirms the activity of the Holy Spirit beyond the borders of the church, and reminds congregations that Christ can be encountered in new and alien ways, for which the congregation needs to be receptive. At a contextual level, congregations that grow organically will tend to have deep partnerships with a variety of secular agencies that complement its work and mission, so that the 'common good' and the blessing of social capital becomes an enlarged and shared task.

Third, ministry has a Sacrificial-Receptive dynamic. Obviously, priesthood, as with other forms of ministry, is costly. But the cost is often found not in the output, but in the receptivity to the input. We observe that, as priests, individuals will confess and confide all kinds of things that go no further. Here, the priest has a role as absorber of pain; of receiving knowledge that cannot be shared; of taking upon themselves burdens that are being finally deposited, once and for all. There is some salvific and cathartic here, to be sure. But we also note how, when individuals finally feel 'they can tell you anything' (and not be judged, but simply loved), they finally feel free to belong to the body of Christ. The costly ministry of sacrificially receiving people's lives and stories allows individuals to be grafted into the church.

Fourth, ministry is a also a delicate combination of the Pastoral-Prophetic. The old English adage expresses it well – clergy are there to comfort the afflicted and afflict the comfortable. The imperative to offer love, nurture and tenderness has to be balanced with the responsibility to speak out, which can be costly. We are mindful that, sometimes, growth and popularity must be sacrificed to truth and justice. Natural, organic church growth sometimes requires heavy pruning and an interventionist cultivation. In all of this, we remember that it is God alone who gives the growth. We know that it can be engineered, and we know that such engineering can be effective in terms of numerical growth. However, we remain convinced that the only true growth is the natural and deep kind that God invariably bestows upon a faithful, hopeful and joyful people.

PART III
Ministry – Practising Theology

Having explored sacraments and ecclesiology in the fist two sections, the third part of this study asks how an understanding of implicit theology changes the way in which leadership should be perceived and formed within the Anglican Church. Chapter 7 reveals the challenge to conventional models of leadership posed by the complexity of the church that emerges under this kind of analysis. This is not simply a question of replacing one leadership model with another: because the insights that emerge through analysis of the implicit are, by their nature, theological, the chapter introduces a discourse of spirituality into the discussion of leadership. This leads, in Chapter 8, to the recognition that for those undertaking ordination training in preparation for leadership roles in the church, the primary need is to acquire the spiritual maturity to inhabit a complex and contested social and theological space with sensitivity and nuance. Critical to this is the development of emotional and spiritual intelligence. This is the subject of Chapter 9, which argues that attention to the emotional life is needed at the highest levels of church leadership. This skill enables the insights that emerge through attentiveness to the implicit to be helpfully and healthily fed into decision-making in the church. This sets the scene for a concluding discussion on the state of the church.

Chapter 7
Herding Cats? Leading the Church (of England) in a New Age

On one level, there appears to be no shortage of resources available for the training of leaders within the Church of England. At least a dozen such organizations have been identified by the Leadership Institute. A comprehensive list of organizations, together with a literature survey, is included in the recent *Creative Church Leadership* (Adair and Nelson, 2004). Yet it appears that the vast majority of individuals and organizations engaged in thinking and training on leadership have a marked tendency to emphasize the individual (and their need for skills, formation, etc), but at the expense of engaging deeply with the complex institutional issues that invariably shape or even determine the context in which a leader must operate.

Besides the tasks and roles that form part of the Episcopal portfolio, there are numerous questions of identity. Given the context of late modernity – replete with secularism and pluralism – many denominations have sought to consolidate and clarify their identity within an era of considerable cultural fluidity. It therefore cannot be surprising that recent Anglican theology has invested more time and energy in deliberating on and defining episcopacy than in any other generation. Indeed, and understandably, there have arguably been more deliberations on the nature, function and identity of episcopacy in the twentieth century than all those that that were penned from the reformation to the end of the nineteenth century. So there appears to be no escaping questions of task, role and identity.[1]

That said, we might say that even an apparently rich theological modelling of the church, such as that attempted by Avery Dulles (1974), fails to come to terms with the actuality of leadership in denominations or congregations. Correspondingly, the resulting analysis of a church or denomination, and suggestions for appropriate reform, emerge as detached ideologies rather than as engaged programmes exhibiting a deep understanding of the actual ecclesial context to be considered. Although interestingly, Nicholas Healy's *Church, World and Christian Life* (2000) has recently offered some focused attention on the problematic gap between 'blueprint ecclesiologies' and the 'concrete church'. He notes that most recipes or formulae that set out to improve or reform the churches fail to come to terms with the grounded reality of denominations and congregations. Thus, the reformers'

---

[1] See Percy (2006) One thinks immediately of Kirk (1946); or more recent reports that have concentrated on senior leadership or episcopacy in relation to contemporary organizational issues: see for example *Resourcing Bishops* (2001), *Working as One Body (The Turnbull Report*, 1996) and *Talent and Calling (The Pilling Report*, 2007).

programme will usually fail as a result, leading to a potentially deeper spiral of despair, and a continual and more intense hunt for that elusive formula that will provide the focused leadership and direction that is perceived to be lacking. Those seeking to improve the church in apparently 'simple' ways do not understand the complexity of the *terroir* that forms that church.

But what, if anything, is the generic 'terroir' of the Church of England? One key insight here is to recognize that the church is an institution, rather than an organization. The distinction between an organization and institution is a classic sociological paradigm. Philip Selznick (1957) argues that organizations exist for utilitarian purposes, and when they are fulfilled, the organization may become expendable. Institutions, in contrast, are 'natural communities' with historic roots that are embedded in the fabric of society. They incorporate various groups that may contest each other, the institution, values and the like. Clearly, in Selznick's thinking, a church is an institution, requiring leadership, not mere management. So the church, when treated like an organization, can only be managed. And such management will, inevitably, be somewhat deficient, since the church is an institution in which only certain types of management will be possible.

A further problem for strategic or tactical reformers of the church is that many of the recipes or formulas that purport to be able to shape the church or improve leadership style actually begin with a deeply deficient ecclesiology: they do not understand the local or regional 'terroir'. Typically, the programmes are too task-orientated, or too simplistic, based on deeply contested aims and objectives. At the risk of a further caricature, one could say that majority of writing and research on leadership in the church is 'functionalist' rather than 'behaviourist'. Most of this is 'applied' in orientation: blueprints, aims, objectives and anticipated outcomes. Most of these fail to read or understand the complexity of the church in its dense and extensive catholicity, or comprehend the kind of local variables that can be located in ecclesial *terroir*. However, some studies do, in part, illuminate the kind of grounded ecclesiological approach we are concerned.[2]

Granted, part of this problem may lie in addressing some fundamental questions within ecclesial polity. Is ministerial leadership essentially a wisdom of the heart? Or is it a science of the laboratory? These questions are far from simple, since preferred answers are likely to be shaped by prior understandings of the church (often held with passion and conviction), which are of course contestable. So if ecclesiologies (or theologies of the church) cannot be easily aligned, it is hardly surprising that a collective vision for leadership in the church cannot be easily achieved, and attain consensus. And if one cannot agree here, it is unlikely that the apparent common problems and issues that might need to be addressed will be easily identified. In practical terms, what we might term the 'descriptive dilemma' in everyday ecclesial polity, lies at the very heart of some of the most infamous cases of leadership or managerial failure in the Church of England.

---

[2]   See for example Torry (2005) and Harris (1998).

Leadership and Episcopacy

Many people, even in assessing the structures and values of a given ecclesial polity, tend to accept the widely held belief that management and leadership are different. The former pertains to organizations that have clear goals and limited horizons; the latter to organizations and institutions that require cyclical interpretation and transformation. Paul Avis puts it quite sharply when he states that 'If the gospels are any indication, Jesus Christ showed scant regard for modern management wisdom … he was not looking for managers, but for learners and leaders – disciples and apostles' (Avis, 1992, p. 96).

But are leadership and management really so different? If one recognizes the church as an institution rather than an organization (see Selznick, 1957), the differentiation may be quite crucial. Avis fruitfully dwells on the distinction in several different ways, pointing out, for example, that in conflict resolution, the role of management is to contain, mediate and reconcile. Whereas in leadership, the leader's calling may be to manage in the first instance, but is also concerned with harnessing conflict to serve the overall mission of the institution. Moreover, because conflict is inevitable, it should be used as a creative force and channelled as such, rather than being allowed to grow unchecked, which risks either paralysing or overwhelming the institution.

Yet as Avis reminds us, many theories of leadership seem to be 'unfashionable' in the church. There is a certain kind of squeamishness around the urgent ecclesiological and hermeneutical task that may face the church in this respect. Because bishops are 'given' to the church, ideally having the necessary Christian character to occupy the role (e.g., sacrifice, commitment, exemplary discipleship; or perhaps the characteristics listed in 1 Tim. 3: 1–7; or the ordinal, etc), and are in one sense there by grace rather than through merit, there is a characteristic reticence in overly prescribing the attributes needed for the role. Avis suggests that 'leadership demands outstanding intellectual ability and outstanding intellectual application' (Avis, 1992, p. 97), which of course on one level is true – but it is not uniformly right for institutions, only perhaps organizations. Avis also considers the bishops as a collation of leadership in the church. Drawing on Medhurst and Moyser (1988), he points out that bishops and archbishops are inevitably drawn into irenic behaviour patterns (as peacemakers and reconcilers, etc), but that this may risk 'cloaking sullen acquiescence' or mask alienation and its loner-term consequences. Thus, he argues, 'the occasional (intellectual) gadfly among the bishops to ask the awkward questions and to bring conflicts into the open' (p. 100) is to be encouraged within the broader composition of collective Episcopal leadership.

Avis further suggests that leadership requires reconciliation with its roles and tasks. First, it has a symbolic role. In ecclesiological terms, the leader is a primary bearer of the institution's values, as well as someone to inspire faith in the common purposes of the institution. Here, the leader, in his or her symbolic role, functions as a catalyst – a major agent of transformation and transcendence. Naturally, this means that leaders will need to be attentive to the projections and unconscious assumptions that are placed upon the role by those within the institution. Second, the leader's priority is to focus the energies of the institution on its primary tasks. This requires the articulation of vision, identifying policies, exploring and implementing strategies, and engaging in tactics. Third, the leader will need to be a problem-solver. This requires the wisdom to distinguish between problems and dilemmas (the latter cannot be solved, usually – they express an endemic tension in the institution); determination to overcome contextual, environmental or institutional issues that inhibit the institution from flourishing; and identification of those factors that need addressing and the issues that need resolving (Avis, 1992, pp. 107–18). Of particular concern to Avis is the 'cognitive myopia' that can develop within institutions: 'responding only to the immediate, the visible, the palpable, rather than searching for the deeper, long-term causes and attempting to deal with them'. Avis quotes Anthony Jay: 'you can judge a leader by the size of the problem [he] tackles – people nearly always pick a problem their own size' (Avis, 1992, p. 118).

One of the more creative and prescient new writers in this whole arena is Simon Western. Western concurs with Avis's observations (borrowed, of course, from secular literature), that 'leaders are authentically transformational ... they increase awareness of what is right, good, important and beautiful ...' (2008, p. 22). Whilst accepting that management and leadership are terms that can be used interchangeably, and that leaders manage, and managers lead, Western nevertheless asserts that the two need to be separated out if one is to understand the theory and practice of leadership within institutions. Western borrows from Bennis and Nanus to highlight the argument relating to management:

> [it] typically constitutes a set of contractual (items) ... What gets exchanged is not trivial: jobs, security and money. The result, at best, is compliance: at worst you get a spiteful obedience. The end result of leadership is completely different. It is empowerment. Not just higher profits and wages ... but a culture that helps employees generate a sense of meaning in their work and a desire to challenge themselves to experience success ... (Bennis and Nanus, 1985, p. 218)

The heart of Western's explication of leadership of institutions rests on seven carefully articulated assumptions. His theory is rooted in social sciences, systems and organization theories, and in theology and religious studies. His observations broadly concur with some of the characteristics identified earlier in Avis's work:

1. *Intellectual* – clear and outstanding articulation of the institution, its traditions and activities. Original and creative thinking, synthesized into coherent programmes that lead to transformation.
2. *Unconscious* – the leader will (somehow) personify the institution. (And also understand notions of projection, etc.)

3. *Corporate* – leadership is collective and shared; maximum involvement, but distance preserved.[3]
4. *Dispersed* – cadres are needed who can also embody the leadership and share in its vision and tasks.[4]
5. *Individual* – understanding and harnessing the interplay and interdependence between the individual and the collective.
6. *Social* – reading and understanding the collective processes that enable the leadership and institution to flourish; cultivating 'active follower-ship'.
7. *Symbolic* – performative acts highlight the possibility of change, resistance, transformation and liberation. (Western, 2008, pp. 72ff)

Western believes these common characteristics of leadership have expressed themselves in three primary forms of discourse during the twentieth century. He proposes a fourth, but the three main ones he identifies are Controller, Therapist and Messiah (Western, pp. 88ff.). Briefly, Controller discourse is closely aligned to social management, and the progeny of a scientific rationalism (born of the early twentieth century). The focus of this discourse lies in efficiency, with transactional behaviour that rests on finding a balance between rewards and deprivation. Therapist discourse is a later development in the twentieth century, and highlights personal growth, well-being and individual concern. Less coercive than Controller discourse, therapist discourse nonetheless represents a subtle form of control, since it feeds off the tensions between individualism and alienation, and personal fulfilment and workplace efficiency. Finally, Western suggests that the latter decades of the twentieth century witnessed the emergence of Messiah discourse. With the elevation of leader over and against managers, Messiah discourse validates charismatic and visionary leadership in the face of turbulent and uncertain environments for institutions. The Messiah discourse feeds off the tensions between salvation and destruction, and hope and despair. Typically, the discourse promises order from chaos.

Western has perceptive and trenchant critiques for each of these discourses. One must, of course, recognize that these categories of discourse are interpretative and artificial, and to an extent have the feel of a 'straw man'. Nonetheless, this careful framing of leadership discourses almost perfectly captures the shape and feel of ecclesial language in relation to the challenges of leading the church over the past century. Early twentieth-century writings on ecclesial leadership were arguably preoccupied with order; a trend that continued right the way through to *Working as One Body* (1996) despite its presenting rhetoric.[5] The more therapeutically-inclined tradition (and to some extent shaped by systems theory and other disciplines) might be said to be represented by Peter Rudge, Bruce Reed, Wesley

---

[3]   Cf. Avis (1992), pp. 126ff.

[4]   For a brief discussion of distributive leadership, see Marturano and Gosling (2008).

[5]   Despite the apparent organic language, the underlying discourse was mechanistic, hegemonic and rationalistic. See Evans and Percy (2000).

Carr and others. The more recent tradition of Messiah discourse can be seen in a plethora of popular and technically-orientated books on Christian leadership. The range of literature here is simply vast. Three preliminary genres can be identified: [a] biblical [b] secular and [c] ecclesial. Much of it is ideologically driven, with romantically-inclined and reformist proclivities that bear some relation to modern self-help books: follow the instructions, and all will be well.

These discourses are not, of course, mutually exclusive. Bishops will inevitably be under some pressure to conform or relate to all three – offering control, therapy and liberation in equal measure. Mercifully, however, Western believes that leadership within institutions needs to pass through these three discourses and enter into something altogether more holistic and engaged. He acknowledges that the search for leadership models and ideas is now driven by several factors: the need to find solutions to changing social, political and economic conditions; the need to sustain the 'leadership industry'; enormous social pressure to modernize ('new sells, old doesn't'); some compulsion to establish perpetual relevance, leading to what Marx dubbed a 'commodity fetish' – the institution, once commodified and marketed, starts to take on an identity that bears little relation to original purpose.

Western proposes, in place of the three models outlined above, a discourse of 'eco-leadership' (Western, 2008, pp. 173ff.). Inevitably, perhaps, this 'model' emphasizes a variety of traits that are already apparent and emerging in twenty-first-century leadership studies, but which perhaps especially draw on our contemporary cultural absorption with organic, natural and sustainable concepts. Thus – and somewhat against the Messiah discourse – Western identifies the 'post-heroic discourse' which emphasizes 'the genuinely human … [drawing] on all their humanity, intelligence and emotions … remember[ing] what they know from their experiences'. Leadership spirit is also identified as a trait, and in particular the capacity of the leader to 'learn from the middle'. So here we could say that Western's plea for the leadership of institutions is more for a portfolio of skills and charisms that may be familiar to those who are deep reflective practitioners: self-awareness, spontaneity, holistic, reframing, vocational, vision and value led, reflexive, compassionate (feeling with) and engaged. Correspondingly, a deep systemic understanding of the institution that is being led is required. Or, and for our purposes here, leadership might be the cultivation of heightened ecclesial intelligence, and its visionary application.

The form of leadership (for institutions) that Western therefore advocates is one that is ecologically sensitive. It understands that:

> solutions in one area may create problems in another … short-term gains may have immediate benefits, but may have longer-term consequences … [thus] there are interdependent parts which make up a whole … it is about connectivity, inter-dependence and sustainability … (Western, 2008, p. 183)[6]

---

[6]   Western quotes Donne's poetic aphorism here: 'no man is an island entire of itself; every man is part of the main'.

Western's appeal to a reticulate, grounded and organic discourse is, of course, a 'fit' for the contemporary cultural aspirations and expectations that many institutions share. It is sensitive to the dynamics of power and authority that both shape and delimit institutions, and, moreover, seems to be more than aware of the kinds of demands that might be placed upon the leader in role. Western suggests that leadership today is:

> *A sponge* – soaking up pressure from within and without.
> *An essence* – epitomizing the institution.
> *A mediator* – addressing tensions and resolving conflicts.
> *A translator* – hermeneutical skills (e.g., for church and world).
> *A buffer* –protecting the institution from internal an external pressure.
> *A mirage* – knowing how much influence or power one actually has.
> *A dynamo* – generating purposeful energy. (Western, 2008, p. 191, adapted)

These associations allow Western to reflect that leaders and leadership are 'formed' within a context and in relations. They are formed through the community they work in. Thus, 'leadership is not a learnt profession or trade or a taught set of skills … [it] is much more complex and goes deeper' (Western, 2008, p. 205). This, however, leads Western to a rather radical conclusion, namely that a concentration on leadership *formation* may need to take precedence over leadership development. He acknowledges that this is complex, since formation is largely unorganized, *ad hoc* and unrecognized. This is a more important insight than it may at first appear. Many institutions, as distinct from organizations, are neither organized or disorganized, but rather unorganized. Moreover, they may have sufficient levels of nascent organization to resist further attempts at explicit organization. All kinds of institutions share this trait: dioceses, as well as certain ancient universities.

However, because Western sees the formation as a holistic process, a focus on the collective is as important as a concentration on the individual. He concludes, therefore, by suggesting three key principles for leadership formation:

1. It must be holistic and embedded in the (institutional) culture.
2. It requires both an informal and formal process.
3. Individuals and teams need a form, containing (paternal) structures and reflective (maternal) spaces for formation to occur. (Western, 2008, p. 206)

Power, Authority, Strategies and Tactics

The question as to what kind of mind the church requires in leadership is, of course, a contested one. There are clearly some dangers when managerialism is incorporated in an uncritical way.[7] Richard Roberts argues that 'the assimilation of managerialism into an organisation whose leaders have been – and remain – in a state of prolonged identity crisis endangers the "care of souls"' (Richard Roberts, 2002).[8] By reference to care of souls Roberts intends 'the fostering of that delicate ecology of spiritual opportunity that constitutes the fabric of real human community, *koinonia* itself'. Roberts argues that this may amount to a betrayal of the church (2002, p. 164).[9]

That said, some would dispute whether such a managerial clarity and concentration is ever achievable in the church. Indeed, one of the more identifiable problems in considering leadership in the Anglican Church is not so much its sharpness of focus as its apparent fondness for ambivalence. Leading the Church of England, it is often said, is a little like trying to herd cats (Cundy and Welby, 2000, p. 26). Precocious and un-biddable creatures, they roam where they will. It is not unlike the oft-quoted quip about trying to pull off a corporate merger: a little like trying to wheelbarrow frogs to market. And when it comes to reflecting on the nature of leadership within the Church of England, one is immediately struck by the complex nature of the body. Identity is contested; so are priorities; and the past, present and future. Bishops, whatever their role, cannot easily impose their agenda or blueprint. They may propose; but the laity and clergy are at liberty to adapt or reject advice or guidance. The circumstances in which anyone or anything can be impelled are few. Leadership is by grace, not law. The very nature of godly, ecclesial and social power is stubbornly contested. This discussion is framed slightly differently by Rudge, who suggests paying attention to the different theoretical paradigms of power and authority found in churches: traditional, charismatic, classical, human relations and systemic (Rudge, 1968).

To help us think a little more about leadership here, let us briefly consider three different *caricatures* of how a diocese might be shaped, ordered and managed under Episcopal leadership. One bishop may see their role and task as primarily *executive*: being a hands-on manager, making key strategic decisions on a day-to-day basis. This view of pastoral power thrusts the bishop into the contentious realm of management, efficiency and rationalization; they operate as a kind of chief executive officer within a large organization. This is a form of *rationalized* authority, and it will typically empathize with reviews, strategies and appraisals.

Another approach is to see power in *monarchical* terms. There are two faces to monarchical power. One is to rule by divine right: the prelate's word is law. But secondly and more commonly it is manifested in a kind of calculated detachment. Like most monarchs, some bishops may elect to rarely intervene in any dispute

---

[7]   This matter was the subject of a special edition of *Modern Theology*, October 1993, Vol. 9, No. 4, 'Ecclesiology and the Culture of Management'.

[8]   See Roberts (2000), pp. 78–96 and in 'Lord, Bondsman and Churchman' (1989), and his more recent *Religion, Theology and the Human Sciences* (2002) and 'Personhood and Performance' (2008). For an alternative view, see Gill and Burke (1996).

[9]   For fuller discussion, see Pickard (2006).

decisively, and thereby remain neutral and above any divisive opinions or decisions. This is not an abrogation of power. Rather, the adoption of the second type of monarchical model proceeds from an understanding that others ('subjects') invest meaning in the power of the ruler, which in turn leads many monarchs and bishops to be 'officially silent' on issues that are potentially divisive. Their symbolic power is maintained through mystique, and ultimately reticence. This is a form of *traditional* authority; power is primarily constituted in the office rather than in the individual charisms of the person holding it.

Another model is more *distributive*, and is concerned with facilitation and amplification. In this vision for embodying power in any office, the bishop becomes an enabler, helping to generate various kinds of powers (i.e., independent, related, etc) within an organization. He or she will simply see to it that the growth of power is directed towards common goals, and is ultimately for the common good. But in this case, power is valued for its enabling capacities and its generative reticulation (i.e., energy derived through networking, making connections, etc); it is primarily verified through its connecting and non-directional capacities. Such leadership usually needs some *charismatic* authority, as the organization requires leadership that is connectional and innovative.

Another perspective on this is offered by P. Nesbitt (Nesbitt, 2001, pp. 257 ff.). He argues that there are four phases of denominational authority: traditional, rational, negotiated and symbolic. Most senior church leadership requires the exercise of all four forms of authority. In the case of symbolic authority, however, there is at least some sense in which there is less power available to those exercising this kind of authority than might be available with, say, traditional authority. Bishops, in many situations and contexts within ecclesial governance, possess authority, but do not have power. This is a relatively well recognized phenomenon.

Whichever models of power or authority are preferred by an individual exercising leadership, it is probably fair to note that office holders move in and out of each model, depending on circumstances. And this leads me to make three brief observations. First, it is probably the case that many aspects of Anglicanism are easier to identify through persons rather than systems: the church is shaped through examples of faith and polity rather than theories of it. In view of this, one could say that the practice of our faith is more of an art than a science, and most especially in relation to problem-solving. Here, the leadership of the church within the context of the challenges of contemporary culture is much more like a 'knack' than a skill; shaping the church is about learned habits of wisdom more than it is about models, rules and theories.[10]

Second, those charged with the ministry of oversight – in both sacred and secular spheres – often speak of *intuition* rather than extended calculation or analysis when dealing with 'unique situations to which they must respond under conditions of stress and limited time' (Schon, 1991, p. 239). This 'knack' or 'wisdom' depends, as Polanyi might say, on 'tacit knowing', where overseers seldom turn to theories

---

[10]   See Schon (1991).

or methods in managing situations, but instead realize that their own effectiveness depends on having learnt (and continuing to learn) through the 'long and varied practice in the analysis of ... problems, which builds up a generic, essentially un-analyzable capacity for problem-solving' (Polanyi, 1962, p. 22). So, one learns by experience in the field.[11]

Third, the outcome of this has important implications for the collegiality of those engaged in the task of oversight. It is in *sharing* – how problems are addressed and resolved, and how individuals and organizations fare in this, and what reflections or analysis one may have about, that 'tacit knowledge' is built up – within relationships based on trust – such that the organization may then experience both stability and a degree of transcendence. Correspondingly, it is how we hold issues, the character we exhibit under pressure, and how we continue to embody being the very best kinds of reflective practitioner, that may help the church as it seeks to address the multiple complexities of being.

For leaders, this, of course, requires a high degree of emotional intelligence. It means, for example, continually listening to the experiences that lead to anger, and trying to see them from the perspective of those with less power. It means humility on the part of those who hold power, and an acknowledgment of the fear of losing power and control. It means continually being open to new ways of looking at power relationships. We are aware that this is one of the most demanding aspects of oversight, namely having the emotional and ecclesial intelligence, patience and empathy to hold feelings, anger, disappointment and frustration – other people's, as well as your own. One aspect of on-going formation in Episcopacy, arguably, is a continually learnt 'deep poise', as much as it is about focusing on strategy and transformation. Change is usually only possible if holding together competing convictions and trying to resolve deep conflicts are achieved at the same time.

With these brief reflections on power and authority in mind, there can be no question that part of the difficulty for most bishops is that, unlike the CEO of a major corporation, they lack the power-base to execute decisive initiatives or decisions.[12] The office of the Archbishop of Canterbury is absolutely not analogous to being the Chairman of a large company. Any Archbishop may venture to suggest what the missiological priorities of the Church of England could or should be. But it is entirely a matter of choice and interpretation as to how such directives are taken up by other bishops, clergy and laity. There is no relationship of compulsion between the leader of the church and the led. Some understanding of this dynamic is important for the study of ministry and its development. Few clergy and bishops have the privilege of being able to be strategic; they only have the possibility of being tactical and pragmatic. Moreover, even when clergy think they are being strategic in leadership, no assumptions can be made about the tactics and pragmatism of the laity.

---

[11] For a more extended discussion, see Hardy (2001).

[12] And as we have noted earlier, the church is primarily an institution, not a single organization.

Michael Certeau offers this account of the context and scope of strategy:

> I call a *strategy* the calculation (or manipulation) of power relationships that
> becomes possible as soon as a subject with will and power (a business, an
> army, a city, a scientific institution) can be isolated. It postulates a place that
> can be delimited as its own and serve as a base from which relations with an
> *exteriority* composed of targets and threats (customers or competitors, enemies,
> the country surrounding the city, objectives and objects of research, etc.) can be
> managed. As in management, every 'strategic' rationalization seeks first of all
> to distinguish its 'own' place, that is, the place of its own power and will, from
> an 'environment' ... A *tactic* is a calculated action determined by the absence
> of a proper locus. No delimitation of an exteriority, then, provides it with the
> condition necessary for autonomy. The space of a tactic is the space of the other.
> Thus it must play on and with a terrain imposed on it and organized by the law
> of a foreign power. It does not have the means to *keep to itself*: at a distance, in
> a position of withdrawal, foresight, and self-collection. ... It does not, therefore,
> have the options of planning general strategy and viewing the adversary as a
> whole within a distinct, visible, and objectifiable space. It operates in isolated
> actions, blow by blow. It takes advantage of 'opportunities' and depends on
> them, being without any base where it could stockpile its winnings, build up its
> own position, and plan raids. What it wins it cannot keep. ... It must vigilantly
> make use of the cracks that particular conjunctions open in the surveillance of
> the proprietary powers. It poaches in them. It creates surprises in them. It can be
> where it is least expected. It is a guileful ruse ... . (Certeau, 1984, pp. 34ff.)

Certeau's account reveals the limited application of strategy in the context of church
leadership. Most senior clergy operate from a (well-informed and theoretically
shaped) tactical base, where it is not possible to directly impose one's will. It is
possible that this is what Jesus had in mind when he exhorted his disciples to be as
wise as serpents and innocent as doves (Matthew 10: 16). It is a call to shrewdness
that recognizes that the power-base from which clergy serve is composed of such
ambivalence (i.e., servant-leader, etc) as to make it almost impossible to have
deep and resolved clarity about the nature of the tasks and roles. This is, of course,
precisely what draws many people into ministry. They do not come seeking power,
but merely to influence in the name of a higher power.

On Formation

The purpose of our brief excursions in the previous section has been to
underline the fact that the church is a complex institution rather than an obvious
organization. Following Selznick, we have argued that organizations exist for
utilitarian purposes, and when they are fulfilled, the organization may become
expendable. Institutions, in contrast, are 'natural communities' with historic roots

that are embedded in the fabric of society. They incorporate various groups that may contest each other, values, and indeed the institution itself. However, it is important to state that this observation does *not* invalidate the proper inculcation of management; and nor does it excuse the church – whether at parochial, sector, deanery, diocesan or national levels – from engaging in purposeful strategies and tactics. Indeed, the church *requires* leaders who comprehend, intellectually and practically, how the mission and ministry can be responsibly reframed and applied in each generation. That said, leaders of institutions will also need to be careful and clear about the nature of the body they have been entrusted with, and also presume to shape and direct.

To lead any institution – such as a comprehensive church – can therefore mean that it will sometimes be necessary to prioritize conversation and quest over precision and absolute resolutions. This will be frustrating for some; but the kind of poise required to lead the institution at this point is, as we have said, different from that of organizations. We, the church, remain open because we see ourselves as incomplete. This means, of course, that the centre ground can also be the *radical* ground. And of course holding to some kind of centre is, to a large extent, evolving into a serious and purposeful leadership task and role which makes the hardest demands upon those charged with oversight. All the more so, because as those who work and study in the field of international conflict resolution remind us, the most difficult and demanding battles are those which involve our own allies or close relationships: what one scholar rather tamely terms 'cooperative disputes'. And such disputes make huge demands on the leadership of the church.[13] Urban Holmes offers a prescient meditation on the dilemmas of leading within Anglican polity, written 25 years ago, with these words:

> … [our] course leads to living in the world as God sees the world. We can debate the trivial points, but the vision is largely clear. To love God is to relieve the burden of all who suffer. The rest is a question of tactics (Holmes, 1971, p. 245).

So arguably, the only transformational strategies for the formation, training and education of senior leaders within the church that will truly prevail are those that read the church deeply. They will be those that engage in a rich and profound audit of our ecclesiology and praxis; those that listen intently to the heartbeat of the body of Christ, sounding the depths of the life of the church. Formation, then, is academic, pastoral, spiritual and human. It is the practice of the presence of God,

---

[13]   Some of these issues are fruitfully discussed in the recent *Communion, Conflict and Hope* (The Kuala Lumpur Report of the Third Inter-Anglican Theological and Doctrinal Commission, London, Anglican Communion Office, 2008). The Report addresses the tension between Anglican ambivalence and catholicity, the limits of diversity, and offers a theological stratagem for resolving conflict hopefully.

holiness and leadership;[14] the delicate blend of education, training, theological reflection and spiritual development that is vital for ministerial maturation. As Kathryn Tanner notes (1997, p. 87ff.), theology is working with materials that don't dictate of themselves what to do with them. The process of theology, rather like that of leadership, is a form of art. The challenge, then, is clear: comprehend the real, raw church in all its complexity, and work creatively from there.

We can build on this further by returning to some of Simon Western's insights, noted earlier. In particular, what does he mean by 'leadership formation'? Apart from obvious skills – the capacity to look awry, think systematically, use depth analysis, and so forth – Western believes that leaders can develop a critical approach to their work that helps to 'co-create with others the social conditions which lay the foundations for emancipatory (work) environments' (Western, 2008, p. 199). He is anxious to move on from leadership formation simply being the development of existing or new competencies, since they run the risk of resonating too easily and quickly with functional and rational discourses that already collude with systemic inertia. Moreover, such approaches also disconnect the leader from their environment – a key insight for us that arguably triggered our research at the outset. Too many of the formulae offered in the various genres of literature on leading the church, and by training providers, lack sufficient ecclesial density and nuance.[15] Too many blueprints for reform may concentrate on micro- and not macro-development. The broad and complex ecclesial ecology is not understood at the outset, which leads to frustration as visions, strategies and tactics continually fall short of their promised goals. This can lead to boredom, collusion, and eventually the onset of deeply embedded institutional cynicism.

A stress on formation, then, is clearly not going to be some kind of 'magic bullet' – for all the reasons that pertain to the deficiency of Messiah discourse discussed earlier. Hence, Western suggests that leadership formation will be achieved 'through a process of collective and individual formation rather than an ad hoc set of developmental opportunities and experiences' (Western, 2008, p. 202). Leadership formation, he adds, needs to hold the whole (institutional) environment in mind, and needs to take a holistic view of that to create a consistent context for learning (i.e., education and training). But the problem here is that the formational process, whilst it undoubtedly takes place, is somewhat *ad hoc* and unrecognized, just as it often is in theological education for clergy. Moreover, to simply adopt a kind of *laissez-faire* approach to formation carries enormous risks for an institution – the kinds that Paulo Freire and others would identify

---

[14]   For an extended discussion on definitions and meanings of formation, see Foster (2006), pp. 120ff.

[15]   For a more detailed and recent discussion of episcopacy in relational community, see Jeffrey Driver (unpublished). Driver effectively argues, towards the end of the thesis, that Episcopal identity, roles and tasks are substantially comprehended in the sphere of ministerial praxis.

in their musings on pedagogy and transformation. In other words, where is the 'education for change'?[16]

How, then, is formation capable of being transformative as well as sustaining? The answer must lie in a formation that is open to creativity, which means that the institution will need to sustain conversations and organizations that challenge the body. Leaders will therefore need to be open to ideas and conversations that may seem counter-intuitive. They will understand that institutions do not have clear boundaries, but are rather comprised of spatial networks and organizations that enjoy a degree of fluidity. Moreover, because each part of the body is capable of innovation and evolution, leaders will need to be receptive to change – holding, not containing. Western suggests one practical idea here – 'laboratories of experience' – which act as spaces for exchange, development and audit (Western, 2008, p. 206). [17] He concludes with a plea that resonates with some of the implications that arise quite naturally from our interviews and research:

> … transformation will be a by-product of leadership formation [but] seeking transformation before formation is premature … it reflects society's preoccupations with immediate gratification. You cannot buy leadership from a quick course, or popular manual. Leadership exists all around us, but much of it presently goes unnoticed and is uncherished, at the expense of organizational success … Leadership formation will reveal many manifestations of leadership that are currently hidden, if we are open to new forms of leadership; like creativity, it will surprise us. (Western, 2008, p. 208)[18]

It therefore follows that any future patterns for developing discrete cultures of leadership formation in the church should be encouraged to immerse themselves in the flow of what is *actually* happening; how the individual in role is being and becoming; and what they will be. We could therefore profitably invest time and energy in trying to develop and cultivate a certain sagacity, shrewdness and wisdom that truly fits with and makes sense of our ecclesial ecology; to say nothing of emotional and ecclesial intelligence that is needed for senior leaders. Transformation can then emerge from formation. In pedagogical terms, this is bound to be more of an art than a science; a world for the reflective practitioner rather than the pure theorist.

---

[16]   See Freire (1998), pp. 51ff and (1973), pp. 51ff.

[17]   The proposal sounds suspiciously like theological reflection and co-mentoring groups, where ideas, innovations, problems and solutions can be discussed and refined.

[18]   Cf. Foster (2006), pp. 120ff.

Conclusion

Given the complexity and density of issues that have emerged in relation to ecclesial leadership – even in this brief essay – what can be said about the possibilities for developing and shaping leaders for the future? We know that all the competencies needed to lead a complex institution are not imparted ontologically at the point of consecration. They take time to be formed. So a turn to sagacity, wisdom, practice and the discernment of the divine offers a helpful foundation from which we can draw some tentative conclusions. First, the distinction between an organization and institution seems to offer some helpful clues as to what kind of leadership the church requires. Leading an organization permits a certain kind of focus and direction that may not be obviously and immediately available to those who head institutions, where continuity with the past, and a highly diverse range of constituencies. It requires equal measures of robustness and suppleness, reflexivity and directionality, intensity and extensity,[19] to name but a few.

Second, senior leaders in the church need to be capable of and enabled to address and hold the 'thick traffic' of ecclesial discourse and praxis that emerges in dioceses. There is, quite simply, an enormous amount of information to absorb – reactively and proactively. Bishops, it is often said, can be conduits through which the church conducts its debates and conversations; the 'speaking in tongues' which is both the unity and polyphony of ecclesial life. Holding this diversity together requires considerable emotional and ecclesial intelligence, as well as skills in absorption, mediation, translation and energizing. It necessitates the development of deep resilience: the capacity to be resistant to and accommodating of the issues, contexts, cultures and traditions that it engages with.[20]

Third, a deeper appreciation of the actuality of the church – in all its depth and miscibility – is required for a formational context in which training, education and development is to flourish. In a series of interviews conducted with senior church figures, it was noticeable that there was a well-articulated absorption with organizational dynamics, especially where problematic issues were very apparent. This suggested evidence of a healthy and deep understanding of the church in many senior leaders, which augurs well for its organization. However, we noted a correlation between inhabiting organizational, managerial and institutional frames of reference, and a decrease in the amount of explicit spiritual and theological discourse. This suggests, possibly, that the more absorbing the managing and leading of the church becomes – especially in the face of complex problems and dilemmas – we find a corresponding loss of overt faith language to express the situation.

Fourth, we sense that in the face of such institutional complexity, there is sometimes a danger that the mission to wider culture is lost. One of the pivotal roles

---

[19] See Hardy (2001) – where Hardy draws our attention to intensity and extensity in ecclesiological development as the 'double movement of God', pp. 41ff.

[20] For further discussion, see Percy (2001).

that bishops have is to evangelize.[21] Our data suggest that the more complex and draining the problems encountered in the church are, the less free the leadership are to proclaim their faith. This in turn runs the risk of the church turning in on itself, with a consequent impact on morale. This is why conflict resolution – the *creative* kind of which we spoke earlier – is so vital to the task of leading institutions. If this cannot be done, the church may find itself mired in the apologetics of ecclesial containment, and unable to proclaim the faith. Put more sharply, a lack of capacity in resolving fissiparous institutional intra-relations will almost certainly blunt the witness of the church to the world. Leaders risk being drawn too much into management, and diverted from leading.

Fifth, we are aware that all the models for leadership discussed and touched on in this essay, together with those pertaining to the church, are inadequate. A single term, or a cluster, cannot be descriptively sufficient for the depth and range of what is being considered. Moreover, the models are interpretive rather than descriptive, and in that sense, are limited insofar as they are only trying to give some hermeneutical account for the miscibility of structures, possibilities and issues that form the nucleus of the discussion. Thus, terms such as controller, therapist and messiah, are less prescriptive than they might appear at first sight, and should be viewed more as frameworks. Similarly, biblical models – such as prophet, priest, king – whilst helpful, cannot operate at any supra-empirical level in a way that will make the task and challenges of leadership in the church either more obvious, or easier. We believe that there are simply no shortcuts to engaging with the concreteness of the church, and leading it in all its complexity.

This may seem like an odd and somewhat downbeat note to end on. But on the contrary, it reinforces the point that the future education, training and development of senior leaders must be securely located, on the one hand, in a deep ecclesiological context. And on the other hand, in an understanding that a developed and open culture of formation is also critical for the enhancement of leadership. This formation is a delicate blend of ingredients: tactical, strategic, pragmatic, ideological, spiritual, intuitive, counter-intuitive, inspiration, creativity, visionary, grounding, and so forth. Moreover, this must be more than (mere) management, since the institution requires, above all else, leadership. And in the church, this means connecting the human to the divine; neither separating the two or conflating the self with one. It is *being* the body of Christ.

Because the church is not an organization, and the Christian faith not an ideology, a focus on Christian leadership cannot be reduced to a kind of crude instrumentality. What the church and her faith offer, above all else, is food for the spirit and everlasting life with God. To paraphrase Aidan Nichols, authentic Christianity, and therefore authentic Christian leadership, is not about us, but about God (2008, p. 131). This is why some of the most sustaining and powerful models we have for leadership formation are both Christological

---

[21]   For an illuminating discussion of how the church might engage with secular culture, see Edward Norman (2003), pp. 103ff.

and pneumatological in character. Nichols, noting the need of the church to correspond to the triplex of Christ's offices (prophet, priest, king), argues that these set the agenda for leadership priorities both now and for the foreseeable future. For Nichols, the prophetic speaks of the intellectual engagement that is required if culture is to be evangelized and converted. The mystical (priestly), in contrast, relates to the salvation and sanctification offered by the church. Whilst the institutional (king) speaks of an ordered-ness and openness that embraces the world; it is not an organization with policy, but rather an institution with polity (Nichols, 2008, pp. 133ff).

Christian leadership has, in other words, a real 'character': the 'stamp' of authenticity that can only come from God, Christ and the Holy Spirit. Leadership is the impression left; the indelible marks of God's presence and leading that point back to their source. So we can perhaps begin to end by saying that leadership formation in the church, and for the future needs to be focused on the language of the Spirit that gives life to the church. As we noted earlier, and borrowing from Western, formation must be holistic and embedded in the (institutional) culture. It requires both informal and formal processes, which include contexts containing (paternal) structures and reflective (maternal) spaces for formation to occur (Western, 2008, p. 206). In other words, pay attention to the implicit. The church is both text and teacher.

Chapter 8
Sacred Sagacity:
The Dynamics of Formation

Introduction

I suppose that the first and most obvious thing to say about the purpose of ordination training – formation and education for ministry – is that it isn't immediately obvious. What, after all, is one being prepared for? As Urban Holmes III presciently observed more than 30 years ago, the roles and tasks of the clergy are not nearly as palpable in the late twentieth century as they might have been 100 years earlier.[1] It almost goes without saying that if the professional status of clergy is somewhat ambivalent, then the training and formation that seminarians (or ordinands) receive is also likely to reflect this.[2] Yet this is not quite so. Students preparing for ordained ministry – in whatever institution they are being trained, formed and educated – can point to a curriculum (usually with a multiplicity of options, but also a 'core'); some kind of disciplined approach to prayer and worship; an ecclesial tradition that (at least) adds some kind of accent to the ethos of the institution; some practical assignments that continue to test the depth and trajectory of a vocation; and a continuous process of theological reflection that links the personal, social, intellectual and transcendent dynamics of formation.

Yet such a sketchy and skeletal outline of the priorities for theological education affords considerable licence to any ecclesial tradition and its training institutions. What then, if anything, can be said about Anglican theological education? Is there anything that might be said to unite the diversity of institutions one encounters within the global Communion? Beyond the superficial obviousness of differences – in terms of resources, history and ecclesial emphasis – is there some kind of trace or sense of a common 'genetic code' that might be said to be distinctive, especially in relation to the rather nebulous concept of 'formation'? Several observations can be made. But before that, it is necessary to make a few more general remarks relating to theological education, and the bearing this has on the kind of preparation for ministry that institutions are inherently responsible for.

For example, over the past three decades, the Church of England has witnessed a number of quite significant sea-changes in the profile and delivery of formation and training for ordained ministry. In the mid-1970's, almost three quarters of

---

[1]   See Holmes III (1971) and Percy (2006).

[2]   See Towler and Coxon (1979); Foster, Dahill, Golemon and Tolentino (2006); Russell (1980); Schillebeeckx (1985).

ordinands were under the age of 30. Today, that figure has dropped to a little over 10 per cent of the total numbers in training – almost the same as those in training over the age of 60. The average of ordination is now around 40. Correspondingly, there has been a significant shift in the expectations provided through training. Ordinands enter colleges and courses with significantly more life experience and maturity. They are also likely to be of similar age to the teaching staff, which has inevitably led to the development of more consensual and negotiated patterns of training, in place of programmes that might have once been (simply) imposed.[3]

To complement this development, the Church of England has also witnessed a significant change in the range of contexts for formation and training. Thirty years ago, more than two-thirds of ordinands trained in residential colleges, with part-time training in non-residential courses a relative novelty. The tables are almost entirely turned at the beginning of the twenty-first century, with the majority of ordinands now being trained on a variety of non-residential courses. So although six of the 11 residential colleges are broadly evangelical (reflecting the popularity of that wing of the church), there are over two dozen regional training schemes and ordained local ministry courses. The latter are ecclesiologically and theologically broad, continuing to reflect the historic strength of and English spiritual proclivity for openness: articulate, conversational and inclusive breadth that serves the whole needs of the parish, rather than a particular confessional stance.

At the core of training and formation – and this will be true for almost all Anglican training institutions – is a commitment to interweaving theology with experience, and usually in some kind of dynamic reflective practice. Often this is done through the exercise of ministry: observing, participating, leading and then reflecting. In such a context, the experiences of ordinands can often be quite turbulent before they become fulfilling. They may undergo a process of 'dis-memberment' before 're-membering', as they encounter a range of experiences and practices that can comfort and disturb in equal measure. The teaching underpinning this activity will most likely be constructive and edifying. Yet the very act of education (from *educare* – to literally 'draw out') can be costly – but an essential prerequisite to the process of trans-formation that ministerial formation is concerned with. James Hopewell observes:

> Rather than assume that the primary task of ministry is to alter the congregation, church leaders should make a prior commitment to understand the given nature of the object they propose to improve. Many strategies for operating upon local churches are uninformed about the cultural constitution of the parish; many schemes are themselves exponents of the culture they seek to overcome. (Hopewell, 1987, p. 11)

---

[3]   Here at Cuddesdon, the average age of ordinands currently in residential training is 38, and those in non-residential training 49. The male–female ratio is 50:50.

So the very nature of contemporary parochial ministry in England can place a demanding onus on institutions preparing individuals for the ministry of the church.[4] This might include, for example, instilling some sort of recognition that the (somewhat dubious) distinction between mission and maintenance is often a false dichotomy in the majority of parochial contexts, where the historic religious resonance of the church building will have a widespread (if sometimes unclear) spiritual significance. Thus, good maintenance of a building ('sermons in stone') is likely to be, *de facto*, good mission in any parochial context. The building may involve and affirm the neighborhood in a myriad of ways (beyond the merely functional operation of providing a place for meeting), thereby nourishing social and spiritual capital. The relationship between a church and its people in many parishes is essentially perichoretic – the 'mutual indwelling' of various cultural and religious currents that blend and inter-penetrate, producing new spiritual meanings, whilst also maintaining distinctive sodalities.

These remarks are perhaps especially suggestive for parochial ministry, but also for formation and theological education more generally, whether in residential or non-residential contexts. Although my comments mostly relate to preparation for parish ministry, the church increasingly recognizes that many engaged in training spend the majority of their ministry in a variety of sector ministries, or possibly new and innovative missiological initiatives that are non-parochial. Whatever the specific context of ministry, quality may need to be valued more than quantity; pace, solidarity and connectedness more than haste, energy and apparent achievement. It may be important to encourage ordinands to see that the worth of affirming the resonance of the past may have a higher spiritual value than the apparent obviousness of the need for relevance and progress. Presence and deep relational engagement may have a greater missiological impact than overt evangelistic schema and initiatives. And clearly, the ministerial 'blend' of being and doing (i.e., the clergyperson as both contemplative and activist) may need to be adjusted in any transition from urban or suburban contexts to rural ministry. Context may have a direct bearing on theological output. In other words, theology can be a rather 'slow' discipline; it takes time to accrue wisdom for the journey. Part of the process of formation is to comprehend the vision for theological reflection, which is attending patiently and deliberately to all kinds of material. This means helping ordinands to 'loiter with intention' in issues and encounters; to consciously and purposefully dawdle in their deliberations, so that clarity and wisdom comes to fruition. Theology is not a discipline for hurrying.

Some Characteristics of Formation

That said, what might some of the common denominators in formation within Anglican theological education be? Here I want to confine my observations to

---

4   See Torry (2004); Markham and Percy eds. (2005); and Percy (2005).

residential and non-residential education and training within the context of an Anglican seminary in England, and make some remarks about the shape of formation as it particularly relates to such institutions, rather than to elucidate the principles of theological reflection more generally.[5] That said, I suspect that these observations will resonate with other parts of the Anglican Communion, and theologies of ministry in most mainline Protestant denominations. Here then, are several suggestions; a list that must be, clearly, far from exhaustive, and is perhaps quite personal. I have listed several characteristics that I would venture are relatively common to flourishing institutions, although they are clearly rooted in my own experiences and expectations.

First, the individual and the institution are set apart for deep and rich composition. There must be some understanding that the person in training, as a character formed within the Christian story and the demands of the gospel, has responded to a vocational call, and has in some sense now been set apart. Ordination is the process and event whereby this calling is recognized, and then established in office. Correspondingly, one of the primary tasks of education and formation for ministry is to integrate the individual character with the catholicity of the office. One of my predecessors at Cuddesdon, Robert Runcie, articulated some of the dynamics within this process, in his inimitable manner:

> (A priest) will not depend on status, nor upon his own abilities, nor upon a system, but upon God. (The primary quality) required is a man's sincerity in prayer and faith and compassion. These may yet be hardly developed, but the relevant signs will consist in obstacles overcome, work voluntarily undertaken and thoroughly performed, and a general attitude of responsibility as a Christian man rather than an interest in the social and ornamental aspects of the priesthood. Then they (the selectors) will look for something which can be described as a love of God's world and his people. Affectation and pretence are danger signs, and the sociability required of a priest consists in a spontaneity of interest in a world and a society of which he feels himself instinctively and naturally a part.[6]

Correspondingly, some understanding of the place or institution set apart for formation and training is also necessary, preferably with some evidence of the capacity to read the dense encryption of the distinctive ethos of the institution they are in, which is usually born out of an alloy of alliances.

There was some opposition to the founding of Anglican theological colleges in nineteenth century England. Unlike the colonies, none existed in England before the early nineteenth century. There was initial suspicion and hostility directed towards the burgeoning number of new institutions that were founded, with fears expressed that education and formation for ministry taking place outside the control of the major universities could lead to elitism and sectarianism on the

---

[5]   See for example Volf and Bass (2002).
[6]   Robert Runcie, *Church Observer*, 1964, p. 11.

part of the church. As late as 1921, Arthur Headlam, the then Regius Professor of Divinity of Oxford and a somewhat ambiguous conservative Churchman, wrote that 'there is a great danger of theological teaching being given in theological colleges ... the students are trained exclusively according to one particular point of view. Their minds, instead of being accustomed to examining and weighing the merits of different opinions, become stereotyped..The tendency of a theological college will be to give a man a set of opinions and to teach him to pass by and ignore those who differ from him. The tendency of a University is to make a man compare different points of view, to form his opinions after weighing alternatives, and therefore to hold the system which commends itself to him with due respect for the opinions of those who differ from him' (Headlam, 1921, p. 22).

Cuddesdon College was founded by Bishop Wilberforce in 1854 as a mainstream Anglican college, 'free from party and sectarian disputes'. Ripon Hall was first established at Ripon in 1898 by the diocesan bishop, William Boyd Carpenter, as a hostel for theological students. His vision for theological training was that 'ordinands had to take on board the new needs of society', and embrace the lessons that were to be found in life and learning outside the control of the church. The two institutions were merged in 1975, and their distinctive and combined ethos remain detectable. A third institution was added in 2006, with the incorporation of the Oxford Ministry Course, a non-party and non-residential training institution, which could legitimately claim to be faithful to the vision of both Wilberforce and Carpenter – broad and non-party in its ecclesiology, and open-minded in its theological outlook.[7] This breadth, of course, is not without complications. Granted, theological programmes are aligned with the spiritual ethos (i.e., open, enquiring, etc). Disagreement can be the price we pay for diversity and depth – as in any rich and cosmopolitan institution. But this is arguably preferable to the comforts of narrow confessional conformity, which can breed its own tensions. So for ordinands, some understanding of the composition of the institution they are in will have a direct bearing on their own formation.

Second, formation is a progressive and subtle journey. Whatever a theological college is, it is not an Ecclesiastical Boot Camp. There is no 39-buttoned-cassock Drill Sergeant to rouse the students to prayer. Most institutions, whether residential or non-residential, will speak quite naturally of 'the discipline of prayer' as foundational. But it will invariably be something that is instilled rather than imposed. Similarly, despite all the assignments and other tasks to complete, institutions will require their students to pay attention to the condition of the heart as much as the head. In that sense, the process of formation requires students to adopt a sense of perspective and pace; to borrow a phrase from Roosevelt, 'make haste slowly'.[8] Discipleship is a marathon, not a sprint. Correspondingly, there has

---

[7]   Cuddesdon currently has more than 120 students training for ordained ministry in the Church of England: 55 per cent are residential, and 45 per cent are non-residential.

[8]   I.e., the Latin motto, *festina lente*.

to be some trust in the continuing process of discernment, and less concern about the outcome: Christ is Lord of the Journey.

It therefore follows that ordinands should be encouraged to immerse themselves in the flow of what is happening; how they are becoming; and what they will be. Institutions invest much time and energy in trying to develop and cultivate a certain sagacity, shrewdness and wisdom for the journey ahead, to say nothing of emotional and ecclesial intelligence. But in pedagogical terms, this is more of an art than a science; a world for the reflective practitioner rather than the pure theorist. One writer (John Paul Lederach) invites us to engage and trust in a process that is sometimes led by the heart as much as the head. His advice provides a good fit for any 'recipe' in the field of theological education, reflection and formation:

> ... the more I wanted to intentionally produce a result, the more elusive it seemed to be; the more I let go and discovered the unexpected openings along the way, at the side of the journey, the more progress was made ... [The] greatest contributions to peace building did not seem to be those that emerged from accumulated skill or intentional purpose. They were those that happened unexpectedly. At a certain time, I came to call this divine naivety ... the practitioners' dilemma of learning more from mistakes than successes. But the reality was that they were not mistakes in the proper sense of the word; they were important things I learnt along the way that were not planned. I needed a combination of [the] divine and naïve. [The] divine pointed to the transcendent and unexpected – but that led towards insight and better understanding. To see that which is not readily planned or apparent, however, requires a peripheral type of vision, the willingness to move sideways – and even backward – in order to move forward ... an innocence of expectation that watches carefully for the potential of building change in good and in difficult times ... foster[ing] the art of the possible ... the key is to [learn how] to build from the unexpected ... to connect [the apparently] accidental with sagacity ... . (2005, p. 115, adapted)

Third, the type of knowledge acquired in formation is also at issue. It is probably the case that Anglicanism is often easier to identify through persons rather than systems: *examples* of faith and polity rather than theories of it. Here, the management of a congregation within the context of the challenges of contemporary culture is much more like a 'knack' than a skill; organizing or shaping the church is about learned habits of wisdom more than it is about rules and theories.

Acknowledging the place of tacit and intuitive knowledge has important implications for teaching those engaged in the task of Christian leadership. There is a valuable repository of spiritual treasure in (dense, and occasionally tense) collegiality, and in the storied communion of shared wisdom. This is why the *character* of the theological college or non-residential course, as a community of fellow learners on the viaticum, is so important in formation and training. Thus, how we teach ordinands to 'hold' complex issues; the character that teachers and mentors exhibit under pressure; and how individuals continue to embody being the very best kinds of 'reflective practitioner' – these are the skills that often make their deep mark in the formational process.

Fourth, openness and vulnerability have a role in learning. Thinking and practising needs to be continually returned to the heart of the vocation, which is, of course, a mystery of risk. Unpacking it takes time and energy, but it also invites seminarians and ordinands to journey deeper into wisdom and wholeness. There is, therefore, a vested interest in encouraging students to engage with and encounter some of the things they might actually fear (e.g., issues, ideas, scenarios, etc). This goes hand in hand with sounding the depths of the complexities of all kinds of encounters, and developing the habit of deep listening, of imagining beyond what is seen, and what presents on the surface. Risking vulnerability is part of the price we pay for love; and this kind of openness belongs to the economy of vocations. In this sense, every truly self-conscious theological college will know, somewhere, that all the members of its community are beginners.

To complement this, there must be the possibility of failure. However, it is also recognized that institutions are often best-judged not by how many stellar scholars they produce, but by how they care for and mentor the weak and the vulnerable. Mistakes happen, and I think the best thing those charged with teaching and mentoring can try to do is encourage seminarians to learn from these things when they happen. Failure is not the worst thing; letting it utterly defeat you is. It takes a special kind of wisdom and courage to face failure and defeat, and then to try and move on from this. But this kind of maturity should perhaps especially be cultivated, in order to help cope with the reality of life's miscibility.[9]

Fifth, the relationships between embodiment, power and wisdom need continual exploration. There is arguably something to be said for a formational process that probes and loosens any relationships with power and privilege. It is perhaps good to be reminded that the gospel is about eternal rewards, not the temporal baubles of the church. Our eyes are to be fixed on Jesus, not on achievement. God is interested in

> much more than a set of competencies. No accumulation of skills impresses God. God is interested in the heart of the priest, more than how impressive his or her curriculum vitae appears to be ... (Pritchard, 2007, p. 4)

Yet there is no substitute for the cultivation of holy wisdom. All of us, I think, encounter projects and persons in ministry that either fail to turn out to be all that we hoped, or can even become arenas of defeat. It is reminiscent of what Graham Greene has to say in *The Power and the Glory*, namely that hatred is the failure of the imagination. Holy wisdom, then, is something related to but 'other' than conventional wisdom. It is an embodied form of spiritual intelligence that is more

---

[9]   On this, see Freire (2006).

than mere shrewdness. It is interpretative, lived and transformative; and those who encounter it will more often speak of an epiphany than mere insight.

And After Ordination?

The stress on formation may seem innocuous and nebulous to some. But given our earlier contention that the church is better understood as an institution and not as an organization, and that its composition is rooted in *terroir*, we are now in a position to establish that leading this kind of body is not necessarily straightforwardly comparable to leading other kinds of institutions and organizations. Moreover, recent research has shown that learning about leadership – as a deacon, priest or bishop in the church – is primarily a formational matter, rather than something derived from formal education or training.[10]

Indeed, much of the research from scholars such as Foster notes the absence of education as distinct from training. Granted, there can be no precise distinction between the two, since there are overlapping definitions for training, formation and education. Nevertheless, distinguishing between the two, although not perfect, may serve us well. But it does seem that *being* a church leader – whether bishop, minister, vicar, curate, priest or deacon – is more often 'discovered' rather than explicitly taught. This is not so surprising. Thus – and to flesh this out slightly – we might say that the 'sense of unevenness' that has been voiced about ministry may be directly attributable to the lack of overt education on the plural, diverse and collective nature of ecclesial governance.[11] It is both lay and clerical; voluntary and paid; static and mobile; structural and spiritual. However, coping with this unevenness is essentially a training issue; and teaching about it, an educational matter. For some ministers, only half the pedagogical formation is complete: they have training on how to cope, but not the education to comprehend the puzzling complexity of the body of which they have oversight. Or, they have that comprehension – but not the tactical skills through training that are needed to manage and lead.

Our attention to the idea of the church as a complex body at this point is hardly accidental. Bodies contain systems and forms of organizations that require meticulous regulative management. Not all of these will be consciously apparent to the mind. But a body is clearly more than one single form of organization. It contains naturally functioning parts that need no conscious instructions; it responds, reacts, grows and declines in relation to different circumstances and environments. It is something that can be trained and educated; yet is also in constant state of complex formations, which may involve instinct, wisdom, memory and innate calculation.

---

[10]   See C. Foster et al (2006).

[11]   I infer here, of course, to the role of Arch-Episcopal responsibility in mediation and in holding together a complex nexus of competing convictions: *primus inter pares*.

A body is a 'natural symbol' (Mary Douglas) as well as a single entity. Its identity, of course, is complex and contestable, yet obvious. It has to come to terms with the multiplicity of meanings that it inhabits, which vary across the range of discourses in which the body engages – medical, anthropological, sociological, spiritual, and so forth. The body is one, yet capable of multiple interpretative possibilities.

Correspondingly, Paul's analogy of the church as the body of Christ allows us to reappraise the richness of the church as an institution (1 Corinthians 12: 12–26.) The human body is a 'natural symbol' by which people often order the systemic nature of their corporate life. The human body is often an image of society; how a group views and values its own members will reflect upon notions of corporate and individual life. Therefore, to contemplate the church as a body is to invite reflection on the sensitivity of the church, its receptivity, its boundaries, barriers and definitions, all processes of exchange, as well as its natural death and replenishment. It is 'osmotic' in character: giving and receiving nourishment, identity and love. The body is inescapably part of its environment, as well as separate and distinct. The body – with all its members – is incarnate in space and time.

Why, though, might any of these reflections matter in terms of the theological leadership of a quite complex institution – whether that is a local church, diocese, mission area or cathedral? Arguably because the leadership of the church requires taking responsibility for a highly complex organism, where obvious clarity of intention and attention cannot be taken for granted, and are not always apparent. The systems and micro-organizations within the institution/body will maintain their foci in a dedicated (even myopic) manner, almost independent of any willed tactics or strategy that the body may consciously have articulated. Thus, the 'head' may well prioritize a range of tasks or opportunities. But the heart will still beat, and other micro-systems within the body will still carry on with their primary functions. This does not mean, of course, that the body is divided, or in any sense schizoid. It is simply the recognition that its complexity is part of its organic and mystical given-ness.

That is why most senior positions of authority within the Anglican Church require that individuals hold (with poise and care) a complex nexus of competing convictions and emotions that cannot be easily resolved on behalf of the institution. Leading a body is not the same as leading an organization.

As the *Common Worship* Consecration service reminds:

> (*Name*), remember always with thanksgiving that God has entrusted to your care Christ's beloved bride, his own flock, bought by the shedding of his blood on the cross. You are to govern Christ's people in truth, lead them out to proclaim the good news of the kingdom, and prepare them to stand before him when at last he comes in glory. You cannot bear the weight of this calling in your own strength, but only by the grace and power of God. Pray therefore that you may

be conformed more and more to the image of God's Son, so that through the outpouring of the Holy Spirit your life and ministry may be made holy and acceptable to God. Pray earnestly for the gift of the Holy Spirit ....[12]

Many diocesan bishops understand the costly nature of this vocation – a kind of servant leadership – in which the body must be both led and served. The slight concern with adopting Greenleaf's servant-leader paradigm (1998) is that the leader *chooses* to be a servant and selects which acts of service to undertake. And whilst one can argue that some service is a matter of obligation and not choice, it is nevertheless the case that leaders can decide on the form of servanthood that they undertake, which suggests that an uncritical use of Greenleaf's equation is somewhat problematic, and even open to a certain kind of abuse. Moreover, this leadership comprehends that much of Anglican polity is open; and although has a shape, is nonetheless unresolved. It is, like a body, replete with creative dilemmas; checks and balances; the reactive and proactive.

So in terms of resolving conflict, and in inhabiting dilemmas, one can see that the desire and need to sometimes reach settlements that do not achieve closure is actually a deep *formational* habit of wisdom that has helped to form Anglican polity down the centuries. It is embodied liturgically, but can also be traced in pastoral, parish and synodical resolutions that cover a range of issues. Put another way, there is a tension between being an identifiable community with creeds; whilst also being a body that recognizes that a whole range of other issues are essentially un-decidable.[13] Essentially, the 'calling' to lead this body is about inhabiting the gap between vocation, ideals, praxis and action. No neutral or universally affirmed settlements can be reached on a considerable number of issues within the church. But settlements have to be reached that allow for the possibility of continuing openness, adjustment and innovation. Inevitably, therefore, consensus is a slow and painful moment to arrive at, and even when achieved, usually involves a degree of provisionality. This is, of course, a typical Anglican habit, embodying a necessary humility and holiness in relation to matters of truth, but without losing sight of the fact that difficult decisions still need to be made. This is the nature of the body.

In this respect, the scriptures are of course helpful and vital in guiding the church through this complex dimension of its polity. Decisions often involve an irrevocable commitment to the future which requires obedience rather than debate. But this, of course, places a further and heightened value on un-decidability, since this allows for the continuance of courtesy and hospitality, which is essential in a Communion that embodies so much diversity. In Rowan Williams's meditations on the aftermath of 11 September 2001, he reflects on Jesus' enigmatic gesture of writing in the dust:

---

[12]   *CW*, 2000.

[13]   On this, see Pickard (2004).

He [Jesus] hesitates. He does not draw a line, fix an interpretation, tell the woman who she is and what her fate should be. He allows a moment, a longish moment, in which people are given time to see themselves differently precisely because he refuses to make the sense that they want. When he lifts his head, there is both judgement and release. So this is writing in the dust because it tries to hold that moment for a little longer, long enough for some of our demons to walk away. (Williams, 2002, p. 38)

The idea that the example of Jesus provides warrant for delaying clarity, precision and resolution has merit. Indeed, one can see the kinds of pleas for ecclesial polity reflected in the pastoral epistles of the New Testament: patience, forbearance and living together in a tense harmony (or communion) are placed alongside or above the need for clarity of purpose. In view of this, it is possible to suggest that part of the task of being a senior leader in the church is somehow to cultivate and embody this deep habit of wisdom – a kind of emotional and ecclesial intelligence which can creatively hold together competing convictions; but in ways that offer direction, yet without necessarily delivering closure. Or, put another way, it is about cultivating the Anglican genius of 'directional plurality': travelling together, and discovering commonality in the pilgrim journey. So here 'directional' does not militate against any kind of willed or clear trajectory. Rather, it sets its face against exclusive resolutions that prevent a participative community of diversity from being itself; it enables 'bonds of affection' to flourish.

Leadership of the body is, then, organic, intellectual, directed, responsive, robust, empathetic, practical and emotional. It is sacred sagacity. It is also a mystical union between leader and led, just as Christ is to his church. It loves the body for what it is – 'his own' – yet wills so much more for it. It is full of realism, but also hope. And these are held together in deep forms of maternal and paternal love. Indeed, the three 'offices' of Christ – prophet, priest and king – may reflect something of this dynamic. This requires a correlation between emotional and ecclesial intelligence. To lead the church requires the development of a deep sagacity: the wisdom of God for the body of Christ, prompted and guided by the Holy Spirit.

An Analogical Coda

In summary, there may be something to be said for theological institutions – of whatever tradition, and whether residential or non-residential – placing a stress on the great Benedictine virtues of hospitality, service and listening. Each of these is vital to the flourishing of the community of learning and the individual in formation. Being open to God, paying attention to others and deep listening – these are the profound spiritual exercises that allow individuals and communities (whether gathered or dispersed) to attend to the cadence, timbre and rhythm of what they are about. So how can we understand the dynamics that take place during ministerial training and formation? Mere description, I think, does not do justice to the depth and richness of the process that takes place. The language we need to capture the journey often comes to fruition by being framed in paradox;[14] of the heart and the soul. And this is where the analogical imagination can be helpful. Thus, one aspect of what takes place in formation is that seminarians learn to find ourselves in what one writer describes as 'God's orchestra':

> Christian leaders are like conductors of God's local orchestra. Our task is multi-layered. We have to interpret the music of the gospel to bring out all its richness and textures and glorious melodies. We have ourselves to be students of the music, always learning, and sharing, with the orchestra what both we and they have learned about this beautiful music. We have to help members of the orchestra to hear each other, and to be aware of each other as they play their 'instrument' or use their gift. Without that sensitivity to each other both an orchestra and a church descend into a cacophony of conflicting noises …
> (Pritchard, 2007, pp. 109ff)

To continue with this analogy, and to apply it more directly to theological institutions, three key observations seem to be particularly pertinent. First, whatever part one plays in the orchestra, institutions have to try and pay attention to the bass-line, and to not get overly distracted by the melody. The bass-line is all about patience, depth and pace. It may also contain the givens of theological discourse. It is about developing sustainable rhythms for the entire symphony – not just the short movements in which one part of orchestra might mainly feature.

Second, teachers and mentors have the task of coaching and conducting. There may be some new scores to teach as well; and the performance of these helps to form the necessary skills in theological and pastoral discernment. In turn, this enables ordinands to develop intuition in relation to knowledge; to become reflexive, yet also sure-footed. Thus, institutions carry the responsibility for developing the natural and given talents, rather than simply replacing them with new instructions. Education is both input and drawing out, to enable spiritual, pastoral and intellectual flourishing.

Third, just as scripture is symphonic in character – many different sounds making a single, complex, but beautiful melody – so it is with God's church, and the institutions that equip ministers for the communities in which they serve. The task of the teacher and mentor is, then, not just to help students understand and critique the scores they read and perform, but also to try and help each seminarian play beautifully and function faithfully – and all within the context of the diversity of the many different sounds and notes that God gives an institution to make.

---

[14]   On this, see Dykstra ed. (2005). Paradoxical images include 'wise fool', 'servant-leader', 'wounded healer' and 'intimate stranger'. These images help frame the pastoral nature of ordained ministry, alongside the classic biblical models ('shepherd') and those drawn from contemporary life (e.g., coach, or manager).

Chapter 9
Feeling for the Church:
Emotion and Anger in Ecclesial Polity

Even in terms of implicit theology, it is perhaps unusual to think of one's denomination or faith in relation to temperature. By this, I do not mean contemplating a cold church on a frosty day, with your breath misting as you say the liturgy or sing the hymns. I mean your faith – or more particularly the denomination to which you belong – in terms of how hot or cool it is. Or put another way, a kind of climatology of religion. The idea is not as daft as it might sound. Scottish Free Presbyterianism is partly born of its host climate; cold, grey and a tad drizzly. Catholicism (much of it, anyway) is born of the Mediterranean; it is a warm, sultry faith, of the passions and of the senses. This is perhaps an unusual way to think about denominations – in terms of temperature and colour. But it is not some kind of new-age fad. We find it in literature all the time. I think especially here of Garrison Keillor's *Lake Wobegon Days* (1985), where the author contrasts his austere Brethren upbringing – plain, whitewashed rooms to pray in; no décor, because 'Jesus is in our hearts'; not warm baths – these might be too sensual – with the Catholic festivals he occasionally glimpses. To a Brethren boy, these processions that he witnesses are an orgy of colour and performance – the very opposite of what he knows to be true faith. His faith is cold, grave and ascetic; Catholics, he thinks, are sunny, colourful and abundant. And one senses a hint of jealousy.

Like many Anglicans from the developed world, we tend to think of our polity in terms of coolness or warmth; but not hot or cold. The classic *via media*; Laodicean, tepid – and proud of it. Anglicanism is born of England, and like its climate, we don't do extremes well. It is a temperate polity; cloudy, occasional sunny spells and the odd shower – but no extremes. But we like to discuss our weather, most of which is akin to our polity. We complain if it is too hot … and too cold. Goldilocks has it right – we look for the warm middle. Anglicans are not alone in this. Even Wesley, as a good Anglican, only had his heart 'strangely warmed' – not hot, then. Indeed, Methodists often celebrate their temperateness. A recent poster for a Methodist church that proclaimed: 'Wesley – the heart strangely warmed: Methodism – warmly strange.'

So what happens in congregations and denominations when things get too hot? Some churches, of course, like intensity and heat; it is a sign of vibrant life and feisty faith. But others who are of a more temperate hue find this disturbing; heated exchanges, anger and passions seem to dismay more than they comfort. Anglicanism, as I have already suggested, is a *via media* – what one of my distinguished predecessors describes as 'passionate coolness'. This is a typically Anglican phrase – the framing of ecclesial identity within an apparent paradox. But you could say that what currently afflicts Anglicanism is not this or that issue – but the heat and intensity that often accompany the debates – because Anglicans are used to temperate, cool debates. We don't do anger well; we don't cope well with excess. So the churches of the global south – used to heat both climatologically and theologically – conflict with the more traditionally temperate culture. And when heat meets coolness, a storm can brew.

But enough, for the moment, of religious climatology. For it is only one way of thinking about churches and their contexts. Here is another:

> In some of my conversations with Anglican theologians ... I have been struck by how much of the coherence of Anglicanism depends on good manners. This sounds, at face value, like an extraordinarily elitist statement. It is clearly not meant to be that. What I mean by manners is learning to speak well, behave well, and be able to conduct yourself with integrity in the midst of an argument ... It is often the case that in Anglicans' disputes about doctrine, order or faith, it is actually the means that matter more than the ends ... politeness, integrity, restraint, diplomacy, patience, a willingness to listen, and above all, not to be ill-mannered – these are the things that enable the Anglican Communion to cohere ... (Percy, 2000, pp. 118–19)

There can be no question that enabling ecclesial polity depends, to some extent, on managing anger. In macro-theological disputes, such as those over the ordination of women, part of the strategy that enables unity can be centred on muzzling some of the more passionate voices in the debate. Extreme feelings, when voiced, can lead to extreme reactions. And extreme reactions, when allowed full-vent, can make situations unstable. Nations fall apart; Communions fracture; families divide. Things said briefly in the heat of a moment can cause wounds that may take years to heal. What is uttered is not easily retracted.

It can be argued that many casual descriptions of Anglican polity are focused on its essentially peaceable and pastoral nature. For T.S. Eliot, the Church of England is the *via media* (Eliot, 1928, p. 14). It is a synthesis of tensions; a delicate infusion of polarities. It is partly protestant, partly catholic, partly evangelical and partly liberal. It is an Episcopally-led church, and yet also one where Synods govern, and also has a supreme governor who is a laywoman (the Queen). It is a church, as one might eloquently put it, which embodies 'passionate coolness'. There are causes and beliefs that it pursues with a righteous intensity. But the communication of such things can often be characterized by reticence, temperance and openness. Any such statements the church may make might be sharp and penetrating, but are often balanced by an instinctive pastoral reflex: to be soft and accommodating as well.

Good manners, then, is not a bad analogy for 'ideal' Anglican polity. In a church that sets out to accommodate many different peoples of every theological hue, there has to be a foundation – no matter how implicit – that enables the Communion to cohere across party lines, tribal borders and doctrinal differences. And just as this is true for macro-theological disputes, so is it also true for micro-ecclesial squabbles. Keeping the peace in a congregation that is at loggerheads over church fabric and fittings, or perhaps unable to agree on an appropriate resolution in a complex ethical debate, is a no less demanding task for a parish priest. Often, congregational unity in the midst of disputes can only be secured by finding a middle, open way, in which the voices of moderation and tolerance occupy the central ground and enable a church to move forwards. In such situations, the cultivation of 'good manners' can be seen to be essential; civility quietly blossoms where arguments once threatened to lay waste.

And yet there are several important pastoral and theological issues that surround this type of narration for a congregation, diocese, church or communion, and question its apparent wisdom. 'Good manners', for example, can be a form of quasi-pastoral *suppression* that does not allow true or strong feelings to emerge in the centre of an ecclesial community, and properly interrogate its 'settled' identity. This may rob the church of the opportunity to truly feel the pain of those who may already perceive themselves to be on the margins of the church, perhaps even disqualified, or who already feel silenced. 'Good manners' can also become a cipher for excluding the apparently undeserving, and perhaps labeling seemingly difficult insights as 'extreme voices'.

Some factors here that are, in all probability, gender-based. Ursula Le Guin makes a helpful distinction between 'mother tongue' and 'father tongue'. The 'father tongue' is the language of power: 'spoken from above ... it goes one way ... no answer is expected or heard ...' (Le Guin, 1989, p. 149). The 'father-tongue' is the clinical language of the lecture theatre or the professions – it distances the emotions, passions and desires. In contrast, 'mother tongue' is the language of the home. It is, according to Le Guin, 'inaccurate, coarse, limited, trivial, banal ... earthbound, housebound, common speech, plebian, ordinary ...' (Le Guin, 1989, p. 149). But for Le Guin, the 'mother-tongue' is also the language of connection and relationships; its power lies in uniting and binding, not dividing. It is Le Guin's contention that much public discourse, especially professional discourse within institutions, is a learned 'father-tongue' that deliberately marginalizes the realm of feelings and the scope of relationality. She argues that a recovery of 'mother-tongue' within public discourse is an essential step for the reconstitution of public life, where 'plain' speaking can reclaim its proper value (or currency) as *bona fide* expression.

Quite naturally therefore, there is the issue of anger itself, and of strong feelings. In the body of Christ, how are these feelings received, articulated and generated? Quite apart from appropriate 'righteous anger' (e.g., on matters of justice), how does a mature church receive and respond to aggression within itself, and to strong feelings such as anger, dismay, passion, rage or enthusiasm? For example, the issue of anger comes to a head in two different places in David Hare's play *Racing Demon* (1990). In the first case, the Bishop of Kingston states that the job of the

Church of England (and especially a bishop), is 'preventing problems turning into issues' (p. 39). In this case, it is the suppression of anger that is paramount, even though it is clear that the underlying feelings are not being addressed. Clearly, the bishop simply hopes that the feelings will 'go away' in due course, and 'everything can return to normal'. But they don't. So second, and by the end of the play, some of the underlying anger about the church and its *via media* and accommodating tendencies simply erupts. A different bishop (Southwark), furious at his lack of power, and the inability of the church to make a decision, and do anything about the apparent incompetence of one of his clergy (Lionel), explodes with rage:

> In any other job you'd have been fired years ago. You're a joke, Lionel. You stand in the parish like some great fat wobbly girl's blouse. Crying for humanity. And doing absolutely nothing at all … you are the reason the whole church is dying. Immobile. Wracked. Turned inward. Caught in a cycle of decline … a great vacillating pea-green half-set jelly … you parade your so-called humility, until it becomes a disgusting kind of pride. Yes, we can all be right if we never actually *do* anything … (Hare, 1990, p. 80)

No-one would want to defend the kind of outburst quoted above. Yet surely there is a right and proper place for anger and aggression and other strong feelings in ecclesial polity and pastoral praxis? An appropriateness in challenging the idea that the interests of the church are best served by the 'silencing of subjectivity'? In place of this, I want to explore how the rightful appropriation of anger and aggression can enable the work of the church, taking pastoral praxis away from the cerebral and peaceable, and into the arena of feelings and desires. I believe this to be important material for the church to be addressing at this time. Rather like a good marital or parent-child relationship, learning to articulate and channel anger can be as important as learning to control it.

It is often the case that in relationships where the expression of anger is denied its place, resentment festers and breeds, and true love is ultimately distorted. Strong feelings need to be acknowledged for relationships to flourish. If strong feelings on one or both sides have to be suppressed for the sake of a relationship, then it is rarely proper to speak of the relationship being mature or healthy. Indeed, some relationships that apparently present as being idyllic and peaceable (e.g., 'we never argue') can turn out to be pathologically problematic. Both parties, afraid of conflict and its consequences, deny their full truth to one another and themselves.

To be sure, feelings such as anger can drive or distort ministry, and their impact upon human organization and process can be considerable. There can be no question that being cool, calm and collected is important in pastoral ministry. But sometimes, being angry, avuncular and ardent can also have its place in a mature church. I can perhaps give one quite personal example by way of introduction. At a diocesan residential conference my wife attended, all the Eucharistic worship had been organized so as not to give offence to any clergy with strong views.

No woman priest was scheduled to celebrate Communion, but neither was any clergyman opposed to the ordination of women invited to celebrate. In this way, the senior staff and conference organizers hoped to avoid an argument.

Of course, the net effect of this policy was that the only people to celebrate Communion were men who approved of the ordination of women. But the women priests and those male priests who would habitually oppose them were far from happy with this apparently peaceable compromise. Silent anger simmered below the surface of an apparently happy conference.

But one woman priest took an interesting initiative. Seeing that her own feelings and those of her colleagues were being 'checked' but never acknowledged, she arranged for the women priests to meet with the male priests who opposed the ordination of women. She argued that neither side could be happy with the enforced compromise, which created a sense of their being 'no argument'. Both sides had a very agreeable meeting over a few drinks, and began to see that proper expression to their true feelings – both their desires and hurts – was being denied. Both sides felt that their genuine, God-given anger (even though they didn't agree), was being muzzled by the hierarchy. Both sides felt that their subjectivity was being suppressed. In not allowing their anger and division to be publicly symbolized (either by men refusing to receive communion from women priests, or women only receiving from men who recognized their priestly ministry), their actual feelings were being ignored.

Both sides, even though they seldom met, and were angry with each other (at least sometimes), felt that it would have been more mature to allow differences and feelings to surface, and thus generate more dialogue, rather than devising a Eucharistic schedule that apparently found a compromise in which no-one was hurt. But in actual fact, all the schedule did was deny people the opportunity to express their hurt, leading to further accusations and pain. Both sides claimed that they were still being marginalized, in spite of assurances to the contrary. Both sides claimed that they were not really being listened to, and that the 'settlement' imposed upon them (for the kindest, nicest reasons – 'to minimize pain', etc) failed to take account of their raw and strong feelings. What then, are we to make of this? I want to pursue three brief lines of enquiry. First, to explore some of the pastoral theology on the subject of feelings. Second, to reflect on the possibility of restoring a concept of righteous anger. Third, to make some remarks about the responsibility for developing ecclesial and emotional intelligence.

Pastoral Theology on Strong Feelings

Gentleness, and love that is detached and self-sacrificing, have often been held up as the virtues that Christians should be striving for. Politeness is certainly an important part of the polity of the church, but often with little acknowledgement that the *form* and *patterning* of manners has normally been established by those in power, so that consciously and unconsciously their privileges are maintained.

At the same time, we may need to appreciate that anger and aggression are often correlated with violence and chaos, and their intimate connection with love is therefore not acknowledged. The expression of passionate feelings, or perhaps of any feelings, is seen as a threat to the manners and politeness that maintain the coolness of rational faith. The danger, as two feminist theologians, Harrison and Robb point out, is that

> We need to recognize that where the evasion of feeling is widespread, anger does not go away or disappear. Rather, in interpersonal life it masks itself as boredom, ennui, low energy, or it expresses itself in passive-aggressive activity or in low moralistic self-righteousness and blaming. Anger denied subverts community. Anger expressed directly is a mode of taking the other seriously, of caring. The important point is that where feeling is evaded, where anger is hidden or goes unattended, masking itself, there the power of love, the power to act, to deepen relation, atrophies and dies. (Harrison and Robb, 1985, p. 15)

Equally, aggression is almost always understood as negative, and often equated with violence. Yet feminist writers such as Kathleen Greider call for a proper reappraisal of aggression and its place. She points that the Latin etymology of 'aggression' lies in the verb *aggredi*, meaning 'to move towards', and she uses an intriguing working definition that is significant for our discussion here. Greider sees aggression as a central part of human nature present from our earliest infancy. It is as important as love in the human capacity to survive and thrive.

> aggression is one primary expression of the life force, of the drive to survive and thrive, embodied in positive and negative movement toward and engagement with goals, persons, objects, and obstacles ... These two primary forces can be seen in infants who have at birth both the sentiment (love) to engage others and the force (aggression) especially through their ability to cry, to influence the powerful others around them to meet their needs ... (Greider, 1996, p. 126)

Thus for Greider, aggression and love are interrelated. They are both deeply connected to the importance of building and sustaining relationships that enable self and other to flourish:

> When functioning in this essential unity, aggression and love cannot be fully differentiated. However, an approximation of their particular contributions might be that love is 'desire' and aggression is 'movement'. ... Aggression enables love to move toward the thing desired, love enables aggression to desire the thing toward which it moves. Love has gumption in it, aggression has affection in it. Without this intermingling, love might be passive, aggression might be only self-serving; with this intermingling, aggression is more likely to be constructive, love is more likely to have backbone. (Greider, 1996, p. 127)

This working definition of aggression alters our perception of the term. It relocates it as a neutral given in human and organizational relating that can be expressed positively and negatively. In its positive form it is about drive; about the activity that moves things forwards so that love and relationship might flourish. In its negative form, it reacts with violence to those things that appear to deny or destroy the self. Thus, 'aggression is used negatively when it is directed toward wasteful and or unconscious violence; aggression is used positively when it is directed toward the affirmation of life and well-being in both its personal and collective dimensions' (Greider, 1996, p. 129).

Greider's 'aggression' is what others might call 'assertion'. Celia Hahn writes that 'assertion means moving outside oneself, reaching out with vigour and initiative, acting on the world' (Hahn, 1994, p. 21). Hahn draws a clear distinction between aggression and assertion, seeing the former as negative; but Greider argues that sometimes it is the very strength of aggression that is needed. She reflects on the fact that on the rare occasions where aggression is defended, it is because it is utilized on behalf of others, or constitutes a creative push. So what is needed is a reappraisal of aggression for the sake of self, and the value of its destructive as well as constructive power: she talks of the possibility of 'creative destruction' (Greider, 1996, p. 113).

These observations lead us to reflect on the type of love within polity and praxis that we are beginning to describe. Love, in Christian terms, has too often been equated with a disinterested detached *agape*, which involves self-sacrifice. The sacrifice of Jesus on the cross has been held up as a paradigm for love but often interpreted as an example of suffering as an end in itself. Of course, self-giving which can be costly and sacrificial is at the heart of the gospel; yet it is a giving that is motivated by love and looks for mutuality. Jesus' sacrifice was not about diminishing self; it is about the cost of his radical inclusivity, as he sought to draw all people into relationship with himself and God. In understanding the Christian calling to be Christ-like and to love God and our neighbours as ourselves, we need to be clear that love is about the flourishing of the self and the other. This way of understanding love stresses mutuality, and this is not possible without a sense that the self is worth something.

A Righteous Anger?

A more systematic and sustained focus on the anger of Jesus may also be helpful as we move forward with our discussion. We often read in the gospels that Jesus, 'moved with compassion', healed individuals. The first healing of a leper recorded by Mark has this rendering of the translation, although 'anger' is clearly implied. Why might this be so? Arguably, because the healings of Jesus, as well as being demonstrations of divine power and actual physical cures, are also politically and socially symbolic. Jesus understands what leprosy does to persons socially: it results in their marginalization and ostracization. The disease renders the victim not only contagious, but also classes them as 'other': labelled as a threat to normal socialization. Jesus' reaction, invariably, is to indict the witnesses, questioning their role in marginalizing and excluding. His healings are therefore often accompanied with anger at the needless additional suffering borne by the victim. Frequently, the ill beg for 'purification' or 'cleansing' rather than healing, since their anti-social treatment at the hands of the 'normal' is arguably worse than any of the physical suffering that they endure (see for example, Mark 1: 40, etc).

Jesus, it seems, is often angry. Later in Mark's gospel (10: 14) when the disciples chide villagers who have brought children to him for a blessing, he loses his temper: indeed, 'boils with rage' is the more faithful rendering of the Greek text. He is indignant and irate with the disciples, but not simply for miscalculating a valuable public relations opportunity. (Which politician or celebrity would resist the attendant publicity and good will generated by the proverbial pressing of the flesh?) In Jesus' care, the anger is centred on his refusal to be narrated as the property of pious right-thinking adults, in a way that excludes him from the lame, poor, dispossessed and broken; not to mention women and children too. The anger of Jesus, then, is directive and purposeful. It is a form of righteous violence that opposes the innocuous, apparently innocent and implicit violence that social and theological constructions of reality perform each day. Usually rooted in class, race or gender, these barriers exclude and marginalize at many levels, and Jesus' hostility towards them can only be expressed in through anger, since there is no other systemic mode of opposition available, other than through philosophy or parables. (He utilizes both of these modes too, of course).

The complexity of Jesus' attitude towards anger also merits further attention when we begin to consider how it can pattern itself in ecclesial polity. Anger in churches is not unusual; and neither are the calls to control or repress it. It is interesting, then to reflect on Jesus' direct treatment of anger in the fifth chapter of Matthew's gospel:

> You have heard that it was said to those of ancient times, 'You shall not murder'; and 'whoever murders shall be liable to judgement.' But I say to you that if you are angry with a brother or sister, you will be liable to judgement; and if you insult a brother or sister, you will be liable to the council; and if you say, 'You fool', you will be liable to the hell of fire. So when you are offering your gift at the altar, if you remember that your brother or sister has something against you, leave your gift there before the altar and go; first be reconciled to your brother or sister, and then come and offer your gift. Come to terms quickly with your accuser while you are on the way to court with him, or your accuser may hand you over to the judge, and the judge to the guard, and you will be thrown into prison. Truly I tell you, you will never get out until you have paid the last penny.
> (Matthew 5: 21–6)

As Lytta Bassett notes (Bassett, 2007, pp. 70ff.), Jesus does not repress the feeling of anger which can often spiral up within us, and finds expression in insults and other forms of aggression. Instead, Jesus' condemnation is of a more distant kind of anger: that which treats another as a 'fool' or as 'mad'. Because this kind of labelling refuses to encounter a person face-to-face, and consequentially maintains the inner violence we feel, since the possibility of an appropriate or equitable relationship is now severed. As Bassett notes, strikingly, Jesus does not say 'you have no reason to be angry'; nor does he investigate whether the anger is justified or not. Rather, what matters is what is done with this boiling rage. And this when Jesus appeals to us to turn to the other person: the object or subject of our wrath. Hence, we are invited – indeed implored – not to offer a sacrifice or gift until there can be some kind of reconciliation with that other. Only then can the sacrifice be liberating.

We are, here, starting to encroach on some fairly familiar Girardian territory. The anger that we have and feel must be purposefully directed and responsibly communicated. It cannot be hurled at those we feel might merit our fury. As Girard explains,

> Instead of giving back more of the same, we must leave the matter at hand to the potential rival. That is the unique role of the Kingdom ... To protect themselves from their own violence, humans ended up channelling it towards innocents. Christ does the opposite. He offers no resistance. He does not devote himself to sacrifice in order to play the sacrificial game, but to put an end to sacrifice ...
> (Girard, 1995, p. 76)

Jesus, in other words does not refute or oppose anger, but rather invites us into his relationship with God the Father, which does not model competitive desire, thereby providing us with a pattern that does not have space for mutual destruction. This allows Bassett to argue that holy anger is therefore *not* an appropriation of God's anger 'in the divine mission against others' (Bassett, 2007, p. 210). For God's anger is something altogether other than human anger. Rooted in judgement and love, and in the overcoming of idolatry and injustice, God's anger is a positive and purposeful force that always seeks justice and peace. Indeed, the quest for perfect love, says Bassett, must always pass through anger (Bassett, 2007, pp. 263–4).

These observations, however, should not be allowed to imply that anger and righteousness – in whatever forms or fusions they occur – can be easily legitimized. To be sure, anger can be the cloak for covering all manner of sentiments and actions that cannot be defended: rash, intemperate and aggressive attitudes that have no place in ecclesial polity, or in the Kingdom of God. The gospels, together with much of the New Testament, preach wisdom and patience in the face of a tendency to judge and act quickly. In fact, very few forms of anger are signs of probity and witness to the prophetic. What is needed in the church, therefore, is the wisdom and character to hold, sift, read and learn from anger; and not be driven by it, or react to hastily to its outpouring. This takes a particular form of grace and patience, as well as resilience and maturity. Often, anger is the messenger, not the message; a flawed vehicle for communicating some important truths.[1]

Towards an Emotional and Ecclesial Intelligence

Presently in the Church of England, the fear of conflict and aggression makes it very difficult to air strong feelings; the neuralgic anxiety is that the manifestation of feelings leads to the loss of poise in ecclesial polity. And yet we live in a world and within a church that are shaped by human failings, and if we truly love these institutions then we will inevitably be angry about the ways they fall short. So what we do with our strong feelings, and how we handle the aggression that moves for change, will depend on whether we can see them as a sign of life and growth, or whether we suppress them for fear they will rock the boat too hard. As Harrison and Robb state,

> The moral question is not 'what do I feel?' but rather 'what do I do with what I feel?' Because this is not understood, contemporary Christianity is impaled between a subjectivist and sentimental piety that results from fear of strong feeling, especially strong negative feeling, and an objectivists, wooden piety that suppresses feelings under pretentious conceptual detachment. A feminist moral theology welcomes feeling for what it is – the basic ingredient in our relational transaction with the world. (Harrison and Robb, 1985, p. 14)

In the Church, the desire to avoid conflict both in parochial matters and in relationships in the diocese can often be a recipe for atrophy. When situations arise which cannot be ignored, the scale of feelings aroused can surprise and disappoint those who believe that if we all try to love each other, we will all agree. To truly love is to take seriously the desire to deepen relationships and work against all that limits and devalues human worth. Harrison and Robb put it like this:

> Radical love creates dangerous precedents and lofty expectations among human beings. Those in power believe such love to be 'unrealistic' because those touched by the power of such love tend to develop a reluctance to accept anything less than mutuality and self-respect, anything less than human dignity, anything less than authentic relatedness. It is for that reason that such persons become powerful threats to the *status quo*. (Harrison and Robb, 1985, p. 19)

---

[1]   On this, and for a specifically Anglican perspective, see S. Pickard, 'An Intelligent Communion? Episcopal Reflections Post Lambeth', *Journal of Anglican Studies*, vol. 7, issue 2, 2009, pp. 127–37 and Bruce Kaye, *Conflict and the Practice of Christian Faith: The Anglican Experiment*, Eugene OR, Cascade Books, 2009.

So discovering how to acknowledge and give voice to strong feelings – in ways that can enable radical working together for the growth of all – is a challenge that the Church needs to heed. In his ministry, Jesus listened to the voices of the marginalized all the time. Indeed, not only did he listen, but he assimilated such voices into his ministry, and often made the marginalized central, and placed those who were central on the periphery, thereby re-ordering society, forcing people to witness oppression and the response of the Kingdom of God to despair, anger and marginalization. So in the Church, we need to allow the experiences of the oppressed to challenge and shape the way we hold power and broker relationships. The churches need to continually learn from the veritable panoply of liberation theologies: that marginalized people should not simply be made welcome in the church, but that their anger and aggressive desire for justice might be allowed to reform the manners of the church. Learning to listen to narratives that convey strong, powerful feelings, rather than seeking to dismiss such stories as 'uncultured' or as 'bad manners', is a major and costly task for ecclesial polity and pastoral praxis. Ultimately, the aggression of those who seek justice may help the churches to move from a 'domesticated' valuing of crucifixion and suffering for its own sake, and work instead 'not to perpetuate crucifixions, but to bring an end to them in a world where they go on and on' (Harrison and Robb, p. 19).

I am more than conscious that an argument for a church in which feelings are allowed to be given their full vent is potentially dangerous and irresponsible. We are all well aware that there is rightful place for reticence, and for the withholding of emotions. All of us understand that a temperate ecclesial polity can, to some extent, depend on finding a non-emotive language for expressing views and communicating across divisions. But I am also struck by how many churches, at local, regional and national level, deliberately disenfranchise and marginalize the proper expression of strong feelings. I find this not only to be poor ecclesial and pastoral practice, but also theologically weak and urbane, rendering the church into some kind of semi-detached realm, in which all the correct probity of manners and politeness are observed, but 'real' feelings are never mentioned or aired.

This cannot be a proper reification of a strong incarnational theology, and neither can it make for the church being an especially genuine community of the redeemed. If one of the tasks of the church is to make it possible for people to truly face one another, then strong feelings must be properly addressed so that they can be appropriately located in the body of Christ, and not suppressed as part of some kind of artful process of subordination.

How, though, do we discern when anger is a legitimate call for justice, and when it is a petulant reaction to not getting one's way? Here we need to look at patterns of power and the motivation of anger. The good news of the gospel is about the accessibility of God: the welcoming in of the religiously marginalized, and the breaking down of barriers. So in any kind of aggression and anger, we need to be clear whether or not it constitutes a move towards a vision of the kingdom, and how it is motivated by the radical mutuality of love. The command to love God and to love our neighbour as ourselves ultimately defines the place of our aggression and anger. It demands action, and that action demands drive, which at times requires generative anger and aggression. The church needs to find a way of holding and utilizing the strong feelings that are part of human loving, remembering, as Harrison and Robb put it, that 'the important point is that where feeling is evaded, where anger is hidden or goes unattended, masking itself, there the power of love, the power to act, to deepen relation, atrophies and dies' (Harrison and Robb, 1985, p. 15).

Part of the ministry of Jesus involved the expression of anger, and was occasionally constituted in acts of wilful aggression. It is hard to imagine some of Christ's words being spoken in anything other than simmering rage. There can of course be something like a *creative* rage – the kind of rage that the poets and the prophets speak of – which is markedly impolite, but utterly godly. The task for the Church, therefore, is to find ways that do not suppress or block out strong feelings of anger, or hurt and the aggression it arouses, but to help discern how to channel the energy they bring into the work of the gospel.

We began by noting how the gaiety and warmth of Catholicism in Garrison Keillor's *Lake Wobegon Days* (1985) contrasted heavily with the solemn coolness of the author's own Brethren upbringing. And in this novel, which is more than semi-autobiographical, Keillor reflects on one of the key debates that divided the Brethren community: namely, should women wear trousers? One group take the Old Testament injunctions literally – that 'a man shall not wear that which pertaineth unto a woman, and neither shall a woman wear that which pertaineth unto a man'. The debate descends into farce as they argue over Jesus being 'wrapped in swaddling clothes' – were his legs wrapped separately, like trousers; or together, like a skirt, indicating that other Christians could follow suit? Yet Keillor the novelist is careful to show that what divides the groups in the end is not the issue, but the passions and feelings that accompany the debate.

This would indicate that as for Lake Wobegon, so for the whole church – we need emotional intelligence if we are to have ecclesial intelligence. We need to be able to cope with deeply held convictions, and the feelings these evoke. To learn to receive, read, hold, discern such feelings – and not to ignore them or rebuke them. Not for nothing did the Early Church Fathers say that, given the choice between schism and heresy in the church, we must always choose heresy. For we can correct heresy over time; but schism can take a long time to heal – and we mostly never get round to it.

So all of this means listening to the experiences that lead to aggression and anger, and seeing them as far as possible from the perspective of those with less power. It means humility on the part of those who hold power, and an acknowledgment of the fear of losing power and control. It means a new way of looking at power relationships that takes the gospel seriously. It means getting in touch with our feelings, and developing an emotional intelligence – the kind that can lead to a new kind of ecclesial intelligence. And this, surely, is what we want from our leaders. People who can receive and handle feelings – even strong ones – and sometimes communicate the same when necessary. People who will be adaptable to the climates they find themselves in. Warm – but still able to be human, wise and loving – no matter how hot or cold the weather actually is.

Conclusion

There can be no question that the current state of the climate within a range of ecclesial expressions is experienced as hot, intemperate and angry. The agenda for implicit theology here is to pay attention to the connection between style and substance; between theology and feelings. They are related at many levels, and the discovery of the capacity to overcome the ensuing turbulence will also lie the practice of a deeper theology that comprehends the relationship between the freedom God gives and the economy of blessing that creation is set within. Bassett notes that God's kingdom – of abundance, overflow and blessing, will, in the end, prevail over all attempts to manage, control, direct or even suppress violence (Bassett, 2007, pp. 253–7). However, grounded ecclesiology must wrestle with the here and now, as much as it pays attention to that which is eternal.

So how might the fusion of emotional and ecclesial intelligence we have been discussing offer some kind of indicative pathway ahead for congregations and denominations that are struggling with strong feelings and intense, hostile expressions of anger? Several things can be said by way of conclusion here. And in order to earth these brief ecclesial reflections more substantially, I am drawing upon the first-hand account of the peace-making process in Northern Ireland, written by Jonathan Powell. In *Great Hatred, Little Room* (2008),[2] Powell hints at several instructive, mediating, yet temporary paradigms that have implicature for theology and ecclesiology. Here again, and for illustrative purposes our attention is drawn to current difficulties in Anglican polity.

First, Powell notes how the uses of 'constructive ambiguity' can help establish conversation and rapport at the early stages of negotiation. In one sense, critics might say that this can mean two sides talking two slightly different languages. Speaking is taking place, but true listening is more limited than it may appear to be. Powell concedes that constructive ambiguity is fine for the beginning of a peace process, but not enough in the middle and end stages. In the end, ambiguity has to be rejected in favour of clarity.

Second, Powell notes how consensus must be built from the centre. Again, this is vital to begin with. But you have to reconcile opposites. So for Anglicans, the Archbishop of Canterbury – or other instruments of unity – may be able to hold together competing convictions for some while. In effect, 'manage diversity'. But in the end, there is no substitute for the ultimacy of Peter Akinola shaking hands with Gene Robinson; or for Peter Jensen sitting down with Katherine Jefferts Schori. Whilst this may be hard to imagine, it is the kind of 'peace' that is

---

2   The title of the book is taken from W.B. Yeats's poem, 'Remorse for Intemperate Speech', 1931.

anticipated in God's kingdom; the end of rhetorical violence, and the ushering in of a community of blessing and consensus that transcends mere consensus.

Third, Powell's insights suggest that the fragmentation and 'Balkanization' of polity are to be avoided at all costs, because it is difficult if not impossible to build consensus out of brokenness. In ecclesiological terms, if you have the choice between heresy and schism, choose heresy. You can correct the former; but it will always be difficult to ever heal the latter. This lays a particular burden on the identity and role for the so-called 'instruments of unity': the Archbishop of Canterbury, the Primates, the Anglican Consultative Council and the Lambeth Conference. The instruments will need to act lightly and precisely, lest they become part of the problem.

Fourth, these instruments of unity and peace may need to triangulate in times of crisis: it is not good hovering between passive-aggressive; liberal-conservative; traditional-progressive modes of behaviours. It will be necessary to get beyond these polarities; and for the instruments to become *facilitators of peace*, not mere persuaders for a temporary cessation in hostilities. The difference is crucial, clearly. But as Powell notes, bringing peace takes time, and necessarily involves setbacks. Underpinning this must be a resolute commitment to talking and listening – without which peace is impossible. And as the church is a community of peace, attentive listening to God, self and otherness is at the core of its very being.

Fifth and finally, the exchange of peace is a central act of preparation and declaration in anticipation of receiving Christ in bread and wine. Communion is centred on companionship – literally, 'those we break bread with'. Because of this, compromise – literally to 'promise together' – is something rooted in the heart of the Eucharist as we pledge ourselves to one another and to God. In accepting the consequential company that our ecclesial belief and behaviour brings us, we commit to a form of unity that is predicated on peace and bound for unity. That form of Communion, of course, does not always mean agreement. Nor does it follow that there will never be anger and division. But because of God's economy of blessing, it remains the case that no 'height or depth' (cf., Romans 8) can separate us from the love of God that is found in Jesus Christ. And because of this – God's ultimate purpose for creation – we cannot be separated from one another.

But the last word in this section belongs to Powell, as he reflects on the long and arduous road to peace in Northern Ireland. His reflections are instructive for all those who seek peace and unity in any context, including those wracked by the pain of ecclesial conflict, where there can often seem to be no hope of peaceful resolution, let alone unity:

> The ambiguity that had been essential at the beginning [of the process] began to undermine the Agreement and discredit the government – the referee for its implementation. We then had to drive ambiguity out of the process ... and insist on deeds rather than words. This process of squeezing out the ambiguity and building trust was painful and it took time, but a durable peace cannot rest on an ambiguous understanding ... . (Powell, 2008, p. 315)

So if there is one lesson to be drawn from the Northern Ireland negotiations, it is that there is no reason to believe that efforts to find peace will fail just because they have failed before. You have to keep the wheels turning. The road to success in Northern Ireland was littered with failures. [But] there is every reason to think that the search for peace can succeed in other places where the process has encountered problems ... if people are prepared to talk ... (Powell, 2008, p. 322)

Conclusion
Shaping the Church

Because it is never easy to say, precisely, where the church begins and ends – let alone Christian beliefs and practices – a proper attention to informal, apparently innocuous and innocent forces that shape ecclesial life is always bound to have significant repercussions for the field and disciplines of theology. As we argued in the first volume of this trilogy, *Engaging with Contemporary Culture* (2005), the dynamics of ecclesial life are often shaped and delimited by operant, grounded, unarticulated and habitual processes, which whilst laced with theological significance, do not of themselves usually count as explicit religious discourse, or are valued as 'official' practice. Professional theologians and church leaders often bear equal blame for this oversight. In attending only to sanctioned sources and authorized traditions, theology always risks missing the emergent theology that is present in informal practices and nascent beliefs; and that these are no less significant, and, in many respects, just as constitutive for the shaping of the church.

Moreover, the miscible nature of the church – which is to say the many sources that form its life, including aesthetics, institutional habits, organizational assumptions and practices, context and so forth – suggests that its hope rests in its hybridity rather than its assumed purity. This is perhaps a surprising remark to come by in ecclesiology, where habitually, much energy is invested in historical or ontological accounts of the church that often suggest otherwise. However, the burden of 'grounded ecclesiology', championed by writers such as Nicholas Healy, and further back still, Edward Schillebeeckx, is rooted in the assumption that the church grows out of both sacred and secular ground. Indeed, the two should not be separated, in some respects. Sociologists such as David Martin have also championed a more sanguine approach to ecclesiology, and more generally to the shape and form of religion in public life. David Docherty, commenting on Martin's prescient *Breaking of the Image*, notes that:

> The fascination of *The Breaking of the Image* (by David Martin) lies not in the opposition between the symbols of natural and transcendental faiths, but in the analysis of the way that the former appropriates the latter only to discover that it has swallowed something alien, something that at some stage will burst out and consume the social order that initially consumed it. Each age may be pregnant with the next, as Marx would have it, but in Martin, each age is pregnant with alien possibilities; the foetus of each age has many fathers, and is the product of many seeds. He points to the ways in which radicalism striving to invent the new world order has to save itself and in the process appropriates the world of blood

and hierarchy from which it seeks to escape. Breaking the image is hard to do because those who seek to break also seek to build ... (Docherty, 2001, p. 81)

There is, here, a kind of attentiveness to what we earlier referred to as 'natural theology' – but not in the sense perhaps intended in the eighteenth century. Rather, our use of the term represents a turn to the grounded nature of the church, which although perhaps more obvious at local levels, nonetheless can also be traced at the meta-organizational level of denominationalism or international Communion. Thus,

> starting with an understanding of the church as a people called into relationship with God and each other, Anglican ecclesiology presents a church that is grounded in society, provisional, inclusive and responsive ... (Thompsett, 1988, p. 253)

Because the church is a body, grounded in a context and social construction of reality, it always reflects and sacralizes values that have yet to be fully processed and comprehended. Thus, an ecclesial movement that is absorbed with concepts of alternative consumerism (i.e., 'fresh', 'local', organic', etc) is simply unsurprising. However, this means that the task for theologians – and perhaps especially those engaged in the study of contemporary ecclesiology – is to bring some illuminating and critical light to bear upon the ecclesial-cultural fusion, and thereby commence a task of discernment that may begin to ask some more penetrating questions about identity, task, role, enculturation and the like. Not every cultural move that the church has aped or absorbed has been missiologically beneficial for the medium and long-term. A wisdom is needed that can draw on the past, and help shape the present and the future. Ecclesiology, then, that is attuned to how culture shapes the church, and how the church shapes culture, has something significant to offer to the field and disciplines of theology. As Rowan Williams observes, most Anglican theologians know:

> ... that as Christians they live among immensities of meaning, live in the wake of a divine action which defies summary explanation. They take it for granted that the believer is always learning, moving in and out of speech and silence in a continuous wonder and a continuous turning inside-out of mind and feeling. (2004, p. 47)

Moreover, to comprehend the church as such a body – living, moving and being in the world – helps us to attend to the ways in which it responds to and reflects its environment. It is here, as we have discussed, that we are we able to locate theologies in ordinary practices. As James Nieman argues, instead of trying to find the places where theologizing occurs at its strongest (e.g., creeds, explicit practices, etc), we would also do well to attend to instances where we are perhaps less conscious of ecclesial shaping. This might include simple ways of gathering: the habitually familiar and social forms for coming together. Or it could include apparently unstructured practices, which nonetheless have a degree of routine, or even predictability about them (e.g., gatherings in charismatic churches that are characterized by a routinized or predictable spontaneity). Or then again, one might focus on the handling of resources, and the ways in which assets and talents are narrated in a congregation, together with the rationalizing and managing of materials. Practices and beliefs can also be conferred through 'soft' traditions: how and whom to visit; what to say; which hymns to sing, and why. Congregations will also negotiate their own maintenance as a body, and have a sense of how to handle transition: either in terms of growth, or how to narrate and make sense out of decline (Nieman, 2004, pp. 204–11).

There will, in other words, be frames of reference for handling change, stability, turbulence, salience, growth and other features of ecclesial life, which will more likely belong to the field of congregational narrative than to its explicit theological frames of reference. To recognize and own this is not, interestingly, to simply collapse theology into a vapid dialogue with sociology or anthropology. It is, rather, the recognition that the theology, even of an apparently homogenous congregation, will be varied, colourful and plural. Michael Battle notes:

> There must be a plurality of theologies, because we do not all apprehend or respond to the transcendent in exactly the same way, nor can we be expected to express our experience in the same way. And this is no cause for lament. Precisely the opposite – it is a reason for rejoicing because it makes mandatory our need for one another because our partial theologies will of necessity require to be corrected by other more or less partial theologies. It reinforces the motif of inter-dependence which is the inalienable characteristic of the body of Christ. (Battle, 2005, p. 71)

As we noted earlier, the issue here for theologians is that the vast majority of theology is implicit. That is to say, it is entangled, entwined and involved in the life of local congregations; that it is engaged in areas of overlap and hinterlands between the life of the church and the world. Implicit theology, as the term suggests, understands that most of what is expressed theologically is implied rather than plainly expressed.

So our focus on implicit theology – and especially in relation to ecclesiology – is essentially an invitation to ponder the myriad of ways in which institutional, belief-based and practice-orientated formation takes place. There is an inbuilt assumption here, that hybridity in ecclesial formation is inevitable; and I am also suggesting, I suppose, that it is probably desirable. Alloys can often be narrated as inferior and debased; the dilution of purity. But alloys are often stronger, more adaptable and supple in their combination: just as compounds can be stronger than elements. Implicit theology, in the service of ecclesiology, recognizes that the socio-cultural elements that are in some sort of fissure with theology, although sometimes problematic, are part of the fundamental nature of the church in terms of its beliefs and practices.

This is why it can be important for some denominations to recognize that, 'truth is not the same thing as the elimination of ambiguity' (Oakley, 2001). Mark Oakley, in his spiritual meditation on truth and ambiguity he suggests that theology is just one of God's invitations for we, as humans, to attentively listen to one another. Oakley suggest that theology is 'also God's opportunity of letting us know, in often tantalizing ways, that he always lies just beyond our reach, forever ancient and forever new'. Thus for Oakley, Christians are 'pilgrims', not 'arrivals'; and in relation to truth, 'explorers', and not 'illustrators'.

The work of James Hopewell adds a further dimension to these ecclesial reflections. Hopewell compares churches to 'househunting', and notes how prospective purchasers of homes pay attention to different aspects and dimensions of the value, situation and meaning of the property (Hopewell, 1988). Thus, those who pay attention to contextual dimensions recognize that no church is isolated from its environment. The neighbourhood is relevant to the potential purchaser, who will explore utility services, climate and social trends. A contextually-astute purchaser will understand that the church is made up of the texture whose weaving reveals something about its context. So in such a scenario, the church should perhaps ideally reflect the concerns of its context.

A more mechanistically-driven purchaser might, on the other hand, pay less attention to context, and more to the inner workings of the building. Mechanistic approaches to ecclesiology are typically task-orientated, with less concern evident about the neighbourhood and more concern expressed about the effectiveness of a distinct body. Here, the church is a collection of (efficient) tools. Mechanistic approaches focus on programmes of effectiveness; and are very likely to have 'aims', 'strategies' and 'goals'. Such churches will not be opposed to the intentions of service, but would normally expect every dimension of church life to be accountable and subject to some rationalization.

In contrast, organic approaches to house-hunting are narrative-based and people-orientated. In this kind of eccesial thinking, individuals and groups will seek to explore how the church portrays and enhances the life of the people. There will be more interest in aesthetic architecture than in functional engineering (mechanistic). Organic approaches typically see the church as 'a gathering of strangers' in need of salvation from alienation. Organic approaches also usually seek to knit together disparate threads of communities: so the parish is a 'potential fellowship', where differences are transcended, and all people can face one another.

Finally, house-hunters may also focus on the symbolic. Here, a church is not just a context, mechanism or social cohesive: it also conveys a meaning. Symbolic approaches place weight on identity. What does this particular church say about who we are and the way we are? How does that enable those who go and those who don't? Symbolic approaches to ecclesiology are concerned with motifs, themes and ideas. They pay attention to the language used, and assess from the inside what the 'construable signs' signify to outsiders. Symbolic analysts reflect on the meanings churches convey – even unconsciously. Like organic approaches, they are deeply concerned with narratives and the internal dynamics of communities.

Clearly, any househunter can possess a combination of these concerns, just as any church can be a collation of these expressions. Hopewell's intention, however, by narrating churches in this way, is to draw our attention to the implicit forms of theology that seep through structures, values and apparently innocuous and innocent practices. Because structure *is* an expression of value, these ways of beholding structural approaches to church life actually refract back subtle and meaning-laden forms of theology that shape ecclesial life. The church, it seems, *is* shaped by what is invested in the contextual, mechanistic, organic and symbolic. These 'features' turn out to be pregnant with meaning: but it is mostly hidden, and implicit.

And so to turn this, slightly, and following Mary Douglas, we might say that the genius of the church therefore lies not in the successful policing of purity and danger, but in its inevitable capitulation to impurity and opportunity. I don't mean by this, of course, that the church is morally or doctrinally compromised. I am hinting, rather, that awareness of the socio-cultural factors that shape ecclesial life and theological priorities – an issue, often, of cadence and timbre rather than re-writing the score, in musicolgical terms – is profoundly helpful for theologians.

Moreover, church history is littered with flawed and failed attempts to rescue the church as a compound and return it to its elemental force. Restorationists have tried this in the British House Church Movement. Anglo-Catholics have sought similar forms of purity through inductive, backward-looking and romantic theological stratagem. More recently, the radical orthodoxy movement has also sought to return the church to age of renaissance that can dominate (or 'out-narrate') the secular in a postmodern world. In some respects, the movement is kind of melancholy for an era that has passed: a post-colonial ethos that longs for the restoration of hierarchical Christendom. But the embedded nature of the church – this body that is 'pregnant with alien possibilities … has many fathers, and is the product of many seeds …' as David Docherty puts it (2001, p. 85) – was not conceived in purity. It was, rather, incarnated in society; a very different theological statement.

So in terms of implicit theology, we might say that each of these 'purist' manoeuvres shares a common trait: a desire to be an intensive and unambiguous element in an extensive world of alloys and compounds. Of course, it is the complexity of the extensity that has produced this wonderment for the simplicity and power of the intense. And I suppose one could say that in the broader ecology of ecclesiology, the intensive and extensive are intra-dependent. However, it should be recognized that the more marginal and less extensive religion becomes in the public sphere, the more likely it is (consequential, indeed) that intensive forms of religiosity will flourish, including types of fundamentalism, revivalism and the like.

Religion, in other words, when un-earthed and de-coupled from social and cultural contexts, has a greater potential to become toxic and self-absorbed. This shift is, at present, detectable in most mainline Christian denominations: the loss of the extensive leads to the heightening of the intensive. That can be beneficial, for a season at least. But unchecked and unchallenged, the pharmacological consequences can be grave. Faith turns in on itself. And churches, here, can then refuse to recognize that their ecclesiology is now a consequence of their marginality, rather than their purity.

Space for the Sacred

If the cultural and social changes of the nineteenth century had any kind of impact on the churches and the place of religion in society, it is perhaps best narrated as a kind of double move: marginalization followed by compression. Or, as we characterized it earlier, it was a move from the extensive to the intensive. This, of course, is not a move against religion *per se*, but rather a deeper cultural pulse that was brought about by emerging industrialization and urbanization. It altered patterns of work, family life, meanings and values, and senses of place and space. As one commentator notes,

> Human society is in permanent motion, change and development. At times and in different cultures [men] perceive and interpret the world in their own fashion, and in their own fashion they organise their impressions and their knowledge, and construct their own historically conditioned worldview. (Sheldrake 2001b, pp. 43ff)

In other words, and to paraphrase Simon Schama, 'landscape' or 'the local' is 'what culture does to nature'. And as another commentator reminds us,

> There is now strong evidence in the archaeological record for contact between [human] groups ... rapid diffusion of elements of learned cultural tradition, and for integration ... through trade and exchange ... (Ingold, 1986, p. 220)

It also seems appropriate to say something about 'place' as a cultural category at this point. Naming a place is power statement, and one that inevitably raises questions of ownership, and therefore fans out into the wider social and political arena. There can never be anything innocent or simple about claiming to be 'local' – even a local minister. Thus, to make the claim to be 'a local minister' is a power counter-claim against a wider ministry, and, therefore, 'the local' is never itself isolated. But it is not as simple as that either. The naming of places and spaces is also a claim on history, identity and destiny.

That said, we must recognize that the identification of the local is often 'a protest against an unpromising pursuit of space ...' (Sheldrake 2001b, pp. 44ff). Simone Weil helpfully points out that 'to be rooted is perhaps the most important and least recognized need of the human soul' (Sheldrake, 2001b, p. 49).

> participation in the life of a community which preserves in living shape certain
> particular expectations of the future … is natural … (Sheldrake, 2001b, p. 49)

Yet even Weil acknowledges that we need to have 'multiple roots' – the local is a construct and a constraint. 'Belonging' must involve not only connection to places, but also to networks of relationships that are trans-spatial. And yet for many people in Europe, the parish once provided both; the geographical and social reality for people was in one place. Born, buried and baptised – all in the same place, as your ancestors were. At this point, even the neighbouring valley was 'other', strange and foreign – and the residue of such sentiments can still be located in many rural and urban communities. The parish dominated human associations, and the senses, albeit implicitly.

This raises an interesting question about our cultural history in relation to ministry and implicit theology. To what extent is it desirable that the minister is 'local' or 'other'? Bear in mind that the otherness of a newly arrived incumbent, in say, the eighteenth century in England, was connected to a sense of place where the priest had come from – a social class. And whilst a new Rector may not have had any connections with a place, a certain organic relationship with the community was assumed.

This observation echoes some remarks made by Philip Sheldrake in his *Spaces for the Sacred*. Noting that the psychological concept of place requires *participation* in a shared sense, he also notes that what is needed is *commitment* to what a place means. When places become full of people that are not committed to its meanings, the place itself loses its identity. Thus, whether it is the club or the village, the church or the community hall, the rhetoric is similar – *they* – the newcomers – don't understand what this is about; they're not from here; we can't tell where they are from; and so on.

In all of this, it is vital to remember that I am not saying that that there is no such thing as place – that it is really all a human construct. Rather, I am trying to show that there is no such thing as *pure* place, just as there is no such thing as 'pure church'. Places and churches exist on many levels, and their boundaries, though real, even perhaps geographical and firmly fixed in culture, are nevertheless subjective and porous. So, it is not that there is no real local – shop, church, minister or otherwise. It is, rather, that there is no *pure* local. Just as one might also say that there is no 'pure theology' and no 'pure ecclesiology' either. And as we noted with Docherty earlier, 'each age is pregnant with alien possibilities; the foetus of each age has many fathers, and is the product of many seeds' (Docherty, 2001, p. 85).

But the theological and sociological response to this plurality and extensity (led by industrialization, emerging technology and mass-migration from rural contexts to new cities), at least in the nineteenth century, was a kind of purposeful withdrawal and specialization. So it was the nineteenth century that saw the rise and definition of the professions, including the clerical profession itself. The eighteenth-century clergymen could not be said to have had a vocation in the sense that we mean today. He would have been a country gentleman, or one who hoped to be one. His very few religious duties left him ample time to mingle in society, to be a magistrate, a naturalist, an essayist or even a sportsman. If he did not much improve his own social world, he was very much part of it.

But the evangelical revival of the nineteenth century, and the comparable revival in ritualism spawned by the Anglo-Catholic movement, created what we would now call the 'serious' Christian. Both movements stressed a definition of the duties of clergymen, and within a space of the generation those duties had absorbed the entire time and energy of clergy. Two sermons on a Sunday, weekday services, frequent visiting of the poor. And to all this, the Tractarians added the sense of a distinct vocation and the separation of the priesthood from the laity. By the 1840's even amongst those clergy who are neither Evangelical nor Tractarian, the professional ideal of the clergy had actually won out. This professionalism came against a widespread Victorian culture of earnestness. From being country squires, they suddenly became a species that neither hunted, nor attended the theatre, nor did any other things that their predecessors had been doing for a few centuries or more. They also started to change the way that they dressed. They wore black unrelieved by the slightest hint of grey, and from the mid-nineteenth century they adopted the ultimate badge of clericalism – the dog collar. Of course, the immediate yields of such a distinctive identification of the clerical profession produced a great deal. Hardworking clergy accomplished much; intensity produces a rich harvest.

But the professionalism also came at a price. Fully occupied by the pastoral, priestly and preaching work was absorbing but specialized, and it meant that the clergy gradually began to withdraw from the wider cultural and intellectual life of England of which they had once been a central part. It is no accident that many of our theological colleges were created in the late nineteenth century in response to this, since universities were no longer entrusted with preparing men for the ordained ministry in the way that they once had. Initiatives such as the Test Act of 1873 were probably more excuses than causes for the creation of individual theological colleges.

There is a real irony here. At the very time that Coleridge was formulating his idea of the clerisy to embrace all the educated classes, the clergy were actually separating themselves from the laity and withdrawing behind the impregnable fortress of the church and its traditions. Of course, the development of a clerical specialization went hand in hand with the secular professions also developing their own distinctive training and functions. However what was different about the development of these professions was the impact that they had on the emerging generations of thinkers in the late nineteenth century. Whereas once, it had been perfectly normal and natural for young men to consider careers in law, teaching, the military or the church as comparable, the church separated itself out from these more than most, and quite suddenly, the church found that it no longer *naturally* attracted the brightest and best minds that were graduating from Universities.

The point of this brief excursion has been to show how social change produced pragmatic ecclesial responses and new ideological and theological rationales for ministry. In the nineteenth century, the world shaped the role and identity of church. The cultural changes of the nineteenth century profoundly altered the senses of place and space, which had wide and deep implications for parochial identity and ministry. In turn, these changes altered the identity and role clergy, and their rationale for ministry. The consequence of this was that the church quickly re-narrated itself, and withdrew into more intense and 'purer' forms of theological constructions of ecclesiology and ministry. These were directly related to the gradual loss of extensive influence, which were now superseded with more intense forms of religiosity. In other words, the church was fashioned by forces it simply could not control. The outcome was the development of a form of implicit theology that continues to shape the church today, which is in turn rooted in some of the profound shifts in the tectonic plates of culture that are traceable to the Victorian era.

The Shape of the Church

Given these brief remarks on cultural-ecclesial formation, we now turn to the shaping of the church in a more theological vein. There are, of course, plenty of 'shapes' and 'models' of the church espoused in academic writings. Dulles' distinctions, for example, come to mind: of the church as herald, community, institution, servant or sacrament (Dulles, 1974). Or, of Lesslie Newbigin's characteristic distinction: between the church as an associational or parochial pattern of mission. However, as we have been focusing on the relationship between context, culture and ecclesiology, and the role of implicit theology in ecclesial formation, a more apposite approach is needed here, which attends to the compound rather than the elements, and the alloy rather than the pure.

Consider, for example, the value and respect afforded to the virtue of patience within Anglican ecclesial polity may have a significant bearing on how unity is ultimately maintained in the midst of potentially damaging divergence. Arguably, one of the chief virtues of living within a Communion is learning to be patient. Churches, each with their distinctive own intra-denominational familial identity, have to learn how to negotiate the differences they find within themselves. For some churches in recent history, the discovery of such differences – perhaps on matters of authority, praxis or interpretation – has been too much to bear: lines have been drawn in the sand, with the sand itself serving only as a metaphor for the subsequent atomization. Yet typically, most mainstream Protestant denominations have sufficient breadth (of viewpoints and plurality) and depth (located in sources of authority and their interpretation, amongst other things) to be able to resist those assaults that threaten implosion. Where some new churches, faced with internal disagreement, have quickly experienced fragmentation, most historic denominations have been reflexive enough to experience little more than a process of elastication: they have been stretched, but they have not broken. This is perhaps inevitable, when one considers the global nature of most mainstream historic denominations. Their very expanse will have involved a process of stretching (missiological, moral, conversational, hermeneutical, etc), and this in turn has led directly to their (often inchoate) sense of accommodation.

This description for the shaping of polity is all very well, however, until one encounters the sharp differences of opinion within churches. No denomination is immune from this phenomenon, and all have slightly different ways of trying to accommodate and ameliorate potentially damaging divisions. Constructions of authority and power, together with idealizations of polity and peace, play a crucial role in maintaining unity. But these do not prevent divisions, even if such fractures are not ultimately inimical for the body. It is at this point that hidden virtues or implicit theology can play a major role in maintaining bodily shape and the actual form of polity. Yet even the broadest and most accommodating ecclesial traditions have their boundaries and limits. But the development of their global identity has involved them in a process of patient listening and learning, and of evolution and devolution.

Speaking as an Anglican, therefore (and one who would locate himself in the broad 'centre' of the tradition), I am still surprised by the amount of passion and rhetoric that has been created by the issue of homosexuality. In three successive episodes, the Anglican Communion has threatened to unravel itself over arrangements in Canada, the USA and England. The historical minutiae of those events in the diocese of New Westminster, New Hampshire and Oxford have no need of reprise now, for they have each, in their own way, been responsible for the production of yet another Commission that attempts to deal with the (apparently) self-inflicted wounds that are said to afflict the Communion. And now that the *Windsor Report* has been published, it is interesting to note that one of its primary tasks has been to point towards the importance of listening to one another in that school of theology, which is the learning church.

Broadly speaking, the *Windsor Report* is a fine piece of Anglican apologetics. Under the skilful chairing of Robert Eames, Archbishop of Armagh – a man who through his own painful experiences of the 'Ulster Problem' knows a thing or two about patience, peace processes and reconciliation – the Report manages to keep open the possibility of a future in which those people who profoundly disagree on some issues can nonetheless continue to regard themselves as being together and in Communion, even if the quality of that belonging is more strained than usual. In the process of its deliberations, the Commission, by any standards, set itself an ambitious question: what do we believe is the will of God for the Anglican Communion? In attempting to address the central issue, the members of the Commission have been well aware that

> since the 1970s controversies over issues of human sexuality have become
> increasingly divisive and destructive throughout Christendom. Within the
> Anglican Communion the intensity of debate on these issues at successive
> Lambeth Conferences has demonstrated the reality of these divisions … Voices
> and declarations have portrayed a Communion in crisis. Those divisions have

been obvious at several levels of Anglican life: between provinces, between dioceses and between individual Anglican clergy and laity. The popular identification of 'conservatives' and 'liberals', and 'the west' as opposed to 'the global south', has become an over-simplification – divisions of opinion have also become clear within provinces, dioceses and parishes. Various statements and decisions at different levels of leadership and membership of the Church have illustrated the depth of reaction. Among other Christian traditions, reactions to the problems within Anglicanism have underlined the serious concerns on these issues worldwide. Comparison has been made with the controversies on women's ordination years ago. But the current strengths of expression of divergent positions are much greater. Questions have been raised about the nature of authority in the Anglican Communion, the inter-relationship of the traditional Instruments of Unity, the ways in which Holy Scripture is interpreted by Anglicans, the priorities of the historic autonomy enshrined in Anglican provinces, and there are also issues of justice. Yet the Lambeth Commission has been aware that consideration within its mandate of any specific aspect of inter-Anglican relationships overlaps and relates to others and has a clear bearing on the sort of Anglican Communion which should enhance the life and worship of our diverse worldwide church family. (From the Foreword by Robin Eames, 2004, p. 4)

Perhaps unusually for a Commission that deals with contested areas within ecclesiology, The *Windsor Report* gives particular prominence to the 'feelings', 'emotions' and 'passions' that the issue of sexuality raises. Even in the Foreword, words and phrases such as 'intensity', 'depth of feeling' and 'depth of conviction' pepper the pages. Eames notes that the 'harshness' and 'lack of charity' that has sometimes characterized the debate is 'new to Anglicanism'. He seems to have an instinct for implicit theology. And perhaps for this reason alone (although there are others), Eames is careful to note that:

> This Report is not a judgement. It is part of a process. It is part of a pilgrimage towards healing and reconciliation. The proposals which follow attempt to look forward rather than merely to recount how difficulties have arisen. (2004, p. 5)

The process proposed by the *Windsor Report*, is of course, one predicated on a shared commitment to patience, listening and learning together. In order to maintain the bonds of affection that are vital to the life of the Communion, it will be necessary for each part of the body to act with restraint and courtesy. Thus, the Report affirms 'the importance of interdependence', whilst also acknowledging that Communion has been breached through particular initiatives, which are specifically identified and spoken of in terms of 'regret'.

The Commission proposes to resolve the ensuing disputes through a period of calm and continued dialogue, with all parties urged 'to seek ways of reconciliation'. The *Windsor Report* concludes on an upbeat-yet-sanguine note, calling for peace, patience, restraint and healing, earnestly setting forth a continued faith in a Communion, in which the participants choose to walk together for the sake of unity, and for its witness to the Gospel. The shape of the church, in other words, is articulated in terms of the present and in terms of ultimacy. There is a real recognition that the Anglican Communion is currently out of shape, so to speak. But at the same time, an appeal to its oft-hidden charisms – its implicit theology, if you will – which values patience, toleration, moderation and space is also called for. Put another way, it is through explicit struggles that the Communion might find its inner strength and implicit theology. And that through an intense period of concentration on a particular set of issues, the Communion may yet find some extensive, widely held values and practised beliefs that are currently implicit.

Interestingly, the election of Gene Robinson as the Bishop of New Hampshire – the first openly gay man to be called by an Anglican diocese to such a position – might just conceivably provide the gateway and opportunity for this kind of reflection. Essentially, this event might lead to the kind of process and reflection that seeks to engage with ecclesial shaping and ultimately its development. Despite the fact that Robinson was chosen by a two-thirds majority of the local electors, his elevation to the episcopate has caused a tidal wave of international debate and disagreement, even threatening the unity and identity of the Anglican Communion. The resulting hullabaloo – even by Anglican standards – could be comfortably described as a hurricane of controversy. Indeed, and insofar as ecclesiastical tempests go, this particular one appears to be almost off the Beaufort scale.

Given that Robinson would be rendered culpable by some for creating the recent inclement ecclesiastical weather that has dogged so much of Anglican polity, even the title of his book seems open to the charge of hubris. Can it really be appropriate to infer that there is any calm place left in which to reflect on the nature of the gospel and the church, whilst in the midst of such heated exchanges on sexuality and biblical authority? Yet *In the Eye of the Storm* (2008) – Robinson's own reflections on the situation – we find an essentially temperate, measured lucid and composed writer. It is a rather touching eirenic memoir, in fact, from a man who despite being at the centre of such controversy, and held responsible by many for the potential dismemberment of the Anglican Communion, is nonetheless keeping his cool.

Indeed, Robinson's book should be understood as a kind of quintessentially Anglican polemic: the very embodiment of fervent detachment – a delicate fission of biblical, personal, ethical, theological and reflective material. And the substance of the text ranges far and wide, covering a familiar litany of topics that are near and dear to the hearts of your average North American Episcopalian. Chapters concentrate on sexuality and justice; faith and life; diversity and exclusion; politics and inclusion; and ending with communion and identity. This familiar terrain is, however, addressed in a manner that is simultaneously moderate and ardent, capturing something of the heart of Anglican polity (at least in style) – as well as neatly expressing its current dilemma (in substance). Here is a cradle

Anglican expressing his mind and heart; baring his soul for the world to read. And read well, it does.

However, the book cannot escape the production and reception of its underlying context. Anglicanism has never considered itself to be a sect or denomination originating in the sixteenth century. It considers itself to be both catholic and reformed, and with no special doctrines of its own. Yet there is something about the style of Anglicanism – its cadence and timbre – that gives it a distinctive feel. Whilst one can never generalize – there are, after all, several kinds of Anglican identity – there is nonetheless a unifying mood in the polity that rejoices in the tension between clarity and ambiguity, decisions and deferral, to say nothing of word and sacrament, or protestant and catholic.

Caught between extremes, critics of Anglican polity have often ruminated that Anglicanism cannot escape its Laodicean destiny. So neither too hot nor too cold – just warm. In other words, the classic *via media*: tepid – and proud. And because Anglicanism is born of England, just like its climate, the polity often struggles to cope with extremities. Anglicanism is mostly a temperate ecclesial polity: cloudy, with occasional sunny spells and the odd shower – but no extremes, please.

Yet in a world where there is a perceived 'coming of age' in the former colonies, and hostility towards the former colonizers, the calmness of the liberal Anglicanism of the Global North has given way to a form of religion that often defines itself against what is regarded as a sell-out to the prevailing culture. So whilst *In the Eye of the Storm* offers us a telling *apologia* for calmness and centred-ness, in which Robinson acknowledges the turmoil around him, he inevitably abrogates any real responsibility for the conditions that have drawn so many into the subsequent storm. In many ways, he is probably right to be so coy, since there have been disagreements for centuries – sexuality was never going to be any different.

But what *In the Eye of the Storm* cannot help Anglicans with is how precisely to face and resolve the divisive dilemmas that threatens the very future of the Communion. Anglicanism, which has traditionally been a *via media* expression of faith, finds itself profoundly troubled by excess. For it strains to embody what one distinguished Anglican has described as 'passionate coolness' – its resources for dealing with the heat of the storm are modest and require consensus.

Herein lies a problem. For the forces of nature that have produced this inclement ecclesial weather are rooted in the unfettered capitalism and rampant individualism that characterizes so much of North American life. The election of Gene Robinson to the See of New Hampshire was, despite whatever personal merits he may have, an example of one small Episcopalian diocese asserting its individualism; and cloaking that decision in the rhetoric of progression, justice and inalienable rights. The trouble with such a decision, however, is the lack of regard for a wider catholicity, and the attendant responsibility this carries. Furthermore, New Hampshire should perhaps have paused to reflect that the (oft overlooked) cousins of individualism are impatience and intolerance.

From the minute that Gene Robinson was consecrated, the unholy and viral trinity of individualism, impatience and intolerance was unleashed, and has inevitably spread to very different quarters of the Anglican Communion, and with unsurprisingly similar results. So that now, each part of the worldwide church, whether liberal or conservative, can claim to be true and right, whilst expressing their individuality, irritation and annoyance with all those they disagree with. The only antidote to this plague of rashness is an old cure: the recovery of those qualities that are embedded in the gospels, and a deeper form of Anglican polity. Namely one that is formed from patience, forbearance, catholicity, moderation – and a genuine love for the reticulate blend of diversity and unity that forms so much of the richness for Anglican life.

Yet perhaps (and ironically), even though the storm in the Anglican Communion was set off by the consecration of an openly homosexual bishop, the book itself offers a model of mild yet ardent temperate Anglicanism. And ultimately, that is the only way in which Anglicans will truly be able to face one another with their manifest differences. So perhaps this is where some of the hope lies for the Anglican Communion. Jesus, after all, did not feed the storm. In one gospel account, he even slept through it, only stilling it when roused by his disciples. But calm it he did. So despite the current storms that bedevil the worldwide Anglican Communion, I predict that the outlook is ultimately calm, and the long-term forecast remains moderate. And I daresay we might discover, when we look back in 50 years' time, that Bishop Robinson's role in the eye of this particular storm will have emerged as something more complex and ambiguous than many currently suppose.

Coda: A Brief Reprise for Implicit Theology

Our attention to a kind of ecclesial climatology is intended to complement the other allusions and illustrations that have helped to sketch the possibilities and promise of implicit theology. By paying attention to the sensed and experienced dimensions of day-to-day ecclesial life, one begins to gain some insight into how style might matter just as much as substance, and behaviours as much as beliefs. The temperate nature of an ecclesial polity has a profound impact of the felt environment, and on the congregation's experience of God. Aesthetics, architecture and music clearly all play a part in this. But as we have been arguing, so do the more inchoate ecclesial practices: the length and structure of church meetings, together with their aims and objectives, is an obvious example.

Implicit theology pays attention to the normally neglected and often overlooked dimensions of ecclesial life that are constitutive for belief and practice. The realization of a relationship between the gentle framing of faith and belief through structures and practices allows us ponder the significance of many things we might take for granted, and their theological weight. Dress codes, manners, the management of strong feelings, the moderation of the collective emotional temperature – all have a bearing on the emerging vision of God within each congregation and denomination. It is not that one causes the other, mind. The emerging task for implicit theology is not to distinguish between God and the world, but rather realize that in a new kind of 'natural theology', even apparently innocuous and innocent beliefs and practices are in fact 'texts' that demand interpretation. This is because the shape of the church is partly brought about by the subliminal as much as by the liminal; and by the implicit as much as by the explicit.

So what of the future shape of the Church of England and the worldwide Anglican Communion? Attention to implicit theology already tells us that the shaping will not entirely be a matter for proponents of explicit theological reasoning. It is said that Henry Scott Holland once stood on the hill at Garsington shortly before his death, and gazed over the valley to Cuddesdon College and parish church, where he had asked to be buried. He noticed a flock of starlings flying past, and remarked how like the Anglican Church they were. Nothing, it seemed, kept the flock together – and yet the birds moved as one, even though they were all apart and retained their individual identity. In an increasingly diverse and cosmopolitan world, of which the Anglican Communion is a part, I suspect that we are going to have to get better at moving together, whilst also at the same time respecting each other's particularity. Birds of a feather still need to flock together, even though each creature is an individual.

There is no doubt that Anglicanism currently stands at an important crossroads for its future identity. The *Windsor Report* is merely a signpost at this juncture (albeit an important one): it anticipates the process that is to come, but it cannot predict the outcomes. I agree with this assessment for the life of the Communion; it is too early to draw conclusions. However, we might say that the there are two very different versions of the shaping of Anglican polity, and the Communion now emerging, which suggest quite different futures.

The first sees the shape of Anglicanism in concrete terms. The polity will be governed by law, and scripture will be its ultimate arbiter. Here, Anglicanism will become a tightly-defined denomination in which intra-dependence is carefully policed. Diversity of belief, behaviour and practice will continue, but they will be subject to scrutiny and challenge.

The second sees Anglicanism as a more reflexive polity; one that has a shape, but is able to stretch and accommodate considerable diversity. Here the polity will be governed by grace, not law, and the Communion itself will continue to operate as both a sign and instrument of unity. Anglicanism will continue to be a defined form of ecclesial polity, but one that tolerates and respects the differences it finds within itself.

On a purely personal note, I pray and hope for the second of these options. But, like many people, I also pray that I will not be divided from my sisters and brothers who favour the first option. I pray that in the midst of our common and diverse struggles, we will discover ourselves afresh in the learning church, within that community of peace we still know as the Anglican Communion. I believe that this may well stretch the Communion to its limits, and test its viability vigorously. But I believe the stretch will ultimately be worth it. And that the shape and the shaping of the church remains a fundamentally collective and catholic enterprise, and therefore often tense and unresolved. For in reaching out just beyond ourselves, and moving outside our normal boundaries and comfort zones, God's own hand is already waiting to clasp our feeble groping. This is often what it is to be Anglican: provisional, incomplete. This is why the church needs a tense diversity to help forge its catholicity; the 'church project' is always ongoing.

To comprehend and practice this kind of polity requires some nerve, and also some faith in the God-given nature of institutional resilience that may be said to reside in churches. Yet at times of crisis and turbulent change, institutions can often be tempted to escape to apparently simple and secure forms of resolution. Some will seek security in hierarchal forms of governance that may simply attempt to repudiate the apparent threat without engaging. Or, institutions may find that they cannot espouse a common response to the crisis, and the nature of engagement quickly atomizes into expressions of individualism. Others may become quite fatalistic at this point, and presume that the institution has reached the end of its natural life and use. Or, some may move into more egalitarian forms of engagement, seeking forms of conversation and exchange that attempt to make some sense out of the cultural changes and crises that appear to be inimical.

Churches – including the Anglican Communion – can be said to model all four of these responses to cultural change and crisis: hierarchical, individualistic, fatalistic and egalitarian. Indeed, alliances between these (caricatured) responses, the most common of which is individualistic-fatalistic. A kind of 'every congregation for itself, because the Communion is already sunk' attitude: 'save yourselves, all else is lost'. Yet a reformed catholicity would continue to persist with faith in an egalitarian model, at least. There is always more to be done through conversation. Not just talking for the sake of talking; but rather, exchange taking place because each actor realizes that they are only part of a bigger picture. They are only one thread within the tapestry; one piece of the mosaic. The whole is greater than the parts. Belonging, therefore, is a partial acknowledgment that we participate in a range of pluralities and existences. There is no single way; but there is a common way. And in travelling together, we learn more of God's grace, richness and truth than if we go it alone.

A more catholic appreciation of tension and conflict, therefore, is long overdue in Anglican ecclesiology. Moreover, we can now see that some of the theological and ecclesiological responses to perceived threats and crises are, in fact, part of a wider cultural picture. The church, as it were, expressing its anxiety about the shifting tectonic plates of culture theologically, whereas other bodies might express their anxieties politically or socially.

Yet it is precisely at this point that reflection on the hidden or implicit drivers in theological discourse becomes important. Conflict – as a by-product of a perceived crisis – may in fact be an underrated theological opportunity, or even gift. Paul Avis puts it like this:

> The deleterious effects of unrestrained conflict are obvious. It reduces collaboration between various components or sub-groups of the organisation. It

leaves the defeated damaged and unfit for production work. It wastefully diverts energy from work to warfare. It polarises conflicting groups or individuals in a way that may take years to overcome. On the other hand, conflict gives vitality to an institution. It allows international interest groups to pursue their aims; which may be for the overall benefit of the system. It opens up the system to its environment as fresh energies are drawn in to replace those consumed in internal conflicts. It clarifies the true interests of the organisation, corrects imbalances and stimulates reform and renewal. (1992, p. 120)

Similarly, the International Anglican Doctrine Commission Report, *Communion, Conflict and Hope* (2008) makes a similar point. The opportunity to regard the usefulness of conflict in enabling deeper reflection on ecclesial identity should not be lost.

Even if the worst fears of Anglicans who value their fellowship and solidarity are realised, the Anglican tradition will not disappear. Communion functions at a number of different levels. IATDC has identified theology, canon law, history and culture, communication, and voluntary commitment rather than coercion, as essential aspects of communion. Yet real communion can exist in many of the elements separately. The Commission is persuaded that 'thick' ecclesiology, concrete experience of the reconciling and healing work of God in Christ, should take priority over 'thin', abstract and idealised descriptions of the church. Communion 'from below', is real communion – arguably the most vital aspect of *koinonia* with God and neighbour – and it is from 'below' that the Commission has worked in its conversations with the churches, and in its reflections in this report. (2008, Paragraph 121, p. 50)

So what of the shape of the church? There is of course no doubt that ecclesial communities look to formal theological propositions, creeds, articles of faith and the like to order their inner life, establish their identity and maintain their distinctiveness in the world. Yet it is also true that moods and manners, informal beliefs and learned (and therefore valued) behaviour, apparently innocuous and innocent practices and patterns of polity, together with aesthetics and applied theological thinking, constitute the shape of the church no less. Attention to the role and vitality of the implicit is therefore vital if one seeks to comprehend the depth, density, identity and shape of the church.

In some respects, this was alluded to briefly in the accompanying and preceding volume. Paying attention to the apparently innocent is vital:

(This is) what behavioural psychologists call 'qualia': subjective but shared experiences and knowledge of the world, such as the smell of coffee, the taste of mango, or the look of love. Or, come to that, the smell of incense, the taste of bread and wine at the altar rail, or the kiss of peace ... . (Percy, 2006, p. 102)

Such things, of course, are not 'learned' in the formal sense: but they are experienced together, and their appreciation depends on comprehending their value and virtue, but often without this ever being formally surfaced. To speak of qualia is to define a certain quality of conscious experience: the ineffable and sublime, for example. This is to say, in other words, that such senses cannot be communicated, or apprehended by any other means than direct experience. Intrinsic, deeply private, yet directly and immediately apprehensible qualia, challenge our sense of where we find our sources for theology.

This invites theologians to ponder the various ways in which practices and beliefs are construed through the various codes and signs that are seldom explicit in congregational and denominational: a kind of ecclesial DNA, if you will. This does not mean, of course, that ecclesial life is utterly determined by hidden forces that programme its inner life. Such a view would be reductionist, and also take no account of pneumatology. The point is that there is something in the (God-given) nature of churches and denominations that is 'natural' to them; implicit, deep and hidden – but of determinative influence, to a degree. And it requires a subtle and nuanced reading of ecclesial life to see how the shape and identity of churches is formed through nature and nurture, in and through the life and work of the Holy Spirit. So to participate in this theological outlook is merely to engage in a form of enquiry that opens up new kinds of 'text' to scholars of religion and practical theologians alike: seeing beyond the formal and explicit, and valuing the informal and implicit.

That said, it surely does not follow that all ecclesial differences and similarities are rooted in proclivity or context. All that can be said here is that such factors, whilst significant, and worthy of theological evaluation, are not necessarily determinative. Although variable ecclesial accents (e.g., Baptist, Anglican, Methodist, etc) sometimes accentuate differences, ecclesial communities cannot evade their intrinsic and extrinsic unity. Equally, they cannot escape developing and diversifying into something of the vision that Paul may have glimpsed for the early Christian church. Twice in his letter to the Colossians, he uses the word 'knit' – first of 'hearts knit together', and then of 'the whole body knit together' (Col 2: 2 and 19). 'Knitting' is a compelling and suggestive concept. It mirrors the density and complexity of the cultures and contexts that ecclesial communities find themselves immersed in; and it invites us to pay just as much attention to the implicit as the explicit. And it also suggests that somehow, different strands of theology, and the variety of threads, materials and colours that make up the whole of the church, can be woven together to make something richer and stronger. This is a mystical vision, of course. And one that is surely only possible in Christ, who interweaves our lives with his own, as the church worships and works together, continually believing and practising to become his body in the world.

Select Bibliography

Adair, J. and Nelson, J. (2004), *Creative Church Leadership*, Norwich: Canterbury Press.

Allen, R. (2005), '3 O'clock Please, Vicar', *Parson and Parish*, Epiphany 2005, no. 163.

Ammerman, N. and Roof, W.C. eds (1995), *Work, Family and Religion in Contemporary Society*, London: Routledge.

Augustine, St. (1961), trans. R. Pine Coffin, Harmondsworth: Penguin.

Avens, R. (1977), 'The Image of the Devil in C.G. Jung's Psychology', *Journal of Religion and Health*, Vol. 16, No. 3/July 1977.

Avis, P. (1992), *Authority, Leadership and Conflict in the Church*, London: Mowbray.

Avis, P. (2003), *Church Drawing Near*, London: Continuum.

Bailey, E. (1997), *Implicit Religion in Contemporary Society*, Kampen: Kok Pharos.

Bailey, E. (1998), *Implicit Religion: An Introduction*, London: Middlesex UP.

Barna, B. (1996), *Index of Leading Spiritual Indicators*, Milton Keynes: Word.

Barrett Browning, E.B. (1857), *Aurora Leigh*, New York, Kessinger Publishing, 2008.

Barth, K. (1958), *Church Dogmatics* vol IV, Edinburgh, T&T Clark.

Barthes, R. (1977), *Image-Music-Text*, New York: Noonday Press.

Bassett, L. (2007), *Holy Anger: Jacob, Job, Jesus*, London: Continuum.

Battle, M. (2005), *Practicing Reconciliation in a Violent World*, London: Continuum.

Becher, T. (1981), 'Policies for Educational Accountability', London: Heinemann.

Bellah, R. (1967), 'Civil Religion in America', Daedalus, 96, pp. 1–21

Bellah, R. (1985), *Habits of the Heart: Individualism and Commitment in American Life*, Berkeley: University of California Press.

Bennis, W. and Nanus, B. (1985), *Leaders: Strategies for Taking Charge*, New York:

Harper & Row.

Berger, P. (1973), *The Social Reality of Religion*, London: Penguin.

Berger, P. and Luckmann, T. (1969), *A Rumour of Angels, Modern Society and the Pursuit of the Supernatural*, London: Penguin.

Bosch, D. (1991), *Transforming Mission: Paradigm Shifts in Theology of Mission*, New York: Orbis.

Brecht, R. (1999), *Believing and Seeing: The Art of Gothic Cathedrals*, Chicago: Chicago UP.

Brichto, S. and Harries, R. eds (1998), *Two Cheers for Secularism*, Yelvertoft Manor: Pilkington Press.

Brooke, G. ed. (2000), *The Birth of Jesus: Biblical and Theological Reflections*, Edinburgh: T&T Clark.

Brown, C. (2001), *The Death of Christian Britain*, London: Routledge.

Brown, M. (1998), *The Spiritual Tourist: A Personal Odyssey Through the Outer Reaches of Belief*, London: Bloomsbury.

Browning, D. (1991), *A Fundamental Practical Theology*, Minneapolis: Fortress Press.

Carr, W. (1992), *Say One for Me*, London: SPCK.

Cavanagh, W.T. (2008), *Being Consumed*, Grand Rapids: Eerdmanns.

Certeau, M. de (1984), *The Practice of Everyday Life* (trans. Stephen Rendall), Berkeley: University of California Press.

Chadwick, O. (1975), *The Secularisation of the European Mind in the Nineteenth Century*, Cambridge: CUP.

Clark, D. (1982), Clark's *Between Pulpit and Pew*, Cambridge: CUP.

Clark-King, E. (2004), *Theology By Heart: Women, the Church and God*, Peterborough: Epworth Press.

Cobb, K. (2005), *The Blackwell Guide to Theology and Popular Culture*, Oxford: Blackwell.

Collins, S. (2000), 'Faith in Young People' in Percy, M. ed. (2000), *Calling Time: Religion and Change at the Turn of the Millennium*, Sheffield: Sheffield Academic Press.

Creedon, J. (1998), 'Designer Religion' in *Utne Reader* (Red Oak, Iowa), July/August 1998.

Cundy, I. and Welby, J. (2000), 'Taking the Cat for a Walk: Can a Bishop Order a diocese?' in G.R. Evans and M. Percy (eds.) (2000), *Managing the Church: Order and Organization in a Secular Age*, Sheffield: Sheffield Academic Press.

Cupitt, D. (1992), *What is a Story?*, London: SCM Press.

Davie, G. (1994), *Believing Without Belonging: Religion in Britain Since 1945*, Oxford: Clarendon.

Davie, G. (2000), *Religion in Europe: A Memory Mutates*, Oxford: OUP.

Dawkins, R. (2004), *The Ancestor's Tale: A Pilgrimage to the Dawn of Life*, London: Orion.

Deacy, C. and Arweck, E. eds (2009), *Exploring Religion and the Sacred in a Media Age*, London: Ashgate.

Desmond, A. and Moore, J. (1991), *Darwin*, London: Penguin.

Docherty, D. (2001), 'Reservoir Gods: Religious Metaphors and Social Change' in M. Percy and A. Walker, eds, *Restoring the Image*, Sheffield, Sheffield Academic Press.

Donovan, V. (1982), *Christianity Rediscovered: An Epistle from the Masai*, London: SCM.

Driver, J. (unpublished), *Anglicanism Beyond Windsor*, Charles Sturt University, NSW, Australia.

Duffy, E. (1992), *The Stripping of the Altars*, London: Harper.

Dulles, A. (1974), *Models of the Church*, New York: Doubleday.

Dykstra, R. ed. (2005), *Images of Pastoral Care: Classic Readings*, St. Louis MO: Chalice Press.

Eagleton, T. (2000), *The Idea of Culture*, Oxford: Blackwell.

Eliot, T.S. (1944), *The Four Quartets*, London: Faber.

Eliot, T.S. (1963), *Collected Poems 1909–1962*, London: Faber.

Elmen, P. ed. (1843), *The Anglican Moral Choice*, Wilton: Morehouse- Barlow Co.

Evans, G.R. and Percy, M. eds (2000), *Managing the Church? Order and Organization*, Sheffield: Sheffield Academic Press.

Fletcher, D. (1997), *The Barbarian Conversion: From Paganism to Christianity*, New York: Holt.

Foster, C., Dahill, L., Golemon, L. and Tolentino, B. (2006), *Educating Clergy: Teaching Practices and Pastoral Imagination*, New York: Jossey Bass.

Fox, K. (2004), *Watching the English*, London: Collins.

Freidberg, S. (2009), *Fresh: A Perishable History*, Cambridge Mass.: Belknapp Press.

Freire, P. (1973), *Pedagogy of the Oppressed*, London: Penguin.

Freire, P. (1998), *Pedagogy of Freedom*, New York: Rowman & Littlefield.

Freire, P. (2006), *Pedagogy of the Heart*, New York: Continuum.

Frye, N. (1957), *The Anatomy of Criticism*, Princeton: Princeton University Press.

Garrett, G. (2007), *The Gospel According to Hollywood*, Louisville, Kentucky, Westminster: John Knox Press.

Gay, J. (1971), *The Geography of Religion in Britain*, London: Duckworth.

Geertz, C. (1973), *The Interpretation of Cultures*, New York: Basic Books.

Gill, R. (1999), *Churchgoing and Christian Ethics*, Cambridge: CUP.

Gill, R. and Burke, D. (1996), *Strategic Church Leadership*, London: SPCK.

Girard, R. (1995), *Violence and the Sacred*, London: Athlone Press.

Graham, E. (2000), '"The Story" and "Our Stories": Narrative Theology, Vernacular Religion and the Birth of Jesus' in G. Brooke ed. (2000), *The Birth of Jesus: Biblical and Theological Reflections*, Edinburgh: T&T Clark.

Greenleaf, R. (1998), *The Power of Servant Leadership*, San Francisco: Berrett-Koehler Publishers.

Greider, K. (1996), 'Too Militant? Aggression, Gender, and the Construction of Justice', in Moessner, J. ed., *Through the Eyes of Women: Insights for Pastoral Care*, Minneapolis: Fortress Press.

Hadaway, C. and Roozen, D. (1994), *Rerouting the Protestant Mainstream Sources of Growth and Opportunities for Change*, Nashville, Abingdon Press.

Hardy, D. (2002), *Finding the Church*, London: SCM.

Hardy, D. (1996), *God's Ways with the World: Thinking and Practicing Christian Faith*, Edinburgh: T&T Clark.

Hardy, D. and Gunton, C. (1989), *On Being Church*, Edinburgh: T&T Clark.

Hare, D. (1991), *Racing Demon,* London: Faber and Faber.

Harris, M. (1998), *Organizing God's Work: Challenges for Churches and Synagogues*, London: Macmillan.

Harrison, B. & Robb, C. (1985), *Making the Connections: Essays in Feminist Social Ethics*, Boston, Beacon Press.

Harvey, S.A. (2006) *Scenting Salvation: Ancient Christianity and the Olifactory Imagination*, Berkeley: University of California Press.

Hastings, A. (1986), *A History of English Christianity, 1920–1985*, London: Collins.

Headlam, A.C. (1921), *Theological Education at the Universities*, Oxford: Blackwell.

Healy, N. (2000), *Church, World and Christian Life: Practical-Prophetic Ecclesiology*, Cambridge: CUP.

Hervieu-Leger, D. (2000), *Religion as a Chain of Memory*, Cambridge: Polity.

Heywood, O. (2007 – new edition), *Revd. Oliver Heywood 1630–1702 V4: His Autobiography, Diaries, Anecdote and Event Books*, Turner, J. Horsfall (ed.), New York, Kessenger.

Hill, R. (2007), *God's Architect: Pugin and the Building of Romantic Britain*, London: Allen Lane.

Holmes III, U.T. (1971), *The Future Shape of Ministry: A Theological Projection.* New York: Seabury Press.

Hooker, R. (1845), *The Laws of Ecclesiastical Polity*, 3rd ed. Oxford: OUP.

Hopewell, J. (1987), *Congregation: Stories and Structures*, London: SCM Press.

Howes, G. (2000), 'Seeing and Believing', *Church Building*, October 2000.

Hull, J. (2001), *In the Beginning There Was Darkness: A Blind Person's Conversations With The Bible*, London: SCM.

Hull, J.M. (2006), *Mission-Shaped Church: A Theological Response*, London: SCM Press.

Ingold, T. (1986) *The Appropriation of Nature: Essays on Human Ecology and Social Relations*, Manchester: Manchester University Press.

James, W. (1960), *The Varieties of Religious Experience*, The Gifford Lectures of 1901–1902, Glasgow: Collins.

Jay, A. (1967), *Management and Machiavelli*, London: Hodder.

Jenkins, S. (1999), *England's One Thousand Best Churches*, London: Allen Lane.

Jung, C. (1974), *Letters*, ed. G. Adler, 2 vols. Princeton: Princeton University Press.

Kaye, B., Macneil, S. and Thomson, H. eds (2006), '*Wonderfully and Confessedly Strange': Australian Essays in Anglican Ecclesiology*, ATF Press: Adelaide.

Kaye, B., *Conflict and the Practice of Christian Faith: The Anglican Experiment*, Eugene OR, Cascade Books, 2009.

Keillor, G. (1985), *Lake Wobegon Days*, USA: Penguin.

Kelley, D. (1986), *Why Conservative Churches are Growing*, New York: Harper & Row.

Kim, S. and Kollontai, P. (2007), *Community Identity: The Dynamics of Religion in Context*, London: Continuum.

King, E.C. (2005), *Theology By Heart*, London: Epworth.

Kirk, K. (1946), *The Apostolic Ministry: Essays on the History and Doctrine of Episcopacy*, London: Hodder & Stoughton.

Klassen, C. ed. (2006), *The Book of Touch*, Berlin: Berg.

LaMothe, K. (2008), 'What Bodies Know About Religion and the Study of It', *Journal of the American Academy of Religion*, vol. 76, no. 3, September 2008, pp. 573–601.

Lears, J. (1994), *Fables of Abundance*, New York: Basic Books.

Lederach, J.P. (2005), *The Moral Imagination: The Art and Soul of Building Peace*, Oxford: OUP.

Le Guin, U. (1989), *Dancing at the Edge of the World: Words, Women, Places*, New York: Grove Books.

Levitt, M. (1996), *Nice When They're Young*, Aldershot: Avebury.

Lindbeck, G. (1984), *The Nature of Doctrine*, Philadelphia: Westminster Press.

Long, E.L. Jr. (2001), *Patterns of Polity: Varieties of Church Governance*, Cleveland: Pilgrim Press.

Luckmann, T. (1967), *The Invisible Religion: The Problems of Religion in Modern Society*, New York: MacMillan.

Lunn, D. (2009), *The Wetwang Saga*, York, Heritage Publications.

McLaren, B.D. (2006), *Generous Orthodoxy*, Grand Rapids, MI, Zondervan.

McClintock Fulkerson, M (2007), *Places of Redemption: Theology for a Worldly Church*, New York, Oxford University Press.

McConnell, T. (1983), 'Anglican Identity' in Elmen, P. ed. (1983), *The Anglican Moral Choice*, Wilton, CT: Morehouse.

McGavran, D. (1970), *Understanding Church Growth*, Grand Rapids: Eerdman.

McLaren, B. (2006), *Generous Orthodoxy*, Grand Rapids, Zondervan.

Mann, A. (1998), *The In-Between Church: Navigating Size Transitions In Congregations*, Herndon: Alban Institute.

Mann, A. (1999), *Can Our Church Live?* Bethesda in Maryland: Alban.

Mann, A. (2001), *Raising the Roof*, Bethesda in Maryland: Alban.

Markham, I. and Percy, M. eds (2005), *Why Liberal Churches are Growing*, London: Continuum.

Marsh, C. (1998), *Popular Religion in Sixteenth Century England*, London: Macmillan.

Martin, D. (1967), 'Interpreting the Figures', in Perry, M. (1967), *Crisis For Confirmation*, London: SCM.

Marturano, A. and Gosling, J. (2008), *Leadership: The Key Concepts*, London: Routledge.

Mead, L.B. (1991), *The Once and the Future Church*, Bethesda in Maryland: Alban; (1993), *More Than Numbers: The Ways Churches Grow*, Bethesda in Maryland: Alban.

Mead, M. (1970), *Culture and Commitment: A Study of the Generation Gap*, London: Bodley Head.

Medhurst, K. and Moyser, S. (1988), *Church and Politics in a Secular Age*, Oxford: Clarendon.

Milbank, J. (2008), 'Stale Expressions: The Management-Shaped Church', *Studies in Christian Ethics*, vol. 21, no. 1, pp. 117–28.

Miley, C. (2002), *The Suicidal Church: Can Anglicanism Be Saved?* Annandale, N.S.W.: Pluto Press

Modern Theology, Oct. 1993, Vol. 9, No. 4, 'Ecclesiology and the Culture of Management'. Special edition.

Moorman, J. (1955), *The Anglican Spiritual Tradition*, London: SCM.

Morris, W. (2008), *Theology Without Words*, London, Ashgate.

Morrise, R.M. (2009), *Church and State in 21st Century Britain*, London: Faber.

Murray, A. (1972), 'Piety and Impiety in Thirteenth Century Italy', *Studies in Church History*, vol. 8.

Nesbitt, P. (2001), *Religion and Social Policy*, Lanham MD: AltaMira Press.

Nichols, A. (2008), *The Realm: An Unfashionable Essay on the Conversion of England*, Oxford: Family Publications.

Niebuhr, R.H. (1929), *The Social Sources of Denominationalism*, New York: Henry Holt & Co.

Niebuhr, R.H. (1951), *Christ and Culture*, New York: Harper & Row.

Nieman, J. (2002), 'Attending Locally: Theologies in Congregations', *International Journal of Practical Theology* 6/2 (Fall 2002), pp. 198–252.

Norman, E. (2003), *Secularisation*, London: Continuum.

Oakley, M. (2001), *The Collage of God*, London: DLT.

Percy, M. (1998), *Ecclesall Deanery Survey*, Rotherham, Diocese of Sheffield.

Percy, M. (2000), *Introducing Richard Hooker and the Laws of Ecclesiastical Polity*, London: DLT Ltd.

Percy, M. ed. (2000), *Calling Time: Religion and Change at the Turn of the Millennium*, Sheffield: Sheffield Academic Press.

Percy, M. (2001), *The Salt of the Earth*, London: T&T Clark.

Percy, M. (2005), *Engaging Contemporary Culture: Christianity, Theology and the Concrete Church*, London: Ashgate.

Percy, M. (2006), *Clergy: The Origin of Species*, London: T&T Clark.

Percy, M. (2006b), *Engaging with Contemporary Culture: Theology and the Concrete Church*, London: Ashgate.

Percy, M. (2007), *Introducing Richard Hooker and the Laws of International Polity*, London: DLT.

Percy, M. and Walker, A. eds (2001), *Restoring the Image: Essays on Religion and Society in Honour of David Martin*, Sheffield: Sheffield Academic Press.

Perry, M. (1967), *Crisis For Confirmation*, London: SCM.

Pickard, S. (2004), 'Innovation and Undecidability: Some Implications for the *Koinonia* of the Anglican Church', *Journal of Anglican Studies*, Vol. 2.2, Dec. 2004, pp. 87–105.

Pickard, S. (2006), 'The Travail of the Episcopate: Management and the Diocese in An Age of Mission' in Kaye, B., Macneil, S. and Thomson, H. (eds) (2006), *'Wonderfully and Confessedly Strange': Australian Essays in Anglican Ecclesiology*, ATF Press: Adelaide.

Pickard, S. (2009), 'An Intelligent Communion? Episcopal Reflections Post Lambeth', *Journal of Anglican Studies*, vol. 7, issue 2, 2009, pp. 127–37.

Polanyi, M. (1962), *Personal Knowledge*, London: Routledge, 1962.

Powell, J. (2008), *Great Hatred, Little Room: Making Peace in Northern Ireland*, London: Bodley Head.

Pritchard, J. (2007), *The Life and Work of a Priest*, London: SPCK.

Putnam, R. (2000), *Bowling Alone: The Collapse and Revival of American Community*, New York: Simon & Schuster.

Rambo, Lewis (1993), *Understanding Religious Conversion*, New Haven: Yale U.P.

Reader, J. (2005), *Blurred Encounters, St. Brides Major*, Glamorgan: Aureus Press.

Riewoldt, O. (2002), *Brandscaping: Worlds of Experience in Retail Design*, London: Momenta Press & Basel: Birkauser.

Roberts, R. (1989), 'Lord, Bondsman and Churchman' in Hardy and Gunton (1989), *On Being Church*, Edinburgh: T&T Clark.

Roberts, R. (2000), in Evans, G.R. and Percy, M. eds (2000), *Managing the Church? Order and Organization*, Sheffield: Sheffield Academic Press.

Roberts, R. (2002), *Religion, Theology and the Human Sciences*, Cambridge: CUP.

Roberts, R. (2008), 'Personhood and Performance: Managerialism, Post-democracy and the Ethics of "Enrichment"', *Studies in Christian Ethics*, 2.1 (2008) pp. 63–84.

Robinson, G. (2008), *In the Eye of the Storm*, London: SCM-Canterbury Press.

Roof, W.C. (1987/1985), *Community and Commitment*, New York: Elsevier.

Roof, W.C. (1994), *A Generation of Seekers: The Spiritual Journeys of the Baby Boom Generation*, San Francisco: Harper.

Roozen, D. and Hadaway, C. (1994), *Rerouting the Protestant Mainstream Sources of Growth and Opportunities for Change*, Nashville, Abingdon Press.

Rowell, G., Williams, R. and Stevenson, K. (2001), *Love's Redeeming Work*, Oxford: OUP.

Rudge, P.F. (1968), *Ministry and Management: A Study of Ecclesiastical Administration*, London: Tavistock Publications.

Russell, A. (1980), *The Clerical Profession*, London: SPCK.

Russell, A. (1998), 'The Rise of Secularisation and the Persistence of Religion' in Brichto, S. and Harries, R. eds (1998), *Two Cheers for Secularism*, Yelvertoft Manor: Pilkington Press.

Scarisbrick, J. (1984), *The Reformation and the English People*, Oxford: Clarendon.

Schillebeeckx, E. (1985), *Ministry: Leadership in the Community of Jesus Christ*, New York: Crossroads.

Schmiechen, P. (2005), *Saving Power: Theories of Atonement and Forms of the Church*, Grand Rapids: Eerdmans.

Schon, D. (1991), *The Reflective Practitioner: How Professionals Think in Action*, London: Ashgate.

Selznick, P. (1957), *Leadership in Administration: A Sociological Interpretation*, New York: Harper.

Sheldrake, P. (2001), *Spaces For the Sacred: Place, Memory and Identity*, Baltimore, Maryland: Johns Hopkins University Press.

Sheldrake, P. (2001b), 'Human Identity and the Particularity of Place', *Spiritus: a Journal of Christian Spirituality*, Vol. 1 Number 1, Spring 2001, pp. 43–64.

Shillington, V.G. (2001), 'Salt of the Earth?' in *The Expository Times*, Edinburgh, T&T Clark, vol. 112, no. 4, January 2001, pp. 120–22.

Snow, C.P. (1959), *Two Cultures and The Scientific Revolution*, Cambridge: CUP.

Spurrell, C. ed. (1998), *The Brightwell Parish Diaries*, vol 62, Oxford: Oxford Record Society.

Stadlen, N. (2004), *What Mothers Do Especially When it Looks Like Nothing*, London: Piatkus Books.

Stark, R. and Bainbridge, W. (1987), 'Typologies of Church, Sect & Cult', in *A Theory of Religion*, New York: Peter Lang Publishers.

Stark, R. and Finke, R. (2000), *Acts of Faith: Explaining the Human Side of Religion*, Berkeley, Calif., University of California Press.

Sykes, S. and Booty, W. (1988), *The Study of Anglicanism*, Philadelphia: Fortress.

Tanner, K. (1984), 'Theological Reflection and Christian Practices', in Volf, M. and Bass, D. (2002), *Practicing Theology: Beliefs and Practices in Christian Life*, Grand Rapids, Eerdmans, 2002, 228–44.

Tanner, K. (1997), *Theories of Culture: A New Agenda for Theology*, Minneapolis: Fortress Press.

Thomas, K. (1971), *Religion and the Decline of Magic*, London: Weidenfeld & Nicolson.

Thompsett, F. (1988), 'The Laity' in Sykes and Booty (1988), *The Study of Anglicanism*, Philadelphia: Fortress.

Thornton, M. (1963), *English Spirituality*, London: SPCK.

Torry, M. ed. (2004), *The Parish – a Theological and Practical Exploration*, London: SCM-Canterbury Press.

Torry, M. (2005), *Managing God's Business: Religious and Faith-Based Organizations and their Management*, London: Ashgate.

Towler, R. (1974), *Homo Religiosus*, London: Constable.

Towler, R. and Coxon, A. (1979), *The Fate of the Anglican Clergy, A Sociological Study*, London: Macmillan.

Volf, M. and Bass, D. (2002), *Practicing Theology: Beliefs and Practices in the Church*, Grand Rapids: Eerdmans.

Walker, A. (1998), *Restoring the Kingdom: The Radical Christianity of the House Church Movement*, London: Hodder & Stoughton.

Ward, M. (2008), *Planet Narnia: The Heavens in the Imagination of C.S. Lewis*, Oxford: OUP.

Wessels, A. (1994), *Europe: Was it Ever Really Christian?* London: SCM.

Western, S. (2008), *Leadership: A Critical Text*, London: Sage.

Weston, P. (2006), *Lesslie Newbigin: Missionary Theologian – A Reader*, Grand Rapids, MI: Eerdmans.

Wickham, E. (1957), *Church and People in an Industrial City*, London: Lutterworth.

Wilkerson, D. (1962), *The Cross and the Switchblade*, New York: Jove Books.

Williams, R. (2002), *Writing in the Dust: After September 11th*, London: Hodder.

Williams, R., (2004), *Anglican Identities*, London: Darton, Longman & Todd.

Woodforde, J. (1999), *The Diary of a Country Parson 1758–1802* ed. John Beresford, Norwich: Canterbury Press.

Woodhead, L. and Heelas, P. eds (2005), *The Spiritual Revolution*, Oxford: Blackwell.

Yeats, W.B. (1974), *Selected Poetry (A Pan Classic)*, London: Pan Books.

Yust, L. 'Teaching Seminarians to be Practical Theologians', *Encounter*, issue 63, 2001, pp. 22–35,

Church and Church of England Reports

Archdiaconal Visitations in 1578 [Bedfordshire Historical Records Society, no. 69. Bedford 1990].

History of the Family of Stanley, Harleian MSS.541, British Museum.

(1990) *Faith in the Countryside, The Report of the Archbishops Commission on Rural Area*s, London, Church House Publishing, 1990.

(1996) *Working as One Body (Turnbull Report)*, London: Church House Publishing.

(2001) *Resourcing Bishops*, London: Church House Publishing.

(2004) *Mission-Shaped Church*, London: Church House Publishing.

(2004) *The Windsor Report*, London: Church House Publishing.

(2007) *Talent and Calling (Pilling Report)*, London: Church House Publishing.

The *Kuala Lumpur Report of the Third Inter-Anglican Theological and Doctrinal Commission*, London: Anglican Communion Office.

(2008) International Anglican Doctrine Commission Report, *Communion, Conflict and Hope*.

Newspaper Articles

Creedon, J., 'The Age of the Do-It-Yourself Religion', *The Guardian*, 05/09/98.

Harries, R., 'Christianity Soldiers Onward', *The Observer*, 26/12/99, p. 17.

Runcie, R., *Church Observer*, 1964.

Vallely, P., *The Independent*, 31/12/99, Review, p. 3.

Index